Durkheim's Philosophy Lectures

In these lectures, given more than a decade before the publication of his groundbreaking book, *The Division of Labor in Society* (1893), Emile Durkheim, the founder of French sociology, sets out to introduce secondary school students to the field of philosophy. Moving easily back and forth between the history of philosophy and the contributions of philosophers in his own day, Durkheim takes up topics as diverse as philosophical psychology, logic, ethics, and metaphysics and seeks to articulate a unified philosophical position. Remarkably, the "social realism" that is so characteristic of his later work – where he insists, famously, that social facts cannot be reduced to psychological or economic ones and that such facts constrain human action in important ways – is totally absent in these early lectures. For this reason, they will be of special interest to students of the history of the social sciences, for they shed important light on the course of Durkheim's intellectual development. But because all members of the French elite would have been exposed to a *lycée* philosophy course similar in certain fundamental respects to the one Durkheim taught, the lectures actually offer something more: a window into the nineteenth-century French mind. Intellectual historians, historically minded philosophers, and scholars of French history will all find the lectures a valuable historical document. Insofar as they speak to the philosophical foundations of Durkheim's thought, they should also be of great interest to social theorists.

Neil Gross is Assistant Professor of Sociology, Harvard University. He writes on classical and contemporary sociological theory as well as the sociology of ideas. His work has appeared in such journals as *Theory and Society, American Sociological Review, Sociological Theory*, and *Annual Review of Sociology*.

Robert Alun Jones is the author of *Emile Durkheim: An Introduction to Four Major Works* (1986), *The Development of Durkheim's Social Realism* (1999), and *The Secret of the Totem: Religion and Society in the Works of McLennan, Smith, Frazer, Durkheim, and Freud* (forthcoming) as well as numerous essays and journal articles on Durkheim and his contemporaries. He has also been editor of both *Études durkheimiennes* and *Knowledge and Society*.

Durkheim's Philosophy Lectures

*Notes from the Lycée de Sens Course,
1883–1884*

Edited and translated by

NEIL GROSS
Harvard University

ROBERT ALUN JONES
University of Illinois

PUBLISHED BY THE PRESS SYNDICATE OF THE UNIVERSITY OF CAMBRIDGE
The Pitt Building, Trumpington Street, Cambridge, United Kingdom

CAMBRIDGE UNIVERSITY PRESS
The Edinburgh Building, Cambridge CB2 2RU, UK
40 West 20th Street, New York, NY 10011-4211, USA
477 Williamstown Road, Port Melbourne, VIC 3207, Australia
Ruiz de Alarcón 13, 28014 Madrid, Spain
Dock House, The Waterfront, Cape Town 8001, South Africa

http://www.cambridge.org

© Neil Gross and Robert Alun Jones 2004

This book is in copyright. Subject to statutory exception
and to the provisions of relevant collective licensing agreements,
no reproduction of any part may take place without
the written permission of Cambridge University Press.

First published 2004

Printed in the United States of America

Typeface Goudy 10.5/13 pt.   *System* LATEX 2_ε [TB]

A catalog record for this book is available from the British Library.

Library of Congress Cataloging in Publication Data
Durkheim, Emile, 1858–1917.
  [Lectures. English Selections]
  Durkheim's philosophy lectures : notes from the Lycée de Sens course,
  1883–1884 / edited by Neil Gross, Robert Alun Jones.
    p. cm.
  "Consists of notes taken by André Lalande" – Translators' note.
  Includes bibliographical references and index.
  ISBN 0-521-63066-5
  1. Social sciences – Philosophy.   2. Philosophy.   I. Gross, Neil, 1971–
II. Jones, Robert Alun.   III. Lalande, André, 1867–1963.   IV. Title.
H61.15D8713   2004
300'.1 – dc22   2003065687

ISBN 0 521 63066 5 hardback

Contents

Foreword	page xi
Translators' Note	xv
Acknowledgments	xvii
Introduction	1

Part I. Preliminary Matters

1. The Object and Method of Philosophy	33
2. The Object and Method of Philosophy (Conclusion)	36
3. Science and Philosophy	41
4. The Divisions of Philosophy	45

Part II. Psychology

5. The Object and Method of Psychology	51
6. Faculties of the Soul	57
7. On Pleasure and Pain	60
8. The Inclinations	63
9. The Emotions and Passions	67
10. Theory of Knowledge	72
11. External Perception and Its Conditions. The Senses	73

12. External Perception. The Origin of the Idea of Externality	77
13. External Perception. On the Objectivity of the Idea of Externality. (1) Does the External World Exist?	80
14. External Perception. On the Objectivity of the Idea of Externality. (2) On the Nature of the External World	82
15. Consciousness. On the Conditions of Consciousness	86
16. Consciousness. On the Origin of the Idea of the Self	89
17. Consciousness. On the Nature of the Self	92
18. Reason. The Definition of Reason	95
19. Reason. The Material of Reason. (1) Principles of Reason	98
20. Reason. The Material of Reason. (2) Rational or First Ideas	101
21. Reason. Empiricism	106
22. Reason. Evolutionism. The Theory of Heredity	110
23. Reason. On the Objectivity of Rational Principles	115
24. Faculties of Conception. On the Association of Ideas	119
25. Faculties of Conception. Memory	122
26. Faculties of Conception. Imagination	125
27. Faculties of Conception. Sleep. Dreams. Madness	129
28. Complex Operations of the Mind. Attention. Comparison. Abstraction	132
29. Complex Operations of the Mind. Generalization. Judgment. Reasoning	134
30. The Object and Method of Aesthetics	138
31. What Is Beauty?	142
32. Prettiness and the Sublime. Art	145
33. On Activity in General. Instinct	148

34. Habit	151
35. On the Will and on Freedom	156
36. On Freedom (Continued). Psychological Determinism	159
37. On Freedom (Conclusion). Scientific Determinism. Theological Fatalism	162

Part III. Logic

38. Introduction. On Logic	169
39. On Truth. On Certainty	172
40. On Certainty (Conclusion)	175
41. On False Certainty or Error	178
42. Skepticism	181
43. Ideas. Terms. Judgments. Propositions	185
44. Definition	188
45. On the Syllogism	190
46. On Induction	198
47. Fallacies	202
48. On Method	205
49. Method in the Mathematical Sciences	207
50. The Methodology of the Physical Sciences	209
51. Method in the Natural Sciences	213
52. Method in the Moral Sciences	215
53. Method in the Historical Sciences	218
54. Language	221

Part IV. Ethics

55. Definition and Divisions of Ethics	229
56. On Moral Responsibility	230

57. On Moral Law. The History of Utilitarianism	232
58. Critique of Utilitarianism. The Morality of Sentiment	236
59. The Morality of Kant	240
60. The Moral Law	243
61. On Duty and the Good. On Virtue. Rights	245
62A. Division of Practical Ethics	249
62B. Individual Morality	250
63. Domestic Ethics	254
64. Civic Ethics	258
65. General Duties of Social Life	263
66. General Duties of Social Life. (1) The Duty of Justice	265
67. General Duties of Social Life. (2) Charity	270
68. Summary of Ethics	272

Part V. Metaphysics

69. Metaphysics. Preliminary Considerations	277
70. On the Soul and Its Existence	279
71. On the Spirituality of the Soul (Conclusion). On Materialism	281
72. The Relationship between the Soul and the Body	284
73. On the Immortality of the Soul	288
74. On God. Metaphysical Proofs of His Existence	292
75. Critique of Metaphysical Proofs of the Existence of God	296
76. Explanation and Critique of the Physicotheological Proof	299
77. Critique of the Physicotheological Proof (Conclusion). Moral Proofs of the Existence of God	303
78. The Nature and Attributes of God	306

79. The Relationship between God and the World. Dualism, Pantheism, and Creation   309

80. The Relationship between God and the World (Conclusion). Providence, Evil, Optimism, and Pessimism   311

Appendix: Biographical Glossary   315

Index   333

Foreword

Another book by Emile Durkheim? Many readers will be surprised to find here a new work from one of the greatest minds in the history of sociology, the true founder of the discipline in France, both intellectually and institutionally, and undeniably, together with Max Weber, the most important continuous source of inspiration for the sociological discipline in the world. Some of the surprised readers may soon feel disappointed, however, when they realize that the present text is not another pioneering sociological work but an elementary course in philosophy. Moreover, it is not a text written by Durkheim himself but a compilation of notes taken in Durkheim's class in 1883–4, one that can reasonably be said to represent the teaching and thinking of Durkheim at a very early point of his career. But although the present text is not an original contribution to the philosophical or sociological literature of the nineteenth century as such, it is extremely helpful for an improved understanding of Durkheim's intellectual development and, above all, for an appreciation of the relationship between Durkheim's sociological project and the philosophy out of which it arose.

For some of the most influential stereotypical views of Durkheim's sociological project, the relationship between sociology and philosophy does not appear to be a problem worth studying. If one takes Durkheim to be an archpositivist, sociology means a complete rupture with philosophy. If one takes Durkheim to be a Kantian, one is certainly closer to his self-understanding but will still consider the philosophical problems as settled in Durkheim's view, just in need of further sociological concretization. Against both these views stands the interpretation that

Durkheim's sociology has itself to be seen as a philosophical project.*
When, for example, late in his life Durkheim called pragmatism and
sociology children of the same epoch, he intended to do more than
note a mere temporal coincidence. Rather, he recognized that there
was a new spirit at work both in parts of academic philosophy and in
the newly emerging discipline of sociology. In both fields, similar efforts could be found to develop solutions for age-old problems through
a new relationship to the methods of empirical science. And "empirical" here meant more than mere reflection on the consciousness of
the researcher. Breaking with the older philosophy thus did not mean
breaking with philosophy altogether. Sociology itself, therefore, could
be seen as a philosophical project, not in the sense of remaining separate
from empirical science but as part of a renewed philosophy based on and
encompassing the empirical disciplines.

The philosophical lectures presented in this volume offer insight into
an early stage of this project of transformation. They cover more than
the areas that are familiar territory for Durkheim readers. It is no surprise
that we find long passages on moral philosophy and epistemology, since
these remained at the center of Durkheim's interests as a sociologist. But
here we also find him talking about aesthetics – a conspicuous absence
in his later writings – and on metaphysics and the philosophy of religion,
which, despite the enormous interest Durkheim had for religion during
all his life, reveals an attitude very different from everything he later
contributed to this subject. Here Durkheim defends conventional arguments for God's existence and the immortality of the soul – arguments
that run counter to what he later had to say on these topics.

There is no doubt that the comprehensiveness of Durkheim's course
and maybe even some of its intellectual thrust are due to the institutional
framework in which it took place. An adequate interpretation thus has
to refer these lectures to the academic setting of late nineteenth-century
French philosophical education.† But beyond that, the identification of
the way in which Durkheim modified the given structure of such a course
and adapted it to his own burgeoning project makes it possible to relate

---

* See Hans Joas, *Pragmatism and Social Theory* (Chicago: University of Chicago Press, 1993), 55–78, 238.
† See the introduction by Neil Gross and the important contributions of John D. Brooks III, above all his book *The Eclectic Legacy: Academic Philosophy and the Human Sciences in Nineteenth-Century France* (Newark: University of Delaware Press, 1998).

Durkheim's sociology more closely to the history of French philosophy preceding his own work. This task not only includes a reconstruction of intellectual influences and of the conditions with regard to which the sociological project had to be legitimated, it also has to draw the precise contours of the philosophical currents out of which the very idea of establishing sociology as a philosophical project could emerge.

A possible starting point for such an attempt that would also lead to a better understanding of the relationship between Durkheim and another philosophical-sociological project of the same epoch is the history of "French Philosophy in the Nineteenth Century" sketched by George Herbert Mead.‡ This text, mostly ignored by sociologists and philosophers alike, traces the history of French thinking after the great revolution and discusses de Bonald and de Maistre, Royer-Collard and Cousin, Comte, Renouvier, Boutroux, and Poincaré, leading up to the thinker Mead obviously considered a main rival of his own project: Henri Bergson. A reader of this text today cannot help feeling that a last chapter is missing, a chapter on Durkheim. But as in the case of the mutual ignorance of Max Weber and Emile Durkheim, there is not a word in Mead's text devoted to Durkheim. Still, we find here an independent contemporary reconstruction of the intellectual field from which Durkheim's work clearly arose.

The publication of Durkheim's early philosophical lectures gives the scientific community rich additional material to reconstruct this field in a fruitful way. The two stereotypes mentioned above – Durkheim as a Comtean and as a Kantian – are certainly more difficult to defend after reading these lectures. Durkheim clearly distances himself from Comte in this early work and is also, again and again, sharply critical of Kant. Although he may not really be attacking Kant but an image of Kant prevalent in France at the time (and although some might even defend Comte against any simplistic picture),§ it becomes clear that a fully contextualized reconstruction of Durkheim's development can be reached only if we see him not merely as conversing with great minds of the past but as fully embedded in the intellectual world of his contemporaries. Bridging the divide between philosophy and sociology

---

‡ George Herbert Mead, "French Philosophy in the Nineteenth Century," in *Movements of Thought in the Nineteenth Century* (Chicago: University of Chicago Press, 1936), 418–510.

§ Johan Heilbron, *The Rise of Social Theory* (Cambridge: Polity Press, 1995), 195–254.

is the other major precondition for such an adequate contextualization, because the different disciplines tend to reconstruct their history as if leading figures had mostly drawn their inspiration from within one or the other. The fuller contextualization of Durkheim's work made possible by the present publication may finally reward us with a new impulse to reevaluate the relationship between philosophy and sociology in our time.

– Hans Joas
(Berlin/Chicago)

Translators' Note

As explained in the introduction, the French manuscript of which the following text is a translation consists of notes taken by André Lalande, then a sixteen-year-old student of Emile Durkheim, in 1883–4. In all likelihood, these notes were never seen by Durkheim, and they could hardly have been edited by him. Our assumption in translating them into English, therefore, has been that while the notes *are* reflective of the various philosophical positions Durkheim intended to advance, these positions are expressed in the text in a manner and with a sensibility that is probably more Lalande's than Durkheim's own. Were the notes written in Durkheim's hand, of course, a more literal translation would be appropriate; but as this is not the case, we have felt free to take a more liberal approach, focusing less on the actual words Lalande used to record Durkheim's arguments than on what we take Durkheim to have meant. In the interests of rendering the text more readable in English, we have not hesitated to reorder phrases or sentences as necessary, rely on synonyms or cognate terms whose English meanings were more suitable, or drop altogether short passages from the text that seemed to interfere with Durkheim's rhetorical thrust. As for Lalande's occasional marginal comments in the manuscript, we retained only those that seemed to shed light on Durkheim's intended meanings. Only rarely, in these comments, did Lalande cite specific texts to which Durkheim referred – as is befitting of lecture notes – and we made no effort to track down the hundreds of citations he did not give. Instead, we opted to include a short biographical glossary that, while falling far short of a comprehensive set of citations, may help familiarize readers with the many thinkers whose ideas Durkheim discusses. Finally, we note that, though we did privilege the intentional over the literal, we tried to preserve as much as possible not only of Durkheim's style of argumentation but of his style as a *lycée* lecturer. Our hope is that the English translation thus retains something of the charm and authenticity of the original.

Acknowledgments

The translators wish to thank, for their assistance with this project, the library of the University of Paris-Sorbonne, where the original manuscript is housed; the Sociology Department of the University of Wisconsin-Madison, which generously paid to have the manuscript microfilmed; the University of Illinois at Urbana-Champaign, which provided the computer resources necessary to make a transcription of the French manuscript available on the Web (at http://www.relst.uiuc.edu/durkheim); and Richard Layton, who helped us with the Greek. For their helpful comments on the introduction, Neil Gross thanks Jessica Berger Gross, Amy Binder, John Brooks, Charles Camic, Barry Glassner, Robert Alun Jones, Warren Schmaus, Jonathan Turner, and Alia Winters.

Introduction

Neil Gross

In the fall of 1882, at the age of 24, Emile Durkheim (1858–1917) was sent by the French Ministry of Public Instruction to live in the provincial town of Sens, a community of 13,000 on the Yonne River, seventy miles southeast of Paris.[1] Having studied for three years at the elite École Normale Supérieure, the traditional breeding ground for French intellectuals, Durkheim had just passed – with low marks – the *agrégation* examination in philosophy that was the stepping stone to a job as a philosophy teacher in one of the nation's *lycées*, or secondary schools. Ambitious young scholars who put in their time at a *lycée* and also completed two dissertations – one in French, the other in Latin – were then eligible to compete for positions at the university level. Such were Durkheim's ambitions, and those who knew him had no doubt that his prodigious intellectual gifts would prove more than adequate for their achievement. His instructors and fellow students at the École Normale were therefore surprised when he placed second to last on the exam, perhaps due to illness.[2] Still, this was enough to secure him a *lycée* post. Like the vast majority of young *agrégés*,[3] Durkheim was sent, not to a prestigious Parisian *lycée*, but to a provincial one. After a month

---

1. Population figure published in *L'Union de l'Yonne*, February 8, 1882, 1. Library of Sens archive.
2. Steven Lukes, *Emile Durkheim: His Life and Work* (New York: Harper & Row, 1972), 64.
3. John Brooks, "The Definition of Sociology and the Sociology of Definition: Durkheim's *Rules of Sociological Method* and High School Philosophy in France," *Journal of the History of the Behavioral Sciences* 32 (1996), 379–407; John Brooks, *The Eclectic Legacy: Academic Philosophy and the Human Sciences in Nineteenth-Century France* (Newark: University of Delaware Press, 1998).

at the Lycée de Puy, he was reassigned to Sens in November 1882. The local Catholic paper, ever eager to ring up anti-Semitic and anti-German points in its polemic against the evils of laicized education, announced with a convenient typographical error in its November 4 edition that a "M. Durckheim [sic], professeur de philosophie, agrégé" was on his way to town.[4] At the *lycée*, Durkheim taught a required academic year–long course that sought to introduce students in their final year of secondary instruction to the field of philosophy – to the questions it posed, the thinkers who comprised its canon, and the range of arguments and ideas in serious consideration by members of the French philosophical establishment.[5] This eighty-lecture course, given for the first time in the 1882–3 school year, was partially repeated in 1883–4 but was cut short by Durkheim's reassignment to the Lycée de Saint-Quentin in February 1884.

Scholars have known for years that the very first lectures given by Durkheim, unquestionably a seminal figure in the social sciences, were these lectures on philosophy given at Sens. Although the content of the lecture course remained unknown until recently, other evidence suggested that Durkheim put on an impressive show for his young charges. Steven Lukes, for his definitive 1972 biography, unearthed reports by Ministry of Public Instruction officials that praised Durkheim's work in the *lycée* classroom as serious and first-rate.[6] The philosopher André Lalande (1867–1963), who was in Durkheim's class during the 1883–4 school year and who took the notes of which the present volume is a translation, observed in an essay published to celebrate the 100th anniversary of Durkheim's birth that "his students, even the mediocre ones, had the greatest consideration for him."[7] And thanks to the diligent archival work of Edward Tiryakian, historians of Durkheim have also had access to the text of a short and quite inspirational address Durkheim made to the *lycéens* at Sens in 1883 on the subject of great men that leaves no doubt as to the cogency of the orator.[8] But the actual

---

4. *L'Union de l'Yonne*, November 4, 1882, 2. Library of Sens archive.
5. "The idea" of the *lycée* philosophy course, Gary Gutting writes, "was to cover the whole of philosophy, both its problems and its history, in a year-long, grand synthesis" (*French Philosophy in the Twentieth Century* [Cambridge: Cambridge University Press, 2001], 4).
6. Lukes, *Emile Durkheim*, 64–5.
7. André Lalande, "Commémoration du centenaire de la naissance d'Emile Durkheim," *Annales de l'Université de Paris* 30 (1960), 22–5.
8. Emile Durkheim, "Du rôle des grands hommes dans la société," *Cahiers internationaux de sociologie* 43 (1973), 25–32.

substance of Durkheim's thought in this early stage of his career remained a mystery.

The Importance of Understanding the Early Durkheim

Not only for those with an historical interest in Durkheim was this a serious lacuna in our knowledge of him. Indeed, there are two reasons why scholars who have sought to use Durkheim's ideas for more presentist purposes have also wished for greater understanding of his early views. First, while it is well known that the entirety of Durkheim's sociological project was closely bound up with philosophical concerns, the nature of the connection remains somewhat murky. Sociology was not a distinct academic field in France until Durkheim helped make it so. As *The Division of Labor* (1893) and *Suicide* (1896) make clear, his effort to carve out its unique domain involved differentiating sociology from economics and empirical psychology. Even more important, however, given the intellectual and institutional realities of the day, was the work Durkheim did to highlight sociology's distinctness from – and importance to – academic philosophy, which at the time encompassed, in addition to more familiar concerns, psychology cum philosophical anthropology, political theory, and methodology. As John Brooks points out,[9] it was philosophers who served on Durkheim's dissertation committee and philosophers who, wielding tremendous power within the French educational system, held the key to the institutionalization of a new discipline. Philosophers were thus a primary target audience for Durkheim's now classic statements about the nature of sociology, his injunctions about the method it should follow, and his substantive efforts to demonstrate the explanatory leverage one could get over a wide range of phenomena by taking account of what he termed the "sui generis" reality of the social. Philosophical interests also lay back of his more general project of mobilizing sociological investigation for the purpose of developing an ethics. Toward the end of his career, Durkheim's attempts to persuade philosophers of the significance of sociology became especially pronounced, as he developed a sociology of religion and a sociology of knowledge in part to shed new light on longstanding metaphysical and epistemological debates. But key questions about Durkheim's engagement with philosophy remain unanswered, not least for those who aim to fold Durkheimian insights into contemporary sociological theory. How

---

9. Brooks, "The Definition of Sociology and the Sociology of Definition," 385.

exactly should we understand the relationship between Durkheim's sociology and his ethics?[10] To what extent does acknowledgment of the external and constraining nature of social facts imply a deterministic vision of the social universe?[11] And how can a sociological account of the origins of the categories of understanding – that is, "time, space, number, cause, substance, personality"[12] – such as that developed by Durkheim in *Primitive Classification* (1903, written with Marcel Mauss) and in *The Elementary Forms* (1912) be articulated from a rationalist[13] standpoint and also square with sophisticated renderings of the apriorist position, which would explain the categories as originating in the very nature of the mind?[14] It would be helpful in answering these and other questions to have a fuller statement of Durkheim's philosophical views. Ideally, such a statement would have issued from the pen of the mature Durkheim as he sought to clear up confusions and misconceptions left by the wayside in the course of his pathbreaking work. Less desirable, certainly, but still of considerable value would be an accounting of his philosophical outlook from an earlier point in his career. For reasons described below, his *lycée* lectures would have been precisely such an accounting.

Second, to know more about what Durkheim's ideas were in the years right after he left the École Normale would be to have considerable information about when and in what sociointellectual context the idea for a genuinely empirical science of sociology was born in France. An important question for contemporary sociological theory, especially various strains of critical theory, is, under what conditions do intellectuals (and those they influence) begin to doubt the atomistic social metaphysics that often passes as common sense and replace it with an empirically informed understanding that the history of human affairs

---

10. For interesting recent discussions of this, see Hans Joas, *The Creativity of Action*, trans. Jeremy Gaines and Paul Keast (Chicago: University of Chicago Press, 1996), 49–65; W. Watts Miller, *Durkheim, Morals, and Modernity* (Montreal: McGill–Queen's University Press, 1996).
11. See Jeffrey C. Alexander, *Theoretical Logic in Sociology*, vol. 2. (Berkeley: University of California Press, 1982).
12. Emile Durkheim, *The Elementary Forms of Religious Life*, trans. Karen Fields (New York: The Free Press, 1995), 8.
13. On the question of Durkheim's rationalism, see Robert Alun Junes, "Ambivalent Cartesians: Durkheim, Montesquieu, and Method," *American Journal of Sociology* 100 (1994), 1–39.
14. See Terry Godlove, "Epistemology in Durkheim's *Elementary Forms of Religious Life*," *Journal of the History of Philosophy* 24 (1986), 385–41.

is in large part a history of how social structures, forms, and processes have shaped people's destinies?[15] Given the power of these entities, to ask the question of when their force comes to be acknowledged is to ask nothing less than what are the preconditions for social autonomy, even if it is recognized that an awareness of the social can lead as easily to heightened control as to autonomization. Among those who are interested in classical theory in part because it represents, as a whole, the premier instance where a number of profound, enduring, and empirically oriented social-theoretical projects crystalized almost at once out of the predisciplinary contributions of figures like Montesquieu, August Comte, and Herbert Spencer, there is widespread agreement as to what conditions brought it about: Classical theory is generally seen as an outgrowth of the process of European modernization that it took as its central problematic.[16]

But this understanding, which identifies various and sundry large-scale social and cultural transformations – industrialization, functional differentiation, urbanization, secularization, individualization, etc. – said to have somehow brought theoretical attention to the social, turns out to be quite incomplete. Not only is the causal argument implied by such an exclusively macrolevel angle of vision called into question by concurrent intellectual trends that ran in the opposite direction (for example, the growth of the entirely atomistic "bourgeois economics" on which Karl Marx heaped so much invective), but the approach ignores the possibility that it might have been in much more local contexts[17] – certain kinds of families, particular educational experiences, participation in social movements, etc. – that the sociological worldviews of the classical theorists actually took shape. To explore the role of such local contexts – which are, of course, themselves structured by larger forces – in the development of classical theory, detailed sociobiographical information about the classical theorists would be required. Especially important would be knowledge of exactly when and in what circumstances

15. For a useful discussion of this point, see Craig Calhoun, *Critical Social Theory* (Oxford: Blackwell, 1995).
16. Anthony Giddens, in *Capitalism and Modern Social Theory* (Cambridge, Cambridge University Press, 1971), xi, thus gave expression to a widely held view when he argued that "if Renaissance Europe gave rise to a concern with history, it was industrial Europe which provided the conditions for the emergence of sociology."
17. For a discussion of this point, see Charles Camic, *Experience and Enlightenment: Socialization for Cultural Change in Eighteenth-Century Scotland* (Chicago: University of Chicago Press, 1983).

they began to attend to the distinctive nature of social reality. But this is a matter that Durkheim scholars, for their part, have had a hard time pinning down. Did Durkheim's dislike for the "dilettantism" and over-interest in classical letters of his fellow students at the École Normale, described in the recollections of his acquaintances, signal already a commitment to empirical social science? Should we follow Mauss in dating this commitment to 1881?[18] Or did Durkheim's vision of sociology, adumbrated in a number of essays published between 1885 and 1892 and then articulated more fully in his Latin thesis on Montesquieu (1892) and in *The Division of Labor* (1893), develop later in his intellectual career, perhaps after his celebrated study trip to Germany in 1885–6 or around the time he arrived at the University of Bordeaux in 1887 to take a position created just for him in social science and pedagogy? Given the lack of first-hand knowledge of Durkheim's early views, it has been impossible to say.

The Unfamiliarity of a New Manuscript

In 1995, however, nearly eight decades after Durkheim's death, a new manuscript surfaced that shed considerable light on what had previously been the great unknown of the early Durkheim. Librarians at the Sorbonne, asked by one of the editors and translators of this volume (Gross) to look through their collection for material relating to a later period in Durkheim's life, came across a neatly handwritten document, more than 500 pages in length, entitled "E. Durkheim – Lectures on philosophy given at the Lycée de Sens in 1883–4 (The end, which he did not give because he was appointed to St. Quentin, was recovered from the notes of a student of 1882–3)." The manuscript was apparently penned in the hand of André Lalande, best known during his lifetime for authoring a philosophical dictionary[19] that went through multiple editions and whose definitions were actively debated by members of the French philosophical community. As mentioned previously, Lalande had been one of Durkheim's students at Sens. He died in 1963. His papers were later donated to the Sorbonne, and it was in this collection that the manuscript was found. Remarkably, the document is transcription-like

18. See the discussion in Jeffrey C. Alexander, *Structure and Meaning: Relinking Classical Sociology* (New York: Columbia University Press, 1989), 126.
19. André Lalande, *Vocabulaire technique et critique de la philosophie* (Paris: F. Alcan, 1928).

in nature; rather than recording mere fragments of ideas, each of the eighty individual lectures of which it consists is a continuous narrative made up of complete and for the most part grammatical sentences. Every lecture is preceded by a detailed outline of its contents.

Shortly after the discovery of this manuscript, it was typed and posted in French to the Durkheim Web site[20] maintained by the other editor and translator of this volume (Jones). Four of the eighty lectures were simultaneously published in the journal *Durkheimian Studies*.[21] Almost immediately, Durkheim scholars began to analyze the lectures. John Brooks, a historian, used them to bolster the argument he had already been developing that despite what conventional histories of sociology tell us, the positivism of August Comte was not the main fountainhead for Durkheim's ideas, or for the French human sciences more generally. Comte argued that study of the relationship between what he called social "statics" and "dynamics" – that is, the relationship between order and progress – would ultimately yield insight into the workings of the mind and usher in a new social and political era. Against the view that the human sciences in France owe their greatest debt to this vision, Brooks marshaled various pieces of historical evidence, including the Sens lectures, to show that another crucial source lay in the "eclectic spiritualism" of philosopher Victor Cousin, whose dual ideas that truth could best be obtained by reconciling the competing philosophical systems developed over the years and that all matter is thinking substance mesmerized the French philosophical field for much of the nineteenth century.[22] Warren Schmaus, agreeing with Brooks's assessment, took the Sens lectures as the starting point for a reanalysis of Durkheim's theory of the origins of the categories of understanding.[23] And Jones himself pointed to one of the most intriguing things about the lectures – the fact that, as is also discussed below, they contain no hint of the social realism that would so soon become synonymous with Durkheimian sociology – as support for his view that it was, above all, Durkheim's exposure to the empirical investigations of psychologist and protosociologist Wilhelm Wundt and other German scholars that allowed him to

20. www.relst.uiuc.edu/Durkheim
21. See Neil Gross, "Durkheim's Lectures at Sens," *Durkheimian Studies* 2 (1996), 1–4.
22. Brooks, *Eclectic Legacy*.
23. Warren Schmaus, *Rethinking Durkheim and His Tradition* (Cambridge: Cambridge University Press, 2004).

advance decisively beyond the intellectual perspectives on which he had been reared.[24]

That more researchers still have not folded a reading of Durkheim's Sens lectures into their understanding of his corpus is probably a function of two things. First, the vast majority of the lectures have never appeared in print, and none has ever appeared in English translation. Second, even those scholars who read French and who might have examined the version of the lectures published on the Web would have found them extremely challenging to get through – not because of the complexity of the language but because of their rather cumbersome style. There is no evidence that the lectures were ever intended for publication or edited in any way by Durkheim. Moreover, there are very few corrections in the handwritten manuscript, which leads one to assume that Lalande wrote it out on the basis of shorthand notes taken in the classroom. It is therefore likely that the writing style is more Lalande's than Durkheim's own. Lalande's subsequent stature as a chronicler of philosophy offers some reassurance that the notes of this very young man accurately record the substance of Durkheim's course, but no one who has ever graded a freshman college essay – and Lalande would have been about two years younger than a freshman at the time – should be surprised to find that the French notes are often repetitive and their style formal and stilted, if nevertheless charming.

But this is not the only thing about the lectures that might surprise readers. Indeed, even after they are edited for style, as they have been in the present volume, something disconcerting about them remains: namely, how utterly strange they are as compared to Durkheim's later work. Whereas the characteristic feature of Durkheimian sociology is the attempt to explain social phenomena as a function of social morphology – Durkheim's term for social organization – the Sens lectures contain no reference whatsoever to functional relationships of this kind. In fact, except for a few entirely conventional remarks about the division of labor and the family, there is almost no discussion of social structures at all, and not a single mention of sociology, in the entire text. Whereas Durkheim is known as a forerunner in the use of statistical and ethnographic data to formulate and empirically ground social-theoretical claims, the Durkheim of the Sens lectures endorses no more than what I term below a "pro forma" empiricism, insisting

---

24. Robert Alun Jones, *The Development of Durkheim's Social Realism* (Cambridge: Cambridge University Press, 1999).

early on in the lecture course that philosophy is a science and that all sciences should study their subject matters experimentally, but then retreating into introspection or argument by anecdote when actually advancing substantive claims in such areas as psychology and ethics. Whereas Durkheim would later offer a provocative and controversial theory of the social wellsprings of religious sentiment, thereby indirectly proclaiming his own atheism, in the Sens lectures, as Schmaus points out,[25] he is quite willing to throw his weight behind a philosophical proof of God's existence. Finally, the Sens lectures find Durkheim, who is widely – though not necessarily correctly – heralded as an important precursor to poststructuralism and its insistence that there is a significant social component to reason, espousing essentialism and fully supporting an apriorist view of the origin of the categories of understanding.

This shocking unfamiliarity raises two important questions. First, how confident can one be in the authenticity of the notes? Perhaps the Sens lecturer appears so un-Durkheimian because he was someone other than Durkheim. Second, even if the question of authenticity is answered in the affirmative, how certain can one be that the views expressed in the lectures were actually Durkheim's own and that he was not simply teaching according to some preestablished formula?

The Matter of Authenticity

With respect to authenticity, there is no way to be absolutely certain. In his address on the centennial of Durkheim's birth, however, Lalande did – without mentioning the notes – say a few things about the lecture course at Sens that are consistent with the manuscript discovered at the Sorbonne. First, he recalled that Durkheim's teaching was characterized by "a systematic order in investigations and a strong organization of ideas."[26] Of course, this describes the pedagogical style of every good teacher. But it is not irrelevant to observe that this recollection is at least consistent with the style of the present volume. Although, as noted earlier, the lectures can be repetitive, on the whole the text does a remarkable job of proceeding systematically and thoroughly through the topics it takes up, typically considering and rejecting numerous alternative

---

25. Warren Schmaus, *Review of Durkheim's Sens Lectures*, http://www.relst.uiuc.edu/durkheim/Reviews/Sens.Schmaus.html
26. Lalande, "Commémoration du centenaire de la naissance d'Emile Durkheim," 24.

theories before going on to propose one of its own – a style of argumentation for which Durkheim's published works are also well known. Second, in the same address, Lalande noted that Durkheim had a habit of going to the blackboard at the end of each lesson, "and there he reconstructed [its]... outline, consisting of titles or short hierarchical formulas which concretized for his listeners the structure of what he had just explained freely and in a continuous fashion."[27] This recollection, too, is consistent with the document found at the Sorbonne. To save space, these outlines have not been included in the present volume, but they are there in the original manuscript and neatly synopsize the author's main points. Interested readers are encouraged to examine the version of the lectures posted on-line.[28] Third, Lalande said not only that Durkheim's students had been fond of him but also that, after Durkheim left Sens in 1884 for the Lycée de Saint-Quentin, "most of those [students] who remained borrowed the class notes compiled by comrades from the preceding year, and copied the lessons they lacked."[29] This is precisely what the title page of the manuscript also states. Finally, Lalande remembered that "in one of his early lessons [Durkheim]... cited on several occasions the name of Schopenhauer, completely unknown to almost all his young listeners."[30] Sure enough, lecture 7 of the manuscript contains a discussion – a quite critical discussion – of Schopenhauer's pessimism. None of this definitively establishes that Durkheim and the Sens lecturer were one, but it does create a very strong presumption in favor of this conclusion, especially given that we are not aware of anyone else who is even a plausible candidate for authorship.

At the same time, there are features of the lectures that *do* appear to be foreshadowings of Durkheim's later views. For example, the philosophy of science Durkheim endorsed in 1883–4 anticipates in certain respects the social realist perspective that would be articulated most fully in *The Rules of Sociological Method* (1895). In that book, Durkheim urged would-be sociologists to treat social facts as real "things," subject to their own laws, and argued that a field of inquiry (like sociology) deserves to be called an independent science if the object and laws it studies are

27. Ibid.
28. The outlines, still in French, are at http://www.relst.uiuc.edu/Durkheim/Texts/1884a/00.html
29. Lalande, "Commémoration du centenaire de la naissance d'Emile Durkheim," 25.
30. Ibid.

distinct from the objects and laws studied by all the other established sciences. Scholars have long argued that Durkheim's thinking on this matter was influenced by the ideas of one of his teachers at the École Normale, the neo-Kantian philosopher Emile Boutroux.[31] Boutroux insisted that each science studies a unique realm of being. Although he conceived of these realms to be interdependent, his position was that each is relatively autonomous, operating according to its own principles – a position he took as a way to counter various forms of determinism, for if what happens in one realm is not strictly determinable by what happens in the next, then the world must not consist of endless and unbreakable chains of necessary cause-and-effect relationships but must rather be a place open to indeterminacy and contingency. In the Sens lectures, as was pointed out earlier, Durkheim makes no move in the direction of recognizing that the social, too, is a distinct realm of reality that deserves to be studied by its own science – sociology. But he does throw his support behind a conception of science quite similar to that advanced by Boutroux – and by himself in *The Rules*. Not only, Durkheim observes, must a science study an object that is subject to either the law of causality or the law of identity and have some method it uses to gain access to this object, but "a science must have a suitable object of explanation. By suitable, we mean that the object isn't the focus of any other science, and that it is well defined" (lecture 3). To be sure, Boutroux was not the only thinker in the history of philosophy to have taken such a position; nor, given his influence, would it have been unusual to find any young *agrégé* at the time arguing along similar lines. Still, if the lectures were given by Durkheim, we would expect to see at least *some* points of overlap with his later thought, and this appears to be one such point.

It is not the only one. The essential analytic procedure of Durkheim's sociology of religion, which began to take shape after 1895, was not to dismiss outright the convictions of believers and explain religious sentiment as mere error or fantasy but rather to demand that the analyst take the phenomenology of those convictions as a point of departure and attempt to identify the social conditions that could have generated

31. Lukes cites the following from a 1907 letter by Durkheim: "I owe [Lukes adds: the distinction between sociology and psychology] in the first place to my teacher M. Boutroux, who, at the École Normale Supérieure, often repeated to us that each science must explain by 'its own principles,' as Aristotle put it: psychology by psychological principles, biology by biological principles" (*Emile Durkheim*, 57).

them. This approach, Durkheim argued, held the greatest promise for locating the true social forces and dynamics at play in religiosity. The Sens manuscript contains no such sociology of religion. Yet the Sens lecturer, like the author of *The Elementary Forms*, is at great pains to convince his audience to forgo the urge simply to dismiss commonsense beliefs as erroneous. Mounting a critique of certain aspects of Cousin's philosophy, the lecturer argues – against the position, inspired by Thomas Reid, that philosophical disputes can always be decided by common sense – that while common sense has no "philosophical rigor" and is "nothing more than a collection of prejudices," still it must be "respected as a fact – one that has some rational foundation for existence. We might decide [a philosophical dispute] against common sense, but only on the specific condition that we show how its ideas developed and became popular" (lecture 2). Later in the course, in a discussion of certainty, the lecturer indicates that he regards religious conviction as falling within the domain of common sense. There are some matters, he argues, including "some of our political or religious opinions," where the strength of our certainty is much greater than the "purely logical considerations" that lay behind them. In such matters, which are the "most common in everyday life," our views are profoundly influenced by our "sensibility," which is a product of our "temperament, education, habits, and heredity" (lectures 39–40). So to explain a commonsense belief – an essential step in challenging it – is to show how the sensibility disposed so many minds toward believing it. It would hardly seem an impossible leap from here to the later position that would explain religious common sense as a function of a sensibility shaped by the experience of sociality and dramatized in moments of collective effervescence.

And it would be easy to multiply examples: The Sens lecturer has not discovered the language of social norms but clearly recognizes that not all of human behavior consists of a quest to rationally maximize one's utility; the Sens lecturer is far from considering the social correlates of suicide but, in arguing that suicide violates the moral law, acknowledges – as Jones points out[32] – that not every suicide is cowardly and driven by egoistic preoccupations, thus implicitly drawing the distinction between egoistic and altruistic suicide that would be so important in Durkheim's later work; the Sens lecturer, like the later Durkheim, is critical of Jean Jacques Rousseau's conception of society as an artificial construction on the grounds that humans are by nature social creatures; and so on. These

---

32. Jones, *Development of Durkheim's Social Realism*, 140.

points of continuity (and discontinuity) are enumerated not out of a desire to offer even a preliminary interpretation of the course of Durkheim's intellectual development but simply to show that the overall pattern of adumbration is consistent with the image of a slowly maturing intellectual vision, thereby bolstering the presumption that Durkheim was in fact the lecturer whose words are translated here.

Institutional Constraints on Durkheim's Freedom of Speech

But there remains another issue to consider: Even if (as seems likely) the Sens lecturer was in fact Durkheim, were the lectures given in an environment where he would have been free to express his own opinions? To answer this question, and also to provide a rough sketch of the context in which the lectures were delivered, something more will have to be said about the *classe de philosophie*.

The *lycées*, and within them the *classe*, played an important role in the nineteenth-century French educational system. The system had been charged with the task, since the Revolution, of advancing the Enlightenment causes of literacy, vocational training, the promulgation of democratic values, and the pursuit of learning and science. But it performed latent functions as well, including the intergenerational reproduction of class inequality. For nonaristocratic students whose socioeconomic backgrounds and gender destined them to occupy positions of social or cultural power, a *lycée* education was essential. Part and parcel of a developing system of credentialization, it prepared them for, among other things, taking the *baccalauréat* examination that was required for entry into the *université* or into any of the *grandes écoles* (e.g., the École Normale), which functioned as parallel institutions of higher education.[33] Credentials like the "bac" and the university diploma became the keys for entry into the ranks of the "state nobility"[34] and the growing French professional and managerial class. At the same time, the *lycées* legitimated the inequality they helped reproduce by endowing students with the cultural capital thought appropriate and necessary for those in the higher echelons of French society.

The *classe de philosophie* was particularly important in this regard. Theodore Zeldin has observed that the characteristic feature of an educated nineteenth-century Frenchman was "the way he used language,

33. Brooks, *Eclectic Legacy*.
34. Pierre Bourdieu, *The State Nobility: Elite Schools in the Field of Power*, trans. Lauretta Clough (Oxford: Polity, 1996).

the way he thought, the way he argued."[35] And this, in Zeldin's view, could be attributed to the education he had received in the *classe*. It was here that the French elite acquired "their characteristic abstract and pompous vocabulary, their skill in classification and synthesis, in solving problems by rearranging them verbally, their rationalism and scepticism – paradoxically conformist – and their ability to argue elegantly and apparently endlessly"[36] – all features that indelibly marked them for high stations in life.

It was in their final year of schooling that *lycéens* would enroll in the *classe de philosophie*, if not exempted from the requirement by virtue of aiming for a career as a scientist or engineer. The *classe* was a kind of capstone course in which students would be asked to mobilize all the knowledge and skills they had acquired up to that point for the purpose of understanding the contributions that philosophers had made over the centuries to the most pressing questions of human existence.

The *lycée* philosophy class took the form it would have in Durkheim's day in the 1830s and 1840s, during the so-called July Monarchy. It was then that political moderates – led by Cousin, who had first come to philosophical prominence in the 1820s – set their sights on the *classe*. For them, it would be a strategic point for the transmission of moderate liberal values and civic virtues to future members of the French elite, a safeguard against both radical republicanism and reactionary monarchism.

The key to control over this ideological state apparatus was centralization, which had been built into the system by Napoleon, during whose reign the *lycée* and *baccalauréat* structure emerged. Handpicked professors of philosophy in Paris would not only design questions for the philosophy portion of the exam but also put together the official syllabus that all *lycée* professors in the country were to follow. The latter would be evaluated on a regular basis by a corps of official inspectors – former *lycée* professors who traveled to various schools to make sure that the young *agrégé* teachers, or those who were teaching without proper credentials, were living up to their responsibilities.[37]

When Cousin assumed the only philosopher's chair on the Royal Council of Public Instruction in 1830, and subsequently became minister

---

35. Theodore Zeldin, *France, 1848–1945*, vol. 2, *Intellect, Taste, and Anxiety* (Oxford: Clarendon, 1977), 205.
36. Ibid., 207.
37. W. D. Halls, *Education, Culture and Politics in Modern France* (Oxford: Pergamon, 1976).

of public instruction, the director of the École Normale, and a member of the Acadamie Française, he set out to make sure that the philosophy syllabus reflected his own views. A constitutional monarchist, Cousin was no obvious son of the French Revolution. Yet his political philosophy insisted that rights are meaningless unless all individuals fully respect the rights of others, which, in a secularizing society, is to put a premium on the ethic of tolerance. The basis for this ethic, he believed, had to be established on nonreligious, philosophical grounds. His aim was thus "to create a society which rested on common and fraternal principles, without excluding the diversity of opinions and beliefs."[38] It was, in other words, to lay the groundwork for a secular morality.[39] Paul Janet has noted that for Cousin "the establishment of an independent philosophy curriculum was not only the consequence of the secular state; it was at the same time an instrument of propaganda for the principles of secularism."[40] His "middle-of-the-road" philosophy was "meant to offend neither Catholic nor atheist"; although "liberal," "proclaiming the principles of the French Revolution," it "would be opposed to republicanism."[41] Eclecticism meant moderatism:

> The nineteenth century, according to Cousin, was to avoid the extremes of the two preceding centuries, while carrying on to completion their lessons in truth. The excellence of the seventeenth

38. Phyllis Stock-Morton, *Moral Education for a Secular Society: The Development of Morale Laïque in Nineteenth-Century France* (Albany: State University of New York Press, 1988), 31.
39. Durkheim, of course, was deeply interested in the same project. He noted in *Moral Education*, trans. Everett Wilson and Herman Schnurer (New York: The Free Press, 1961), 3, that "[t]he last twenty years in France have seen a great educational revolution, which was latent and half-realized before then. We decided to give our children in our state-supported schools a purely secular moral education. It is essential to understand that this means an education that is not derived from revealed religion, but that rests exclusively on ideas, sentiments, and practices accountable to reason only – in short, a purely rationalistic education. Such a change could not take place without disturbing traditional ideas, disrupting old habits, entailing sweeping organizational changes, and without posing, in turn, new problems with which we must come to grips." See as well his extended discussion in *The Evolution of Educational Thought: Lectures on the Formation and Development of Secondary Education in France*, trans. Peter Collins (London: Routledge & Kegan Paul, 1977).
40. Paul Janet, *Victor Cousin et son oeuvre* (Paris: Alcan, 1885), 281–2.
41. Walter Vance Brewer, *Victor Cousin as a Comparative Educator* (New York: Teachers College Press, 1971), 30.

century – the emulation of the great qualities of character and the contemplation of the omnipresent God – and those of the eighteenth century – the awareness of man's free will, the concept of man's great role of progress on earth – must be combined in the nineteenth. This could be done under the aegis of a reign of political compromise, a constitutional monarchy.[42]

Despite the fact that many Catholics did perceive his philosophy to be a threat, Cousin and his followers – owing no doubt to their centrism and willingness to adjust to shifting political circumstances – managed to retain control over the philosophy syllabus for much of the remainder of the nineteenth century. The syllabus Cousin designed was divided into five sections: an introductory section followed by sections on psychology, logic, ethics, and the history of philosophy. In later years, the history of philosophy was folded into the other sections, and metaphysics, which on the 1832 syllabus had been included under ethics, came to compose a section of its own. The syllabus specified what topics or questions were to be treated under each of these headings. For example, the syllabus of 1880 indicated that the treatment of ethics was to cover speculative ethics, practical ethics (including domestic ethics, social ethics, religious ethics), and the elements of political economy. The syllabus also indicated what books should be read in conjunction with the class. In 1880, these included Plato's *Republic*, Aristotle's *Nicomachean Ethics*, Seneca's *De Vita Beata*, Cicero's *De Legibus*, Descartes' *Discourse on Method*, and Leibniz's *Monadology*.[43] In what now seems like an ingenious scheme, students were strongly encouraged to study for the philosophy portion of the *baccalauréat* by reading textbooks written by Cousin, his student Janet, or others who shared their views.

Cousin's program proved remarkably successful, not least in raising the status of philosophy, which had long been associated with theology but which, under his guidance, became an increasingly professionalized affair. With the establishment of the Third French Republic in 1870, however, new pressures arose that would greatly modify the curriculum Cousin put in place. Republicans had demanded for years an end to Catholic influence over education, but when the dust finally settled from France's humiliating defeat to Germany in the 1870–1 war, more

---

42. Ibid.
43. See Brooks, *Eclectic Legacy*, 252–4.

than half of all primary schools in the country remained Catholic.[44] Republicans laid the blame for the outcome of the war at the feet of Catholics and monarchists. In their view, the loss could be attributed to France's industrial and scientific backwardness relative to Germany, and Catholic involvement in education was seen as the stranglehold that had kept the country from moving forward.[45] The educational reforms called for by the Revolution had never been fully carried through, Republicans charged, and the ignominy of defeat was the price to be paid.

When Jules Ferry was appointed minister of education in 1879, he set out to construct the educational infrastructure of which Republicans had long dreamed. This was no small task. There were more than four million school-age children in France at the time, and to educate them all in free public schools would require the formation of thousands of new classes.[46] Under Ferry's direction, new schools were opened and existing schools expanded.[47] Some 70,000 new classrooms were built between 1882 and 1900,[48] and the teaching corps grew by nearly 14,000.[49] As a result, according to Halls, "by the turn of the century, no child, however remote his home, had to walk more than 2 kilometers to the nearest primary school."[50]

Hand in hand with infrastructural expansion came new legislation. A law of March 28, 1882, made school attendance compulsory for children aged 6–13 and established a system of fines for parents who refused to comply.[51] Legislation and administrative decrees further centralized control of the teaching curriculum, forbade teachers from engaging in any sort of religious instruction, and placed an emphasis on the teaching of ethics and civic morality. Church authorities were also denied the right, which they had exercised since 1850, to inspect and supervise public school teachers.[52] By 1886, members of the clergy were prohibited from teaching in public schools altogether.[53]

---

44. George Male, *Education in France* (Washington, D.C.: Department of Health, Education and Welfare, 1963), 16.
45. Halls, *Education, Culture and Politics in Modern France*, 7.
46. John Talbott, *The Politics of Educational Reform in France, 1918–1940* (Princeton: Princeton University Press, 1969), 29.
47. Ibid.
48. Male, *Education in France*, 17.
49. Talbott, *The Politics of Educational Reform*, 29.
50. Halls, *Education, Culture and Politics in Modern France*, 8.
51. Male, *Education in France*, 16.
52. Ibid.
53. Halls, *Education, Culture and Politics in Modern France*, 7.

Most of these reform energies were centered on primary education. But the *lycées* did not escape attention. Here Ferry pursued a two-pronged approach: "He tried to bring students in classical *lycées* in closer contact with those in the special secondary system by introducing 'modern' studies (science, history, geography, and modern literature) to the classical curriculum; simultaneously he sought to raise standards in the special secondary system by making studies more theoretical and less vocationally-oriented."[54] These reform efforts were not pursued out of an idle interest in change; they were based on the perceived exigencies of a shifting class structure. Ferry hoped that "both the traditional bourgeoisie and the emerging industrial and commercial middle classes would be exposed to a judicious mixture of literary studies – which developed moral, aesthetic, and spiritual qualities – and science, which taught observation and critical thinking. The combination would enable the elite classes to resist the attractions of inflamed political passions."[55]

Reform of the classical curriculum was tied to reform at the university level. A pressing need emerged for teachers who had been trained at the university or in the *grandes écoles* in "modern" subjects, and this required considerable expansion of the higher education infrastructure. State funding for higher education increased by more than 150 percent between 1869 and 1883;[56] more significant, under Louis Liard, director of higher education, a plan was put forward to decentralize the university system and to encourage local faculties to seek private funding for research and institution building. These increases in resources led to a gradual but uneven increase in the size of the faculties. With support from sectors of the business community, which hoped for immediate returns in the form of marketable technology, the faculties of science grew especially, but the social sciences fared well too, particularly as members of the law faculties began to reconceive of themselves as empirical social scientists. Empirical psychology, and then later sociology, expanded also, as competition for chairs in philosophy – where early practitioners were housed – lessened with the overall growth of positions.[57]

These institutional transformations had an important impact on the relative status of the various philosophical traditions and approaches that were jockeying for prominence within the French philosophical field. The major effect was a privileging of those strains of philosophy

54. George Weisz, *The Emergence of Modern Universities in France, 1863–1914* (Princeton: Princeton University Press, 1983), 127.
55. Ibid.
56. Ibid., 131.
57. Brooks, *Eclectic Legacy*, 142.

that purported to take the findings of the empirical human sciences seriously; in the new environment, these were coded as being on the side of progress. Eclectic spiritualism came to seem rather old-fashioned. To be sure, Cousin had conceived of philosophy as a science and insisted that its point of departure was psychology. But for him the proper method of psychology was introspection. And while he made gestures in the direction of incorporating some kind of observational procedure into the study of ethics and logic, his assumption was that these domains of inquiry were "in principle independent of the contingencies of human history and society."[58]

In part for these reasons, attacks on eclectic spiritualism mounted, and non-Cousinians stepped up to offer their own approaches as alternatives. Comtean positivists, who had been sidelined during Cousin's tenure, sought to replace absolute laws of ethics with the laws appropriate for societies given their stage of development in Comte's tripartite philosophy of history, wherein they were said to progress from being theologically to metaphysically to positivistically oriented. Positivists of a more psychological persuasion, like Théodule Ribot, argued for the empirical study of consciousness, a consideration of its relationship to physiology, and a discussion of the philosophical implications of psychopathology. And even neo-Kantians like Charles Renouvier, eager to preserve the notion of freedom of will in the face of scientific advances that might bolster the case for determinism, called for more empirical investigations of psychological phenomena. Renouvier's caveat, however, was that such investigations must recognize that there is an ineliminable element of indeterminacy built into consciousness at the moment when the mind decides under what "category" of relation it wishes to subsume the object of consciousness.[59] Not only did each of these positions gain adherents at eclecticism's expense, together they signaled a growing diversification of the philosophical field.

Such were the institutional and intellectual realities that Durkheim would have had to navigate in preparing his lecture course of 1883–4. Among the philosophers who composed his professional reference group, empirical social science was very much in the air, but eclectic spiritualism, though under attack, remained the entrenched position. At the same time, insofar as the lessons he was to teach offered instruction in civic morality, they would have been quite controversial in Sens, where "local life between 1880 and 1914 was constantly marked by the

---

58. Ibid., 63.
59. Ibid., esp. 151–2.

clerical question,"[60] and where everyone associated with the Republican program was accused by the vocal Catholic press of undermining the morality of the country by creating a "Godless school." In this unsettled disciplinary field and charged local environment, Durkheim would also have realized how important it was for his career to walk a tightrope between originality and conformism: career advancement depended in part on showing creativity in the presentation of classroom material as assessed by ministry inspectors, but originality could not come at the cost of failing to fulfill one's responsibilities as a teacher of an established curriculum. How constrained would he have felt, under pressure to prepare his students to take the standardized exam, to rein in his own philosophical views and toe instead what he might have perceived to be the philosophical party line?

The safest assumption is that he would indeed have felt constrained both topically and substantively. As for topical constraints, it is clear that he had to cover all the topics listed on the syllabus, even if they were not ones in which he himself had much interest. This is a major constraint, not least because the limited duration of the course would have meant that other topics to which he might have wished to devote greater attention would necessarily have been squeezed out. It cannot be known what these topics, if any, would have been, but it is certainly possible that if Durkheim had unlimited time he might have given greater attention to, among other things, the nascent social sciences and their relationship to philosophy.

With regard to substantive constraints, it is likely that the major pressure Durkheim was under was to avoid expressing views that were too radical or idiosyncratic. Despite the fact that the tide of positivism was already beginning to rise, this pressure might well have been enough to dissuade Durkheim from discussing at great length any sociological identity he might have then had, especially given that at such an early stage of his career he would not yet have developed a sophisticated and credible way of doing so.

But while these constraints together may have kept Durkheim from making sociology a central focus of the lecture course, it is doubtful – had sociology been for him a major preoccupation at the time – that they would have kept him from mentioning it at all, or that they would have prevented him from endorsing one position rather than another

---

60. Louis Cailleaux and Denis Cailleaux, *Sens de la Belle Epoque à la Libération* (Le Mée-sur-Seine: Editions Ammatéis, 1995), 11.

from within the slate of more or less conventional philosophical views under consideration by his contemporaries. For example, it is hard to see how it would have been out of place for Durkheim to briefly mention something about the difference between mechanical and organic solidarity – if he had had the idea at the time – when discussing the division of labor, or at least to touch on the notion of variation in social conventions when asserting, as he does in lecture 64, that the Germans, French, Spanish, Italians, and Swiss each have their own "ends" that it is their duty to pursue. In both instances, Durkheim veers close enough to a social-scientific point of view that it is difficult to see how going one or two steps further could have made much difference in how his lectures would have been received. To take another example, it is difficult to imagine how Durkheim could have gotten in trouble with the inspectors for endorsing a fuller version of the still important eclectic spiritualism rather than, as he actually does, embracing only the spiritualistic and introspective sides of Cousin's philosophy while rejecting the view that philosophical moderatism and common sensism hold the key to unlocking truth. Neither position would have seemed extreme or bizarre, given the increasing heterogeneity of the philosophical field at the time. These examples, which could easily be multiplied, thus tend to suggest the same thing: that the constraints of Durkheim's institutional position would not, in all likelihood, have prevented him from injecting *something*, if not something substantial, of his own views into the lecture course. Indeed, if Durkheim had zero degrees of freedom, and if all *lycée* philosophy classes were essentially the same, it becomes tough to explain why students like Lalande so hung on his every word or how Durkheim could possibly have demonstrated the kind of originality that was expected of aspiring academics. This assessment is consistent with that of Jean-Lous Fabiani, who has argued that nineteenth-century *lycée* professors did in fact have considerable latitude in how they covered the material specified on the official program.[61]

At the same time, the fact that Durkheim did experience topical constraints must be seen as a double-edged phenomenon from the standpoint of Durkheim scholarship. While Durkheim scholars would certainly be interested in knowing what philosophical topics he would have lectured on at that point in his career had it been entirely up to him, the fact is that the syllabus represented a crystallization of everything on which

---

61. See Jean-Louis Fabiani, *Les philosophes de la République* (Paris: Les Éditions de Minuit, 1988).

young philosophers were supposed to have views. So to have a record of what Durkheim likely thought about each and every one of these topics – which range from the nature of philosophy itself to the objectivity of the idea of externality to evolutionism, the unconscious, aesthetics, habit, logic, the origins of language, Kantian ethics, etc. – is to have a fairly complete indication of where he stood vis-à-vis his philosophical contemporaries. It therefore seems reasonable to view the lectures as a kind of murky baseline in relation to which Durkheim's subsequent intellectual development can be measured. Where the Sens lecturer seems especially un-Durkheimian – for example, in his discussion of metaphysical proofs of God's existence – one might be tempted to suspect that here Durkheim was running up against the constraints faced by a young *agrégé* trying to prepare his students for their exam; but it is possible, too, that these really were his early views. We will never know for sure. What is clear is that, given these constraints, readers should be circumspect in interpreting the lectures contained in the present volume without allowing their interest in preserving an unvarnished image of Durkheim to keep them from entertaining the possibility that his views underwent even more change over time than is usually acknowledged, and not simply in the direction – as has often been noted – of placing greater analytic weight as his career unfolded on the cultural rather than material dimensions of social life.

Central Themes in the Lectures

Given the somewhat sprawling nature of Durkheim's course, it may be useful at this point to identify some of the thematic chords that are struck in it repeatedly and to which readers may wish to pay special attention. Three such chords stand out for their centrality, though a fuller interpretation of the lectures than can be offered here would no doubt identify others as well.

The first has already been touched upon: Durkheim's empiricism. As he would do later in his career as well, Durkheim in the Sens lectures strongly rejects the empiricism of John Stuart Mill on various grounds: that its emphasis on the observation, recording, and classification of facts is inattentive to the active role played by the creative mind in formulating hypotheses; that its argument that the fundamental principles of reason have their origin in experience actually rests on that which empiricism seeks to challenge, namely, the apriori givenness of those same principles; that there is no justification for its reductionism vis-à-vis sensory stimuli, and so forth. Yet Durkheim also strongly endorses a more generic form of empiricism: the view that philosophy must take account of the actual workings of the aspects of the world of interest to it and that observation is the key to doing so. More specifically, Durkheim holds that philosophy is the study of the states of consciousness and their conditions. For him, "inner man" is the axis around which all philosophical questions turn (lecture 1). But inner man, Durkheim insists, cannot be understood merely through the abstract positing of essential qualities. For these qualities follow their own laws, which can be ascertained only through experimentation.

Durkheim means something quite specific by experimentation, however. Although he views psychology as an essential component of philosophy, he does not mean to insist that philosophical experimentation be reduced to psychological experimentation, at least where the latter is understood to center on the quantitative measurement of sensation and its correlates. In fact, he is extremely skeptical in the lectures of the approach to psychological research taken by scholars like Gustav Fechner, Ernst Weber, and even Wundt, who were all very much concerned to carry out such measurement in laboratory settings. The problem with the work of Fechner and Weber, according to Durkheim, is that psychological phenomena, unlike physical and physiological phenomena, occur only in time, not in space, which makes measurement of the intensity of sensation impossible, because the measurement of forces ultimately reduces to the measurement of movement, which cannot occur outside of space. Wundt's approach, for its part, is subject to the criticism that it is concerned only with the relationship between psychological phenomena and the physiological environments in which they transpire and thus fails to reveal much of anything about the specific nature of psychological phenomena in themselves. These latter, Durkheim argues, are best studied not by means of measurement but by "observation through consciousness," which qualifies as experimental inasmuch as it aims to test preconceived hypotheses and which has as its goal to get to know psychological phenomena "intimately, make an exact inventory of them, describe them, and reduce them to a certain number of general types" (lecture 5). Durkheim goes to great lengths to defend the notion that introspective observation is a valid way to obtain knowledge about states of consciousness, showing his indebtedness to Cousin by arguing that the effective use of introspection by writers, poets, and artists over the centuries is a testament to the fact that its acuity may be honed. He also allows, however, that philosophy may supplement observation through consciousness with the materials of history, broadly understood, for these may furnish the philosopher with information about the workings of consciousness under conditions so extraordinary that they permit certain fundamental questions to be resolved. This is what he has in mind when, in his critique of Herbert Spencer's evolutionary account of the genesis of reason, he refers to the fact that the "uncivilized peoples" of which Spencer has knowledge do not lack the principles of reason "or possess ... them to a lesser degree" than do Europeans; that this is so shows, in a way that introspection never could, that these principles are universal and given by the very nature of the mind (lecture 22). Durkheim makes a similar move in his discussion of morality, where he uses material on the history of the family to support his theory of domestic ethics and also makes passing reference to the ineffectiveness of punishment as a deterrent to crime in order to lend credibility to the approach to civic ethics he wants to advance.

The important thing to point out about Durkheim's empiricism here is that it is very different from the sociological empiricism to which he eventually turned, where introspective observation by consciousness gives way to the privileging of statistical data, much more detailed historical information, and ethnographic observation. In fact, given Durkheim's emphasis on introspection – an observational procedure that would seem to be intrinsically subjective – it is fair to describe his empiricism in the 1883–4 lectures as pro forma in nature, as was suggested above: an empiricism that claims the mantle of science without burdening itself with the rigors of methodical data collection. That this is so suggests that Durkheim's methodological views underwent a rapid and profound change in the second half of the 1880s. Whether this move was independent of his move toward social realism, or closely bound up with it, is difficult to say.

Moving from methodology to substantive theorizing, a second theme becomes evident: the irreducibility of consciousness to intelligence. Although Durkheim rejects altogether the idea of unconscious psychic phenomena, he does take the view that consciousness is not simply an intellectual or cognitive affair, a matter of having ideas, but also comprises the faculties of activity and sensibility. In the perspective he lays out as the lectures unfold, intellectual life occurs alongside the tendency of human beings to seek pleasure in "free and varied activity" (lecture 7), to give expression to altruistic inclinations (lecture 8), to experience and share the "disinterested" pleasure of beauty (lecture 30), to be guided by instinct (lecture 33) and habit (lecture 34), and, as discussed below, to fulfill the functions for which they were made.

What is striking about this view from the standpoint of contemporary sociological theory is not simply that we can surmise, on the basis of it, that Durkheim would have disapproved of the more cognitive versions of rational choice theory, which explain many different aspects of human behavior by treating them as functions of a utilitarian intelligence at work.[62] More surprising, in light of how his sociology has come to be viewed through the prism of Talcott Parsons' *The Structure of Social Action* (1937), is Durkheim's staunch refusal to court any form of reductionism with respect to the nature of action. Parsons argued that Durkheim and Max Weber, among others, had converged in their efforts to found sociology on the study of "residual categories" of action – that is, those forms of action in which calculations of utility, the purview of economics, are not entirely determinative. According to Parsons, the residual category to which Durkheim paid the greatest attention is that of action influenced by social norms, and, on the basis of this induction of Durkheim into the sociological canon, one of his greatest contributions to sociology has been seen to lie in his emphasis on action's normative dimension. As has been repeatedly stressed, norms are not yet a part of Durkheim's theoretical vocabulary at the time of the Sens lectures, but what is equally remarkable in this early stage of his career is how far he is from focusing his energies on any single category of action, much less any category understood as residual. To the contrary, Durkheim insists on preserving the complexity and richness of the action situation. If this is a correct interpretation, and if the later, more sociological Durkheim retains any trace of his earlier thinking on the matter, it would suggest that his emphasis on norms in *The Division of Labor* and elsewhere may have been an example, not of an insistence that norms are the be-all and end-all for explaining human behavior, but simply of the kind of "analytical" reduction Parsons himself often tried to employ – that is, a reduction in the complexity of

---

62. In his discussion of Kantian morality (lecture 59), Durkheim does aver that "giving the word 'interest' an expansive definition... it's clearly impossible for man to act without having some interest in his actions. A maxim of action that doesn't work on us through some motive will necessarily be ineffective." But here "interest" means no more than a motive of some kind. There is no suggestion that human beings always or even usually act in accordance with calculations of their interests.

the action model that is performed for specific heuristic purposes only and that should give way when fuller accounts of the phenomenon are attempted.

But the implication of this is certainly not that Durkheim was opposed in principle to developing simplified scientific models of the world. Although he argues in the lectures that "everything we know leads us to believe that multiplicity and diversity are the nature of the world," he also holds that "the mind finds great satisfaction in bringing unity to things. Multiplicity goes against its nature, and there's nothing it finds more displeasing" (lecture 22). More than simply a philosophy of mind, however, this credo gives expression to a larger metaphysical stance that represents a theme no less central than the two previously mentioned: namely, Durkheim's finalism. On topic after topic he falls back on the metaphysical claim that each entity has an end for which it has been made, not necessarily by an intelligent designer but simply as a result of how the universe has come to be arranged. "Nature has a certain plan," he observes in his discussion of the method of the natural sciences, a "design," and the basis of this design is the "principle of finality," according to which nature "assigns" to all "things" certain ends (lecture 51). Given indeterminacy and contingency in the universe, things do not always move toward the ends for which they have been made. On these grounds, Durkheim rejects the principle of "immanent finality" (lecture 77). But they would do best *to* move toward these ends, Durkheim is often at pains to argue, for when they do, they achieve the best that is possible for them. In the Sens lectures, Durkheim thus gave expression to an essentialist philosophy that had its roots in antiquity.[63]

Traces of Durkheim's finalism can be found scattered throughout the lecture course, but one place where it has an especially important role to play is in his discussion of the origins of reason, where he insists, against the empiricists, that "the mind could never have been a *tabula rasa*, now or centuries ago. It's always had its own nature and, as the expression of this, its own laws – not to mention reason, which is the totality of these laws. There's something innate in the mind – itself,

---

63. For a discussion of Durkheim's essentialism in his later work, see Warren Schmaus, "Explanation and Essence in *The Rules of Sociological Method* and *The Division of Labor in Society*," *Sociological Perspectives* 38 (1995), 57–75; Douglas Challenger, *Durkheim through the Lens of Aristotle: Durkheimian, Postmodernist, and Communitarian Responses to the Enlightenment* (Lanham, Md.: Rowman and Littlefield, 1994).

its nature" (lecture 22). To be sure, in *The Elementary Forms*, where Durkheim advances the argument that our conceptions of the categories of understanding such as time, space, and causality bear the imprint of social experience, he never denies that there are some qualities all minds have in common by virtue of their very nature. Yet no one familiar with that book could fail to observe the tremendous distance between the position staked out there and Durkheim's stance in the Sens lectures, which seems much closer to the apriorist view he was later at such pains to argue against. "Since reason can't be derived from experience," Durkheim notes in 1883–4, "rational ideas and principles must be innate within us" (lecture 22). But this early apriorism does not appear to be derived in a straightforward way from the philosophy of Immanuel Kant. Whereas Kant's transcendental idealism – as Durkheim understands it, anyway[64] – holds that the principles of reason have only subjective value because they inevitably denature sensory experience, placing the noumenal world beyond our experiential grasp, Durkheim argues that the mind, whose greatest satisfaction lies in "understanding," would simply not have been made in such a way as to have its intellectual goals continually frustrated. From the vantage point of Durkheim's finalism, it is unthinkable that there should be "an antinomy rather than a harmony between the mind and things." The distinction between the noumenal and phenomenal worlds is therefore untenable. Although "the mind is something definite whose forms are immutable," and although "there exist objects whose nature is no less determined," the proper conclusion to be drawn "is that knowledge is a synthesis of these two constitutive elements" (lecture 22). It is thus Durkheim's finalism that, for him, gives objective value to the principles of reason.

But it is not only in this context that finalism makes a significant appearance in the lectures. As Jones has insisted,[65] finalism is also fundamental to Durkheim's ethics. Indeed, finalism is the very basis for his understanding of the moral law, discussed in lecture 60:

> What is our duty? It's to do that for which we're made. Here I don't mean an end determined by some higher power, only that we're fashioned in a certain way, disposed toward some actions and unfit

64. Warren Schmaus, in *Rethinking Durkheim and His Tradition*, argues convincingly that this represents a fundamental misinterpretation of Kant, one that was passed down to Durkheim by way of Cousin and the German philosopher Friedrich Heinrich Jacobi, with whom Cousin briefly studied.
65. Jones, *Development of Durkheim's Social Realism*.

for others. The same is true of us as of other things, that we should do what we're good at. So the question we have to ask is: What is man's proper employment? The answer to this question will be the moral law itself.

But what, Durkheim asks, is the end of a person? It is to develop her or his personality, which means actualizing to their fullest all the potentialities one is endowed with by nature. This in turn presupposes the capacity to act freely. So the moral law demands that all individuals be given the opportunity – that is, the freedom – to develop their personalities and commands each person to prioritize this development when confronted with a problematic moral situation. This is not, Durkheim argues, a recipe for egoism and selfishness, because the development of our personalities cannot be allowed to interfere with the development of the personalities of others and because our own development is contingent upon the maintenance of a sustaining web of social relationships – principally relationships with members of our family and our fellow citizens. In all situations, therefore, it is incumbent upon the individual to strike a balance between developing her or his personality and acting in such a way as to facilitate such development in others.

In light of Durkheim's emphasis elsewhere in the lectures on the intrinsic creativity of the human mind, it might be tempting to read his call for enabling the full development of the personality as akin to Marx's call for a redistribution of wealth that would make possible the fulfillment of our "species being." But the Sens lectures yield little evidence of a "radical Durkheim."[66] Substantively, his teleological ethics issues mostly in quite conventional moral prescriptions: Do not commit suicide, work hard, show respect for your family, obey the law, pay taxes, vote, and so on. And in fact, where his ethics does depart from these familiar homilies, it is to move in a direction Marx would have detested. Not only does Durkheim reject the "socialism" of Rousseau on the grounds that it "undermines the personality of the individual" by regarding the "individual's personality as simply a means, an instrument employed by society to achieve its ends" (lecture 64). In addition, he argues, consistent with the thought of G. W. F. Hegel and others, that respect for the personality demands the preservation of the institution of private property. Our "duty," he asserts in lecture 66,

---

66. See Frank Pearce, *The Radical Durkheim* (Boston: Unwin Hyman, 1989).

is to develop our activity and personality. But how could we develop our activity if we couldn't exercise it on external objects, if we had to keep it enclosed in the narrow walls of our person? We must add to our being, by extending it under the form of exterior objects. Such objects store up our actions, so to speak, and keep them from disappearing. So they're an indispensable condition for the development of the individual, and for this reason property is a right.

Interpretive Possibilities

Durkheim's finalism, his insistence that there is more to consciousness than intelligence, and his pro forma empiricism, are certainly at the core of his overall philosophical position. But they are far from exhausting it. As readers make their way through the lectures contained in the present volume, they will find Durkheim weighing in on all the major philosophical questions of his day and trying to construct a coherent response to them.

However uncomfortable it might have made Durkheim, were he alive today, to find his earliest, unpolished ideas in print in a foreign language and subject to careful scrutiny, it is likely that once he got over the initial shock he would have seen present-day consideration of them as all to the good, and not simply out of vanity. Although Durkheim is sometimes depicted by positivists as someone who had more of an interest in theorizing about the empirical world than in commenting ad nauseum on the work of other theorists, he was clearly of the view – as these lectures and many of his books and essays and reviews attest – that there are some figures in intellectual history whose ideas are so profound and pathbreaking that an engagement with them may well help us understand the intellectual problems of the present. Durkheim himself is one such figure, and that he remains so recognized is evidenced by the considerable renaissance that scholarship on Durkheim, including efforts at developing new sociological theories around Durkheimian themes, has undergone in the last fifteen years or so.[67] It can only be hoped that

67. Important edited volumes include Jeffrey C. Alexander, ed., *Durkheimian Sociology: Cultural Studies* (Cambridge: Cambridge University Press, 1988); Stephen Turner, ed., *Emile Durkheim: Sociologist and Moralist* (London: Routledge, 1993); W. S. F. Pickering and H. Martins, eds., *Debating Durkheim* (London: Routledge, 1994); Geoffrey Walford and W. S. F. Pickering, eds., *Durkheim and Modern Education* (London: Routledge, 1998); W. S. F. Pickering, ed., *Durkheim and*

the publication of the present volume will provide the community of scholars engaged in this collective undertaking with a new textual resource they can use to shed light on some of the interpretive debates surrounding Durkheim's ideas; and that this illumination, in turn, will prompt new readings of Durkheim that will contribute to our understanding of the intellectual problems that occupy sociologists and scholars in cognate fields today.

Representations (London: Taylor and Francis, 2000); W. S. F. Pickering, ed., *Emile Durkheim III: Critical Assessments of Leading Sociologists* (London: Routledge, 2000); and W. S. F. Pickering, ed., *Durkheim Today* (Oxford: Berghahn Books, 2002).

PART ONE

Preliminary Matters

ONE

The Object and Method of Philosophy

What is philosophy? The word is used often, and this suggests something about its meaning. To philosophize is to reflect on specific facts in order to reach general conclusions. Philosophy, in other words, is reflection and generalization. This is what we mean when we speak of the philosophy of art or the philosophy of history. The philosophical spirit – the kind of reflection that philosophy involves – can be defined as follows: The philosophical spirit is the need to justify all opinions, together with a strength of mind more or less sufficient to satisfy this need. The defining quality of the philosophical spirit is free reflection and examination. To reflect freely is to eliminate from our thinking every influence but logic, to reason according to the rules of logic alone. So the two main characteristics of the philosophical spirit are the tendency to reflect in order to generalize and freedom of reflection. From this second characteristic, it follows that philosophy is different from religion. Reason plays a role in religion, but religion also recognizes the authority of historical tradition. Philosophy is concerned only with matters of reason. So their domains are quite distinct.

If we look back on the history of philosophy, we see that philosophical reflection has proceeded in two different ways, taking two different forms. Sometimes philosophy proceeds by analysis, using the method of mathematics. This involves beginning with an obvious idea (or one accepted as such) and connecting it to a number of derivative ideas, thus forming an uninterrupted series. From the first idea we derive a second, from this second a third, and so on, so that once the first idea is shown to be true all the others follow as a matter of course. Cartesianism, for example, proceeds in this way.

The other form of the philosophical spirit is synthetic and affords much more room for inspiration and imagination. Philosophers working in this vein feel no need for mathematical order. Rather, they see facts holistically and tie them together in special ways – that is, they prefer broad hypotheses that group facts together rather than the analysis that dissects them. Instead of arranging their ideas in a series, they introduce a whole that can be grasped instantaneously. This is the style of Platonic philosophy.

Now that we know some of its external characteristics, let's define philosophy by its object. Various definitions have been proposed. Bossuet says, "Philosophy is the science of man and God." Cicero defines philosophy as "the science of things divine and human." Aristotle calls it "the science of first causes and first principles." Finally, it's been said that philosophy is "the science of the absolute."

All these definitions amount to the same thing. To show this, let's begin by defining the term "absolute." By the absolute we mean that which is by itself, independent of space and time, depends on and is related to nothing. Knowing this, we can show that all these definitions offer the absolute as the object of philosophy. The first cause is the being (or beings) out of which all reality develops. The first principle is the most general law that governs this development. So to look for the first cause and the first principle is to look for the primitive, the absolute, as much in the world of knowledge as in that of existence. What is the absolute in the world of knowledge? It's the mind of man. In the world of existence? It's God. So all these definitions come down to this: Philosophy is the science of the absolute.

The problem with this definition is that it takes as the object of philosophy something – the absolute – whose existence philosophers debate. The notion of the absolute might be necessary to make sense of certain facts, but it can't be assumed at the beginning of our inquiries. So it shouldn't be a part of our definition of philosophy. There are, after all, important philosophical systems – for example, positivism – which don't recognize the existence of the absolute. Our definition of philosophy can't exclude systems that raise the same questions as all the others and differ only in the way they answer them. In short, we can't give philosophy an object whose very existence is in question.

So how should we define philosophy?

Let's examine the facts with which this science is concerned. All these pertain to human beings, and more specifically to nonphysical aspects of human life – aspects not studied by the positive sciences. Philosophy's domain is therefore the inner man. By this we mean the realm of facts not perceptible to the regular senses but known instead through a sort of intimate sense that we call consciousness. The perception of these inner facts modifies consciousness, just as the perception of material objects modifies the other senses. So these inner facts can be called states of consciousness.

We can therefore say that philosophy is the science of states of consciousness.

But this still won't do. The psychological facts we're calling states of consciousness are relative, at least in relation to time. By definition, then, philosophy would be restricted to the realm of the relative. The study of the absolute would be excluded. Metaphysics, mistakenly imposed on us by the earlier definitions, would – equally mistakenly – be excluded by this definition. So we have to modify our definition: "Philosophy is the science of states of consciousness and their conditions."

This definition covers every philosophical system. Isn't the absolute one of the conditions of states of consciousness? We'll have to consider this later. But regardless, the definition we've given allows philosophy to raise this question if it deems the hypothesis essential.

TWO

The Object and Method of Philosophy (Conclusion)

We've now determined that the object studied by philosophy consists of the states of consciousness and their conditions. But how should philosophy proceed? What should be its method?

Different philosophical systems have advanced different philosophical methods. A contemporary school – the eclectic – maintains that the best of these methods is to reconcile the competing systems. In antiquity, eclecticism – although not yet organized as a school – was championed by Cicero and the New Academy, and more recently by Leibniz, who often recommended its basic principles. But eclecticism didn't become a distinct school of thought until Victor Cousin made it so. This famous philosopher gave eclecticism both a method and – what had not yet been coherently laid out – a set of principles to follow. Here's what Cousin's eclecticism is all about.

According to Cousin, there's no longer any need to search for the truth, because it has already been found and is dispersed among the various philosophical systems. All we need do is extract the fragments of truth – scattered and intermingled with error – from these systems and then reunite them to form a system whose doctrines will be truth itself. For this, of course, we need some criterion that will allow us to distinguish truth from error. What is this criterion? According to Cousin, existing philosophical systems have erred by being too narrow-minded. The things they affirm are true, but the things they deny are often true as well – for example, the idealists claim that mind is the sole source of knowledge, while the sensualists say that it comes solely from sensation. The eclectics believe that the error lies in the words "sole" and "solely." As they see it, knowledge comes from both the senses and the mind.

Because its views are so broad, eclecticism at first seems to be a great system. But actually it's quite problematic. Aside from the fact that, by its very principle, eclecticism denies the future progress of philosophical science, the proposed criterion is too vague. How are we supposed to determine where affirmation ends and negation begins? In many cases, this distinction is purely arbitrary. So the eclectics propose a second criterion – common sense – claiming that this criterion derives from the first (that is, if the answers of common sense are superior to those of philosophy, it's because they're broader): "If common sense doesn't adopt the systems of philosophers," Jouffroy says, "it's not because the systems say one thing and common sense another. It's because the systems say less and common sense more. Were we to plumb the depths of every philosophical opinion, we would find there a 'positive' element that common sense has adopted, such that philosophy has been assimilated into human consciousness." Note in this passage the use of the word "positive," indicating the relationship the eclectics believe exists between the two proposed criteria – breadth and affirmation.

So this method subjects philosophy entirely to common sense. But common sense doesn't have any philosophical rigor. It wasn't formed by the rules of logic and is constituted of opinions that have developed under myriad influences (climate, education, heredity, habit, etc.). Common sense isn't reflective in the least and in the end is nothing more than a collection of prejudices.

To be sure, we need common sense to guide us in everyday life, and in fact it's precisely this that distinguishes it from philosophy. Common sense is practical, while the distinctive feature of philosophy is that it involves reflection. For this reason, common sense often results in error. When Galileo announced that the earth moved, for example, common sense – seeing the earth as immobile – couldn't go along. So as a philosophical criterion, common sense surely ought to be rejected.

Does this mean we should ignore common sense altogether? Of course not. Common sense should be respected as a fact – one that has some rational foundation for existence. We might decide against common sense, but only on the specific condition that we show how its ideas developed and became popular. If common sense contradicts some hypothesis, there must be some reason, and though the hypothesis rests solidly on all the other facts, it remains on shaky ground if it can't explain how common sense has been so thoroughly misled.

There's also a second objection to eclecticism. Common sense is broad and might very well embrace contradictory ideas from different philosophical systems. And who would decide which is correct? But even if this didn't happen, how could a solid, well-ordered system be put together from the pieces and scraps of philosophy torn from here and there? The different elements that go to make up common sense weren't designed to be compatible, and it would be an arduous task – for which, in any event, we haven't yet developed a method – to combine them. So eclecticism can't produce a well-built system based on a stable foundation, and the proof of this lies in the fact that, though its criteria have settled specific questions, Cousin himself never tried to build a complete philosophy with them.

Since eclecticism doesn't provide the true method of philosophy, where else should we look?

Another school – the idealist – proposes the deductive or a priori method. According to the idealists, we should find the initial, most general idea upon which all later ideas depend. Then, just as the mathematician deduces all subsequent definitions from those with which he begins, showing that everything is contained in the first definition, so from this first idea the philosopher should derive all the other ideas. Spinoza gave us the most striking example of this method, and his philosophy contains all the trappings of mathematics – definitions, theorems, corollaries, etc. Spinoza's method was later revived by Fichte, Schelling, and Hegel, who dispensed with his mathematical form.

The deductive method, however, has a serious defect – it renders experience completely extraneous to philosophy. But in the sciences, we have to explain the facts as they are, not invent a whole series of ideas, deduced and inferred from one another, unconcerned with whether they correspond to reality.

The deductive method might be appropriate for mathematicians, who work on ideal figures that might or might not exist outside the mind. But the philosopher works in an entirely different way, studying states of consciousness – and these are facts. Facts aren't invented but have to be observed and studied. The idealist method – which tries to do away with facts and reason about their purpose – must thus be rejected.

This critique of the deductive method shows us how important the study of facts is to philosophy. But is this all there is to philosophy? Is the method insisting that all knowledge derives from sensation more legitimate than the one claiming that all knowledge comes from the mind?

The empirical school thinks so. According to the empiricists, philosophy should be content to observe phenomena, classify them, and make generalizations about them. It should restrict itself to this study and identify the general laws that govern these phenomena.

But we can't accept this. Philosophy is a science, and no true science can survive by observation alone. In itself, observation – if not a completely sterile activity – is no more than fact-finding and doesn't tell us very much. Generalization – the necessary complement of observation – is what enables us to identify the common characteristics of phenomena. These characteristics might be very clear, but even when they are, they yield only simple laws – for example, observation shows us that bodies are heavy but can't yield the law of gravity. As soon as the facts become even slightly complex, observation loses its capacity to discover the law, and then the mind has to intervene and formulate what we call a hypothesis.

This brings us to the true method of philosophy. The law that observation alone was unable to discover must be invented by the mind and stated as a hypothesis. Once formulated, the hypothesis must then be verified before it may be considered a law. Here we discover the characteristic operation of this method – experimentation. To experiment is to observe with the goal of verifying a preconceived idea, to make sure that the facts confirm what the mind assumed to be true. If they do – if the facts are all consistent with the hypothesis, and above all if the hypothesis helps us discover new facts that were previously unknown – then the hypothesis gradually loses its hypothetical character. It never loses this character altogether, of course, for it's obvious that we can never observe all the relevant facts, and a single contradiction is enough to require that it be revised. All the sciences proceed in this way, and hypotheses have led to the greatest advances in science (for example, those of gravitation, of electrical currents, etc.).

So the true method of philosophy is the experimental method, which has three parts:

1. the observation, classification, and generalization of facts;
2. the invention of hypotheses;
3. the verification of the invented hypotheses by means of experimentation.

This method takes the middle road between its deductive and empirical counterparts. According to the idealists, the mind is everything.

According to the empiricists, observation is everything. In contrast to the idealists, the experimental method begins with observation. In contrast to the empiricists, it asks the mind to invent a hypothesis – one it then verifies against the facts. So while the facts have the first and last word, the mind is the soul of the method. It's the mind that creates and invents, but in doing so it doesn't fail to respect the facts.

THREE

Science and Philosophy

It's often been asked if philosophy is a science; if so, to what extent; and what the relationship is between philosophy and the other sciences. To find answers to these questions, we must define science. The first thing that comes to mind when we think of science is a system of knowledge. But this system has some special characteristics. To identify these, let's examine the goal of science. Actually, science has two goals. It should satisfy a need of the mind and make human life better. This need of the mind is the instinct of curiosity, the passion to know. But in the end, science always has – if not for its explicit aim, then at least as its consequence – the improvement of the material conditions of existence, for advances, even in theoretical matters, often result in an improvement in human life. Science achieves these two goals by a single means – explanation. Through explanation, the instinct of curiosity is satisfied in the most complete and perfect way possible. To know what the facts of a given case are brings us immediate pleasure, but to know why they exist – to understand them – brings a satisfaction of a higher order. Science should be seen as a struggle between intelligence and things. Depending upon whether intelligence wins or loses, it is satisfied or suffers. Intelligence is happiest when it can seize in its entirety the thing it studies, understand it, and, so to speak, make the thing its own. This is the ideal of explanation, so to explain something is the best way to satisfy the instinct of curiosity. It's also the best way to achieve the second goal of science – the goal of making life better. When we really understand the nature of something, we put it to better use than if we simply know that it exists. For example, the laws of heat are well known to us, so we've been able to put heat to very good use. But we're ignorant about the laws of electricity, and as a consequence our use of it remains almost entirely experimental. Since the best way for science to achieve its goals is through explanation, we can say that the goal of science is to explain.

But science can take two different forms, and, correspondingly, there are two different ways to explain things. Mathematicians explain through demonstration – by showing that some theorem to be proved is included in another which has already been proven, so that to state one is to state the other; in short, that one is identical to the other. To demonstrate something mathematically, in other words, is to establish a relationship of identity between what is known and what is sought. So we can say that mathematicians explain by means of relationships of identity. For example, how do they show that the three angles of a triangle are equal to two right angles? By showing that:

1. the alternate internal and corresponding angles of the triangle are equal to one another; and
2. the sum of the angles made around the apex of one right angle is equivalent to two right angles; and
3. to say that the sum of the angles of a triangle is equivalent to two right angles is to say the same thing.

Since the first two propositions are true, it follows necessarily that the third, which is identical to them, is also true.

The physical sciences, by contrast, explain things differently. These sciences are concerned not with relationships of identity but instead with causality. If we don't understand the causes of a fact, then it hasn't really been explained, and the mind is not going to be satisfied. Once the cause is revealed, however, the mind becomes satisfied immediately, and the fact can be considered explained. From this we can generalize and say that the goal of science is to establish relationships of identity or causality (since we've established that the goal of science is to explain) and that to explain is to establish relationships of identity or causality between things.

Knowing all this, let's examine the characteristics any system of knowledge has to have in order to be considered a science. First, a science must have a suitable object of explanation. By suitable, we mean that the object isn't the focus of any other science and that it's well defined. How could we explain something if it weren't well defined?

Second, the object must be subject to either the law of identity or the law of causality, because without these no explanation – and consequently no science – is possible.

But these two characteristics alone aren't enough to make a system of knowledge a science. In order to explain an object, it must be somehow accessible to us. If the object were inaccessible, then obviously we couldn't study it scientifically. The term used to describe the means used by the mind to study an object is "method." So the third characteristic of a science is that it has a method for studying its object.

Guided by these principles, let's see if philosophy can be called a science. First, it has a suitable, well-defined object – the states of consciousness – that no other science studies. Second, the facts that philosophy studies exist in determinate relationships to one another – it can't be said that states of consciousness escape the law of causality. Third, philosophy has a method – experimentation. So philosophy has all three of the characteristics of a science and can rightly be regarded as one.

But this raises another question: If philosophy is a science, what is its relationship with the other sciences?

In antiquity, philosophers, having too much confidence, believed that their science contained all others – that philosophy was universal knowledge itself. The other sciences were thought to be parts or chapters of philosophy.

But the definition of philosophy we've given, and the proof that it's a distinct science, show that this theory can't be accepted.

More recently, some philosophers have come up with another idea – the argument that philosophy doesn't exist independently of the other sciences and is only the concluding chapter of the positive sciences, the synthesis of their most general principles. This is what August Comte believed.

To refute this theory, all we have to do is mention again the definition of philosophy we've given. Philosophy studies its own distinct object – the states of consciousness – and this object is independent of the objects of all other sciences. When it studies states of consciousness, philosophy is at home, and although it might sometimes borrow from the other sciences to explain its object, this doesn't make it any less independent from them, or any less distinctive.

What, then, is the relationship between philosophy and the other sciences? There are two kinds of relationships – general, which are the same with all the sciences, and particular, which differ depending on which science we're talking about. Let's begin by taking a look at general relationships. The objects studied by all the positive sciences must somehow be known, and the science that studies the laws of knowledge is philosophy. So philosophy is at the center of all the other sciences, because the mind itself, which philosophy studies, is at the center of the world of knowledge. Let's suppose, for example, that philosophy decides that the human mind, as Kant argues, has no objective value – that the mind doesn't have access to real objects. This decision would condemn all the positive sciences to subjectivity.

Next, let's examine particular relationships. There are two kinds, for philosophy takes from the other sciences and gives to them as well.

From the other sciences, philosophy borrows a large number of facts that it reflects on and that help it explain its own object. It's impossible to study psychology, for example, without incorporating the lessons of physiology. Likewise, when we speculate about the nature of external phenomena, we have to draw on knowledge of physics and chemistry.

On the other hand, all the positive sciences rely on various explanatory procedures. Mathematics, for example, uses deduction; physics, induction; natural history, classification. But who studies these procedures? It's philosophy, which develops theories about them and asks about the conditions they have to fulfill in order to generate accurate results. Philosophy also asks how these different procedures might be combined to study the different objects of the various sciences, thus searching for the best method for each science. In fact, this project makes up an important part of the study of logic – what we term methodology.

FOUR

The Divisions of Philosophy

Now that we know what the object studied by philosophy is, it's not hard to see that this object, by its very nature, will be quite complex. This is so because states of consciousness involve quite diverse types of phenomena. In order to study them all, we'll have to divide the science of philosophy into several specific sciences.

Different philosophical systems have proposed different ways of dividing philosophy, and this is entirely natural, for these divisions are tied to the general spirit of the system in question. In the earliest days of Greek thought, philosophy wasn't divided. It was said to be the whole of human knowledge. Philosophy was thus confused with physics and, until Socrates came along, all philosophical treatises bore the title: Περὶφύσεως (On Nature). We don't know if Socrates divided philosophy or how he divided it. Plato, who more than anyone else made Socrates' philosophy known to posterity, didn't divide it. So it's unlikely Socrates himself did. For Plato, philosophy is synthetic. Rather than discussing a distinct part of his system, each dialogue touches on many different questions, which seem to be only randomly connected.

Aristotle, who saw philosophy as comprising quite different sciences, was the first to divide it neatly: "All human activity," he said, "can take three different forms – knowing, acting, doing.[68] From this we get three sciences: theory, whose object is speculation; practice, which is equivalent to what we today call ethics; and finally, poetics, whose object is art."

---

68. Written above the word "faire" is the word "créer," followed by θεωρεῖν, πράττειν, ποιεῖν (to contemplate, to act, to make). Eds.

This division eventually fell into disuse, however, and was replaced by another, accepted by the two major philosophical schools of the day – Epicureanism and Stoicism. This new division also saw philosophy as comprising three parts: the physical science of external nature, the logical science of the laws of mind and knowledge, and ethics or morality.

Descartes, for his part, never divided philosophy in this way. Yet he too made an attempt at a division – one more concerned with the whole of human knowledge than with philosophy alone. "Philosophy is like a tree, whose roots are metaphysics. The trunk of the tree is physics, and the branches which stick out from the trunk are all the other sciences, of which there are three principal ones – medicine, mechanics, and ethics."

Note that not one of these divisions can square with the definition of philosophy we've set out, for each refers to a far greater field of inquiry.

But Cousin proposed a new division, dividing philosophy into four parts: psychology, logic, ethics, and metaphysics. This division is the simplest and has become very popular. It's also the best and the one we'll adopt.

The definition of philosophy we've proposed contains two parts – states of consciousness and their conditions. So we need at least one division of philosophy that corresponds to each. But states of consciousness can't be studied by just one science alone. Right away, therefore, we'll need to decide what the various types of states of consciousness are, to identify the different species and properties of each. This inventory complete, we'll then have to study the states of consciousness from another point of view. One of the states of consciousness revolves around intelligence. The purpose of intelligence is the pursuit of truth. If it's to avoid making mistakes, intelligence has to follow rules; and these rules form the second part of philosophy, which we call logic. Logic differs from psychology, for it studies some rather than all states of consciousness, and because psychology is purely descriptive where logic explains the laws of knowledge.

There is also another category of facts – activity. Here we ask: How, and under what circumstances, does activity take the form it should? What are the laws that govern it? This is the subject of ethics. This science, by its very nature, is different from logic and psychology.

Finally, we are left with the conditions of states of consciousness, or metaphysics.

The different parts of philosophy should be treated in the order just set out.

Before studying the states of consciousness in detail, we obviously have to examine them in their totality and then fully describe them. So the first thing we should study is psychology.

For the same reason, metaphysics should be studied last, for to study the conditions of states of consciousness, we must understand them thoroughly, and this is the goal of the other three divisions of philosophy.

Logic, which deals with the most important questions of all, should be placed before ethics. We're able to reason only because we understand the laws of reasoning, so if we could, we'd put logic first. But since psychology necessarily comes first, we must at least give logic the very next place, and this is why we've put it before ethics.

So in philosophy, there are four sciences we have to study:

1. psychology;
2. logic;
3. ethics;
4. metaphysics.

PART TWO

Psychology

FIVE

The Object and Method of Psychology

We've already indicated that the aim of psychology is to describe the states of consciousness and develop a typology of them.

But the phenomena that psychology studies are almost indistinguishable from certain other phenomena that don't fall within its proper domain. Leaving for later the question of whether there's merit to the philosophical viewpoint known as materialism, it's clear that the body and soul are closely related to one another. We might almost say that nothing happens in the body that doesn't find its echo in the soul, and vice versa. For this reason, we have to be clear about the difference between physiology and psychology.

Physiological phenomena have the following characteristics:

1. They occur in space, occupy a certain part of extension, and can all be reduced to movements. In addition, we can depict them by means of figures — for example, to depict a stimulation of the nerves, it's sufficient to draw its different phases.
2. Because physiological phenomena occur in space, they can be measured. We can mathematically estimate the quantity of space they occupy.
3. Physiological phenomena are unconscious. We're often conscious of their result, of course, but not of the phenomena themselves — for example, we're not aware of the nervous stimuli that flow through our bodies when we injure ourselves. We only know the result — pain.
4. Finally, we don't attribute physiological phenomena to the self. We might say, "I suffer," but suffering is just the psychological manifestation of a physiological wound. Only the body endures suffering, and the expression "I endure" is misleading.

Psychological phenomena have precisely the opposite characteristics:

1. They don't occur in space and so can't be reduced to movements. We can't depict a psychological sensation in the same way that we can depict a stimulation of the nerves – that is, figurally. Sensations aren't spatially perceptible and occur only in time.
2. Since they don't occur in space, only the duration of psychological phenomena can be measured.
3. All psychological phenomena are conscious and are known to us only through consciousness. We become aware of their birth and development through consciousness alone, not through our senses.
4. We attribute all psychological phenomena to the self, which isn't always their cause, although we think of it as such. When someone is injured, it's not as though the self has caused the injury to the body, but still we say that the pain is that of the self.

So these two sciences, physiology and psychology, are quite distinct. Each has its own unique object. There's no reason to confuse them.

Now, of all forms of explanation, the mathematical method is the one best suited to the study of the mind. This is why many thinkers have tried to apply it to psychology, including Weber, who founded the psychophysical school in Germany. The central concern of this school was to measure the intensity of sensation (it being easy to measure duration).

Fechner – one of the main thinkers working in this vein – argued as follows. In order to measure something, two things are necessary:

1. a standard of measurement distinct from that which is measured;
2. the thing to be measured must be measurable.

What standard of measurement is appropriate for sensation? Fechner calls this standard excitation – the external cause that produces the sensation. We sense that there's a precise relationship between excitation and sensation whenever we try to lift something heavy. Psychophysical research tries to calculate this relationship exactly.

But is sensation really measurable? To answer this question, we must distinguish between the quality and the intensity of sensation. Consider visual sensations. One sensation may be red, another blue. This is a qualitative difference. But if one is bright red and the other pale blue, they also differ in intensity, which is what Fechner wants to measure.

But there's a problem. We can vary the quantity of excitation and know exactly how much it varies. But we can't do the same thing for variations in sensation. These we can measure only indirectly, by taking note of "the least perceptible differences of sensation."

Here's what we mean. Imagine that I have in my hand something that weighs 100 grams. I add one gram and sense no difference. I add two grams but still sense no difference. So I keep adding weight until the difference in weight from the initial 100 grams becomes perceptible. This experiment shows that, for the difference to become perceptible, we have to add, on average, a third again to the initial weight. This is the least perceptible difference.

Now let's try to depict this mathematically. We'll assign the number 1 to the first sensation and also to the corresponding excitation, and continue the experiment until we again experience a sensation of difference. This sensation – the sum of the first and the second sensation, each equal to 1 – would, according to Fechner's logic, be equal to 2. Proceeding in this way, we would eventually arrive at the following table:

Sensations – 1:2:3:4:5:6:7:8 . . .
Excitations – 1:2:4:8:16:32:64 . . .

From this table, we can derive the following law: Sensation varies as the logarithm of excitation.

But this law has been challenged, for Fechner's calculations are inaccurate. Even more problematic, however, is the reasoning behind the calculations. Why should we assume that if the sensation produced by the smallest perceptible difference equals 1, then the sensation produced by double the smallest perceptible difference equals 2? Why should the two sensations be added together rather than multiplied in some way? Fechner's approach assumes that sensations are measurable, but we certainly can't know that one sensation is double the other. Mathematics – like all sciences – measures only lines and movements. When we say that one force is double that of another, what we mean is that, applied to the same object in motion under the same conditions, if the first force makes the object move with velocity a, then the second will make it move with velocity $2a$. Were we to do away with the object and with space, then we'd be unable to measure these forces in relation to one another. We can only measure results, or movements.

Some claim that we can measure sensation directly. But this is impossible, because sensations are outside of space. Only their duration can be measured. Sensations do differ from one another, but this difference isn't such as to allow them to be measured directly.

There's another objection to the psychophysical method – it ignores the physiological basis of psychic phenomena. Fechner and Weber do attempt to measure the relationships between psychic phenomena and their physical antecedents; but they pay no attention to the physiological phenomena occuring between them that are the immediate antecedent of the psychic phenomena. If the body were a passive environment that didn't change nervous stimuli in the course of transmitting them, we could safely disregard it, as the psychophysical method does. But the body isn't passive at all, and as it transmits such stimuli, it modifies them a great deal, and it does so differently depending on the individual and the circumstances. This would certainly have to be taken into account by any acceptable method, and the relevant relationships established – first, between the physical and physiological phenomena, and second, between the physiological and psychical phenomena.

For all these reasons, we can't accept the psychophysical approach. To respond to this last objection, however, another school – that of Wundt – was established, calling itself the psychophysiological school. Wundt's school sees states of consciousness as directly connected, not to physical phenomena but to physiological phenomena. So Wundt argues that physiology provides the means for studying psychology.

According to Wundt, the mind is dependent on the body – that is, the conscious life of the mind has its roots in the unconscious life of the body. The immediate antecedents of all psychic phenomena are physiological phenomena. To this Wundt adds that without measurement no science is possible. The philosophers who've followed in Wundt's footsteps have applied this principle. Recognizing the futility of efforts to measure intensity, however, they've been satisfied with measuring duration. So it can be said that this school has two principal characteristics:

1. The relationship with which it's concerned is not that between psychology and physics but that between psychology and physiology.
2. It studies duration and not intensity.

This school claims that the only way to study the mind is to study its relationship to the body. But here it errs. Of course, we have good reason to be interested in this relationship. But research of this kind, however useful, can't substitute for a science that studies psychological facts themselves. What we need is to know these facts intimately, make an exact inventory of them, describe them, and reduce them to a certain number of general types; and this is the goal of pure psychology. The need for this type of study is absolutely clear and can't be eliminated by a science concerned only with the relationship between mind and body.

We wouldn't do away with psychophysiology or any similar science. But psychophysiology can't proceed until:

1. an independent science has been established that studies only the mind;
2. an independent science has been established that studies only the body;
3. both of these sciences have reduced all the phenomena to the study of one or a few principal facts, types, and origins.

Sometimes people speak of reducing physics to mechanics. What does this imply? A science of mechanics, whose sole object is movement, and a science of physics that reduces all physical phenomena to movement alone. Only if these two sciences existed independently could we demonstrate the identity of the phenomena with which they're concerned. It's the same with psychic and physiological phenomena.

Even if we eventually wanted to develop some kind of psychophysiology, we'd first have to establish a special science of the mind – pure psychology.

From this study of psychophysics and psychophysiology comes a positive conclusion – we have to study the states of consciousness in and for themselves. The only method that makes this possible is observation through consciousness.

But this method too has been criticized. It's been said that observation of this sort is too difficult, that psychic phenomena are fleeting and remain for only a moment in the field of interior vision. This fact keeps them from being studied in detail. And then there's the gaze of consciousness itself. Isn't it crude and imprecise? This gaze reveals to us only the general outlines of phenomena, not their details and essential characteristics.

There's a second objection as well – that observation of this sort is not only difficult but impossible, because it requires that the mind observe and be observed at the same time. The mind has to be both actor and audience, and this is impossible.

Here's a third objection. Even if this method were easy, it couldn't produce scientific results. For exactly what does this kind of method observe? Individuals, who are very different from one another. But this means that the resulting observation would lack generality and be accurate only for particular cases. So this method would make psychology nothing more than a collection of case studies.

These objections can be easily refuted.

To the first, we respond that the observation of psychic phenomena by consciousness isn't as difficult as claimed, since it's done every day and yields incontestable results. After all, this kind of observation has been cultivated by the greatest minds – moralists, comic and satiric writers, and artists. All have found it possible to grasp the most delicate nuances of the interior world and to illuminate them. And while it's true that psychological phenomena are fleeting, it's easy to bring them back to consciousness through memory, which gives us the means to study them carefully and at leisure – as we do external objects. So while observation by consciousness certainly involves difficulties, by no means are these insurmountable.

As for the second objection, it's merely a quibble over words. Certainly the same subject can observe and be observed at the same time. One can't be simultaneously an actor and a spectator, but one can definitely be an actor and watch oneself act. One can watch oneself in a mirror! And to "listen to oneself speak" is a common expression. So the second objection fails.

Finally, to the third objection we respond that we study in each particular man only that which is common to all men, in the same way that in a particular triangle a mathematician is interested only in the properties common to all triangles. Besides, we always compare the results obtained in our research to those obtained from other research, and the result of this comparison is that only common characteristics remain in our observations. Nor do we remain content just to study those who live around us and under similar conditions, for we also study documents about great men of the past left to us by history. Here, of course, there's another danger to avoid. One system has tried to base psychology on historical documents alone. This takes things too far. History records only the deeds of great men, and their psychological level shouldn't be taken for that of all humanity. Besides, we can't even understand the ideas and passions of great men without first studying those more familiar to us. So history can serve only as a complement to our method of observation.

SIX

Faculties of the Soul

We now know the object of psychology as well as its method. It's time to apply the method to the object.

This object, as we've seen, is to enumerate, describe, and classify the states of consciousness. But this should be done methodically, so we'll divide the states of consciousness into a certain number of classes and examine each more closely. We won't let ourselves be discouraged by the apparent diversity of states of consciousness but rather will search for the common characteristics that might serve as the foundation for such a division. There'll be as many faculties of the soul as there are perceptible classes.

A faculty is a specific mode of conscious activity, and there are as many different faculties as there are forms of the inner life. The soul has faculties in the same sense that inorganic bodies have properties and that complex living bodies have functions. The only difference is that a faculty refers to a larger sum of activity than a function and that a function refers to a larger sum of activity than a property.

How many faculties (or classes of states of consciousness) can be identified? There are three:

1. Activity: We act on the external world through the intermediary of our bodies and on the inner world through simple will, by directing our intelligence, exercising our thought, etc.
2. Depending on whether our activity is unencumbered or encounters obstacles, we feel what is called pleasure or pain. But pleasure and pain aren't activities. In fact, they're fundamentally different than activity, for, while our actions might lead to pleasure and pain, pleasure and

pain can't be directly willed. Concerning phenomena of this kind, we're largely passive. This second faculty is called sensibility.
3. When we act, we know that we act. When we suffer, we know that we suffer. When we think, we know that we think. But this knowledge is neither action nor sensation. Here we encounter that category of states of consciousness called ideas. The faculty concerned with these ideas is intelligence.

So there are three principal faculties: activity, or the faculty of acting; sensibility, or the faculty of experiencing pleasure and pain; and intelligence, or the faculty of knowing.

To identify these three categories, we classified the states of consciousness because, outside these states, the faculties have only a latent existence. But while the faculties are closely bound up with their corresponding states of consciousness, we shouldn't think that they exist only as generic terms for them or that they're just labels for states of consciousness. Without these states, of course, the faculties wouldn't have any concrete reality. But they are still real powers of the soul, with a foundation in its very nature. The states of consciousness are derived from the faculties just as the faculties themselves are derived from the nature of the soul. Faculties both precede and survive states of consciousness, which proves that they're distinct from them.

Some people ask if we can't simplify the number of faculties, reducing them to one. Condillac tried to do just this, reducing them all to sensibility, by which he meant the faculty of knowing by means of sensation. For him, everything in the soul depends on sensation. In the same way, Maine de Biran reduced everything to muscular effort, or activity. Finally, for Spinoza, all faculties of the soul could be reduced to intelligence.

But we've shown clearly that the faculties differ too much to be conflated in this way. Activity is characterized by action, sensibility by passivity, and intelligence by representation.

There's also another pitfall to avoid – that is, conceiving of the faculties as distinct entities, as Plato did. Not content merely to grant the faculties a material reality, he actually assigned them distinct homes in the body, putting the νοῦς (mind), or rational intelligence – which he believed to be the immortal part of man's soul – in the head; the θύμος (passion), which represents man's noble appetites, in the chest;

and the ἐπιθυμία (appetite), which represents the needs (base and vulgar desires), in the abdomen.

But it's a mistake to make entities of the faculties in this way. The faculties are properties or powers of a single being – the self. They're the distinct forms taken by our activity, but the self remains one, the point around which all the faculties converge. Moreover, the faculties always act in conjunction with one another. No psychological fact depends on one faculty alone. We act according to the motives provided by reason or the incentives furnished by sensibility. This proves that the three faculties are united. As Aristotle says, we live not by one faculty but with the entire soul (σὺν ὅλητῇ ψυχη).

SEVEN

On Pleasure and Pain

Earlier we defined sensibility as the faculty by which we experience pleasure and pain. But what are pleasure and pain? We can't give a perfect answer to this question, but we can seek out their essential characteristics and try to identify their causes.

These states of consciousness have three main characteristics:

1. Pleasure and pain are affective phenomena – we experience them without having to do anything at all. Where pleasure and pain are concerned, we're passive. Of course, there's no complete passivity in psychological life – we certainly react in order to decrease pain or increase pleasure. Nevertheless, when it comes to pleasure and pain, we're mostly passive.
2. The second characteristic of these phenomena is their necessity. We can't stop ourselves from experiencing pleasure and pain. They're the necessary consequence of the prior event that brought them about, and the only way we can modify them is by modifying that event. Through an exercise of will, of course, we can avert our consciousness from pleasure and pain, or make them more intense by giving them our attention. By doing so, we can even take some pleasure in pain, as when we feel melancholy. But while we can have some influence over these feelings, we never control them completely. This was the illusion of the Stoics and the Epicureans, who thought they could eliminate pain by sheer willpower.
3. The third characteristic of pleasure and pain is relativity. In the realm of sensibility, everything is relative. What's pleasurable to one person is painful to another. The manual laborer takes pleasure in working with his body, while the intellectual hates it.

So passivity, necessity, and relativity are the three characteristics of pleasure and pain.

Now let's search for their cause. Some philosophers maintain that pleasure is simply the absence of pain, so that we can't experience pleasure without first having experienced pain. In short, we can't have one without the other. This was the view taken by Plato and recently revived by Schopenhauer in his book *The World as Will and Representation*. According to Schopenhauer, pain is the more basic fact, and pleasure simply its cessation. In order to experience the pleasure of possessing something, for example, we have to start with the desire for it, with the painful realization that we lack it. So pleasure begins with pain.

But this doctrine leads to some pretty sad consequences. If pleasure is only the absence of pain – if we have to buy the slightest enjoyment at the cost of prior suffering – then life is a somber affair indeed, as obtaining pleasure is scarcely worth the effort required. At the very least, this situation should lead to indifference. But is pleasure even adequate compensation? Is it as great as the sufferings required to obtain it? Schopenhauer thinks not. Is life worth the effort? The German philosopher, ever faithful to logic, doesn't hesitate to respond: No.

Eduard von Hartmann, author of *The Philosophy of the Unconscious* and a disciple of Schopenhauer, reaches the same conclusion, even though he contests certain aspects of his theory. Life isn't worth the trouble, he says, not because pleasure doesn't exist independent of pain, but because the sum of all pains surpasses the sum of all pleasures.

But we don't accept Schopenhauer's theory. There are many pleasures that we experience without having suffered first. Of course, if the need that preceded the pleasure was violent, then yes, we've suffered. But if it's not violent, and if we're certain we'll be able to satisfy it, then we're really talking about one pleasure preceding another. For example, if the pleasure of eating has been preceded by starvation, then obviously there's suffering involved. But if we've only had time to develop a healthy appetite, then there's nothing but pleasure in the act of eating. There are also pleasures that are preceded by no need whatsoever – the announcement of good news, for example, or the pleasures of art or science. On the basis of these objections, it's perfectly reasonable to reject the doctrine that gives only a negative value to pleasure.

According to another doctrine, the cause of pleasure lies in free activity. This theory goes back to Aristotle but was more recently taken up by the Scottish philosopher Hamilton and then again by Francisque Bouillier in his book *Of Pleasure and Pain*. According to this theory, we're absolutely delighted when our activity unfolds freely, and we suffer when it's constrained. Where else should we expect to find a cause of pleasure if not in freedom? "Being takes pleasure in its proper action," οἰκεῖον ἔργον (proper function). This theory explains many facts quite well. Muscular exercises, bright colors, and intellectual pursuits bring us pleasure because in them our diverse modes of activity are allowed to unfold unencumbered. So free activity is at least the principal cause of pleasure.

But is it the only cause? The theory we've just considered doesn't account for the pain we experience after we engage in a lot of the same kind of activity. Avoiding obstacles isn't the only condition for pleasure. Pleasure comes about when activity is not just free but also varied. Activity is agreeable only if it's allowed to change forms. This alone explains the keen pleasures associated with change. In addition, it explains the pleasure we experience when we're at rest. When we're inactive, activity hasn't yet taken any specific form, and we're able to imagine it taking an infinity of forms. It's the imagining of this variety that makes inactivity pleasurable. This also explains the pleasure of youth – the young are able to imagine themselves engaging in a variety of forms of activity, as their lives have not yet taken a particular course.

Free and varied activity are thus the two causes of pleasure.

EIGHT

The Inclinations

Strictly speaking, sensation (as we've defined it) refers only to experiences of pleasure and pain. But the self also makes certain movements related to pleasure and pain – if an object causes pleasure, for example, we tend to move toward it, or in the opposite case away from it. In actuality, these movements fall more in the domain of activity than sensibility per se, but they're so closely related to sensibility that it's really quite impossible to separate them.

The tendency of the self to move in the direction of an agreeable object is called an inclination, and this definition also gives us a classification – that is, there are as many different types of inclinations as there are types of objects leading to such movements. Of these, there are three major classes: the self; other selves (our peers); and finally, certain ideas or conceptions of the mind, like the good or the beautiful. This also yields three types of inclinations: egoistic, altruistic, and higher.

The self is the object of egoistic inclinations, which are of two types. Some are purely conservative and try to keep things as they are, while others are acquisitive and seek to augment being. To conserve and to augment being are the two tendencies of nature. The first kind of inclination is called the instinct for conservation – the love of life. Whatever occurs, we find life dear, clinging to it even if it brings more pain than pleasure. There are certainly exceptions to this rule, but these constitute but an insignificant minority. For the instinct for conservation, the highest priority is reserved for physical needs, which have the following characteristics:

They're associated with specific parts of the body;
They're periodic – once satisfied, they disappear, and don't reappear until a certain period of time has passed.

Inclinations of the second kind – those whose goal is to augment being – are numerous and complex, for once being is assured, we seek well-being, which is intellectual as well as physical. Hence a number of inclinations that are well characterized by the Greek word πλεονεξία.[69] All of these seek to add to what we already have, including ambition in all its forms – for love, for grandeur, for wealth, etc.

What about altruistic inclinations? We've said that the object of these inclinations is our fellow human beings. It's often been asked whether altruistic inclinations really exist or whether we're rather entirely egoistic – La Rochefoucauld, Hobbes, Pascal, and Rousseau all took the latter view. We won't try to resolve this question here, but there's no doubt that some of our inclinations are directed toward other human beings. By nature, we're so constituted as to be concerned with others and even to need them. Altruistic (sometimes called sympathetic) inclinations can be subdivided into as many different classes (three) as there are different classes of our fellows.

1. Domestic inclinations concern the family.
2. Social inclinations concern society. These have varied significantly over time, having initially been oriented toward the family, later toward the religious community, and finally toward the community of citizens. The idea of "society" has also changed considerably. But in spite of all these changes, social inclinations have always remained the same in principle.
3. Finally there are inclinations oriented toward the most general group – the collectivity of human beings – and hence the love of humanity.

These altruistic inclinations didn't all emerge at the same time. Domestic inclinations came first. In the earliest days, human beings saw

---

69. The term πλεονεξία is used in classical Greek to refer to a specific vice, and is not, to our knowledge, used to refer to impulses as a class. Perhaps the lecturer meant instead to refer to πλεονασμος ("excess"): the Stoics regarded an emotion as an "excess" of impulse. Eds.

only enemies outside the family. Later, numerous families came together, forming cities and societies, and out of this arose patriotic inclinations. Finally, once we knew one another well enough and found our ideas and wills converging, Stoicism and Christianity were among the doctrines that spread the love of humanity.

Some people believe that these three inclinations – for family, society, and humanity – conflict with each other, and occasionally some have demanded the abolition of two for the benefit of the third. Plato dismissed domestic feeling, for example, and thought little of patriotism. Others have gone further, suggesting that the love of humanity is broad enough to encompass the other two. But none of these attempts at combination will do. In addition to having their own reasons for being, these three sentiments support one another. Society is a union of families, humanity a union of societies. It's from love of the family that we learn to love society, and from love of society that we learn to love humanity. Even if universal peace were realized, patriotism – in its largest sense – wouldn't fade away, any more than the establishment of society and country led to the withering of love for the family.

The third or "higher" category of inclinations concerns three ideas – the true, the beautiful, and the good, which together compose what's called the ideal. So we can define the higher inclinations as man's tendency toward the ideal, and when this ideal is personified – depicted as a living, conscious being – the tendency bleeds over into religious sentiment.

Here are the characteristics of the higher inclinations:

1. They're infinite, insatiable. Unlike other inclinations, they never become fully satisfied – the more we know, for example, the more we want to know.
2. They're impersonal. There's no such thing as jealousy when it comes to inclinations of this kind. When we learn the truth, we don't seek to keep it for ourselves but rather feel the need to disseminate it. The same holds for beauty – we willingly allow others to share the aesthetic joys we've experienced.

Having concluded our review of the different kinds of inclinations and their essential characteristics, we're now in a position to generalize. All inclinations seem to be comprised of two phases. In the case of an agreeable object,

1. The self is directed toward the object. Here the inclination is really only a desire or, if the desire is violent, a need.
2. The self attains the object, trying to make the object similar to or a part of itself, to assimilate it, identify with it, appropriate it.

The first phase is a movement of expansion, the second one of contraction – and only in the latter do egoism and jealousy come into play. The self's aim in this second phase is to keep the desired object for itself, to keep it from falling into someone else's hands – entirely consistent with the theories of La Rochefoucauld and Hobbes. Here indeed the self is both the starting and ending point of the movement; but for their theories to be true, all inclinations would have to consist of both phases, while it's clear that some inclinations stop at the first.

The higher inclinations, for their part, never enter into the second phase. We enjoy the ideal without wanting in any way to monopolize it or prevent others from enjoying it. The person who practices the good is happy to see others follow in his footsteps. When we experience beauty, we seek out others with whom we can share it. And learning the truth, we feel a powerful desire to teach it to others.

Some altruistic inclinations share the same characteristic – we often love others for themselves rather than for ourselves, for example, and here too the inclination stops at the first phase. Is there anything egoistic, for example, about maternal love? Of course, there are always exceptions arising from the inevitable mix of different inclinations, and egoistic preoccupations often get in the way of the higher inclinations and steal their impersonal character. But there are at least some inclinations whose conscious or unconscious aim is never to appropriate the desired object for the private ends of the self. In short, there are such things as disinterested inclinations.

NINE

The Emotions and Passions

We've seen that inclinations involve movement toward an agreeable object or away from one that's disagreeable. Depending on whether an inclination is satisfied or not, the result is pleasure or pain. But pleasure and pain are general terms, and in this lecture we want to examine the varieties of more specific affective phenomena called emotions. Like pleasure and pain, some emotions are agreeable and others disagreeable, and they too are passive. But where pleasure and pain are localized, the emotions aren't. When we taste a delicious food, the palate alone – not the entire self – experiences pleasure. A large part of our being remains free, unoccupied. Emotion, by contrast, tends to take over the whole self, absorbing it completely. While the will intervenes to an extent in how emotion is experienced, emotion is by nature invasive.

So we've defined emotion from a double perspective – it's a form of pleasure and pain but is distinct from them because it's expansive rather than localized. Emotion is also an extension of the inclinations, resulting from their success or failure.

A rigorous classification of the emotions is impossible, but the expression "emotion varies with inclination" affords a reasonable starting point. Our method for classifying the emotions is to hypothetically vary the relationship between object and self, so that the latter will pass through different emotions that can be easily observed.

Consider an agreeable object. Depending on whether it approaches or moves away from the self, agreeable or disagreeable emotions will result. So this object will allow us to study all the types of emotions. At an infinite distance, the object exists only in our imagination. We don't know the object but only dream of it. Imagining that we might someday overcome this infinite distance, we experience a certain kind of anxiety in which the predominating element is pleasure. The object approaches, producing another emotion – hope – which increases the closer the object comes. When we possess the object, hope disappears and is replaced by joy. If the possession continues, we experience another agreeable feeling – the joy of possession – more tranquil than that of acquisition. Reserving "joy" for the former emotion, we might call the pleasure of continued possession that of "security."

But now let's assume that possession of the desired object isn't certain and that we fear that the object will disappear. This produces the painful feeling known as anxiety. Assume next that we suddenly see the object about to be taken away from us – the emotion that arises unexpectedly is fear. If we're deprived of the object suddenly, without warning, we're terrified.

The object moves away from us – the feeling of deprivation is one of sadness and, if we've possessed the object, regret. If the object continues to move away, sadness turns to a despair that increases with the distance of the object. Finally – the object having returned to the infinite distance – our powerlessness to obtain it is experienced as despondence.

All these varieties of emotions were studied by Spinoza in his *Ethics*.

Some have thought it convenient to reduce all emotions to just two categories:

physical emotions, or sensations;
moral emotions, or feelings.

We've avoided this division for several reasons. First, it's too crude – it lacks the finesse essential for the proper classification of these phenomena, which are difficult to pin down. Second, it ignores the meaning of the word "sensation," which isn't simply a physiological fact or its resulting impression but all our knowledge of the external world. Defining sensation this way helps us avoid a number of conceptual problems. Let's take an example:

I injure myself and experience pain. This isn't a sensation. But imagine that at the same time I learn what has injured me. This knowledge would be a sensation.

In everyday language, the meaning of the word "feeling" is rather vague, while the quite specific meaning it has here – a moral emotion – would be confusing. Since there's no point in dividing the emotions, we'll simply use the term in its most general sense to refer to sensory phenomena.

The final type, which includes a wide variety of sensory phenomena, is the passions. In his *Traité de la connaissance de Dieu et de soi-même*, Bossuet mixes inclinations and emotions together, suggesting that there are eleven passions. Ten are opposites (love and hate, desire and disgust, joy and sadness, audacity and fear, hope and despair); the eleventh is anger. All, Bossuet says, can be reduced to love and hate; and because the hatred of an object is only the love of its opposite, for Bossuet love is really the only one passion.

Descartes also wrote a treatise on the passions, where he suggested that all passions can be reduced to one – admiration. Descartes considered the passions semi-sensible, semi-intellectual phenomena, produced by means of animal spirits.

In his *Ethics*, Spinoza also devoted a book to the study of the passions. Like Bossuet, he confused passions properly so called with inclinations and emotions, concluding that joy and love are the two basic passions.

Using the word "passion" in its current sense, let's define it as a sensory stimulation of particular intensity, whose key characteristic is violence. This violent intensity can strike all at once or build up more gradually. Certain passions are habitual, their strength lying in their tenacity. Others last for only a moment, exhausting themselves as soon as they're expressed. This distinction is important for refuting the theory that passions are only habits.

But even more can be said of the passions. They have the following two characteristics:

1. Like inclinations, they always exist in relation to some external object – to be passionate is to be passionate for something. Emotions, by contrast, have a cause but no object. Emotions excite the self but don't direct it toward any specific end.
2. Like emotions, passions are invasive, taking over the whole self, where inclinations are localized. While inclinations affect but one small part of the self, passions are far more all embracing and direct all the faculties of the self toward their objects.

Passion thus borrows one of its characteristics from inclination and the other from emotion. For passion is simply a more violent state of inclination or emotion. A very strong emotion is a passion. Mild anger, for example, is only an emotion. But when it becomes stronger and more lively, it becomes a passion. Likewise, fear in itself is only an emotion; but if it becomes so strong that it takes over, it becomes a passion.

Under normal circumstances maternal love is only an inclination; but if it confronts an obstacle, its liveliness will increase, invading the whole self and becoming a passion.

These two characteristics of passion can be expressed simultaneously – on the one hand, passion concentrates the self, and on the other hand, it directs the self toward some object. So we can say that passion concentrates the whole self toward one and the same object. As a result of passion, all our forces are gathered and directed toward the same end. In short, passion introduces an absolute unity into psychological life.

This analysis of passion also allows us to judge its value – the useful or harmful role it might play. Passion has sometimes been criticized as an unhealthy phenomenon. It's been said that the defining characteristic of passion is that it impoverishes the self. This danger is undeniable; but we might ask whether passion always leads to such an impoverishment. Left to its own devices, of course, it often destroys the equilibrium of the faculties. Under the sway of passion, we pursue some object violently, no longer seeing anything else, trying to attain it by any means whatsoever.

In this case, the entire self is consumed by the passion, and its activity takes but one form. The desire to obtain the passion's object is so strong that the self hasn't the patience to seek out the best means for attaining its ends. In fact, the passions of some people are so violent that they must postpone the achievement of their desire until they're less obsessed and actually capable of acquiring the means for its satisfaction. People like this are headstrong or obstinate.

But if reflection intercedes at all, passion becomes conscious of itself and of what it requires, understanding that certain means are necessary if it's to achieve its ends. From this arise secondary passions, which are considerably more useful. Where primary passions attach themselves to some end, their secondary counterparts attach themselves to the means necessary to realize that end.

Consider, for example, the passion for money, which is itself immoral. Undeniably, this passion carries with it the passion for work and economy, both of which are quite useful. Or consider the passion for glory – it too will carry with it the passion for work, study, etc.

Obviously, a passion that has an immoral end is and always remains immoral. But does passion in itself (ignoring for a moment its end) so dangerously disturb the economy of the self? We've just seen that it brings about secondary passions, at least some of which are quite useful. From this perspective, therefore, passion can and should be useful.

In fact, for any activity to be truly productive, it must be concentrated so that its strength is maintained. In short, activity must be moved by passion. To bring a work to life, we must have a passion for it. Artists and writers succeed only if they're passionate about their work. A painter needs not just a passion to paint but also a passion for the people he paints. And the same is true for a thinker. When the object of passion isn't unworthy – and when reason exerts some control – passion is an indispensable condition without which no great thing can be accomplished.

TEN

Theory of Knowledge

Intelligence is the faculty of knowing, and its characteristic activity is thought. Ideas are representational, for each idea represents some object. This naturally provides a way to classify the different forms of intellectual activity – that is, there are as many intellectual faculties as there are types of objects to be known.

Humans can have knowledge of three types of objects – those given to us in experience, those given to us outside experience, and finally those of the inner world. Many people question whether there really are things known by us outside of experience, but (without answering the question here) we'll take the commonsense position that recognizes three different kinds of knowledge.[70] We can always reduce these to two if necessary.

This division yields three faculties of perception – the senses, reason, and consciousness.

There are three other intellectual faculties that deal with objects having only a virtual presence. These are the association of ideas, memory, and imagination, which we'll call the faculties of conception.

Finally, beyond these simple faculties, there are also a number of complex operations formed by the combination of different faculties. These are abstraction, attention, judgment, and reasoning.

Such are the major divisions of the theory of knowledge.

70. The original says "two," but "three" is indicated by the context. Eds.

ELEVEN

External Perception and Its Conditions. The Senses

External perception is the faculty by which the external world becomes known to us. The external world begins where the world of consciousness ends.

In order for external perception to take place, three conditions must be met:

1. Some object must be in our vicinity. This seems obvious, but perception sometimes occurs even in the absence of an object. This is called a hallucination.
2. Certain physiological conditions must be fulfilled. Again, there are three: The object must come to the attention of a sensory organ; the nervous stimuli generated must be transmitted through the body; and this transmission must reach the brain.
3. The self must intervene. Sensory stimuli are multiple and diverse, and unified perceptions occur only through the intervention of the self.

Of these three conditions, here we'll study only one – the relationship between the object and the senses. We won't concern ourselves with the existence of the object or the intervention of the self. Instead, we'll focus on the organs – called senses – that mediate between objects and the brain.

Five senses are typically recognized: touch, smell, taste, sight, and hearing. But it's important not to restrict the word "senses" just to the sensory organs that are the intermediaries between the external world and the self. We define the word more broadly as "sources of information about the external world" because there are some senses that aren't localized. Two senses – known to us only recently – are not associated with a specific organ. The first of these is the muscular sense, which allows us to feel the state, position, and fatigue of our muscles. The second is the vital sense, which gives us access to the general condition of our bodies – its well-being or malaise – regardless of specific location. Lemoine has described it as "like a kind of inner touch." In the Middle Ages, this was called the *sensus vagus*. "When I say that I know by eye or ear that I'm ill, it's not of or by sight, nor is it of or by hearing that I suffer.... These five senses have nothing to do with the production of such sensations. They depend on a different faculty of sensibility." [71]

What is the relative value of the different senses? Some obviously provide us with information that's more precise or more abundant than that given by others.

At the lowest rungs of the ladder are the senses of smell and taste. These are so meager that – except for the sensory emotions they produce – they give us virtually nothing to appreciate. They're purely affective, and only after we've undergone a long education do they yield true knowledge.

On the next higher rung comes the vital sense. This placement disagrees with Albert Lemoine, who invented the term and who claims that it is "thanks to [the vital sense] alone [that] we know the external world." We disagree because, as we see it, all the indications that come to us from the vital sense are on the order of sensory emotions and contain little in the way of precise information.

Higher up still are sight and hearing. These are the two aesthetic senses, which gives them their superiority.

On the fourth rung comes touch, which gives us some very precise notions indeed. Touch can replace sight and sometimes even hearing. The superiority of this sense was well recognized among the ancients – Anaxagoras, for example, said that man is able to think because of the hand.

At the top of the ladder is the muscular sense, which gives us the most precise notions of all. Together with touch, this sense gives us knowledge of extension; and besides, it's muscular effort that makes us different from the world around us.

Smell, taste, the vital sense, hearing, touch, and finally the muscular sense. Such is the natural classification of the senses.

71. A. Lemoine, *The Body and the Soul*. Lalande.

Compared with the kinds of knowledge provided by the other senses, however, what kind of perceptions do these senses yield naturally (rather than through experience)? To put this another way, how should we distinguish between natural perception (that furnished naturally by each sense) and acquired perception (that which we come to have)?

For most of the senses, making such a distinction isn't very difficult. Taste naturally yields flavor, smell gives us odor, hearing gives us sound, the muscular sense yields resistance, touch gives us extension, and finally the vital sense provides knowledge pertaining to the general state of the body.

Things are more complicated when it comes to sight. Properly speaking, what sight allows us to perceive is color. But is this all? Doesn't sight also give us knowledge of extension? After all, how can these two perceptions be separated? But is knowledge of extension only the consequence of experience and education? Or is this sensation part of sight's intrinsic nature?

Some philosophers think that the latter is the case, and because they believe that extension is an innate perception of the eye, we'll call them nativists. By contrast, empiricists believe that this perception is only an effect of experience and education.[72]

There are two components to extension:

1. The idea of distance. Operations performed on those blinded by cataracts from birth prove that sight doesn't give us the idea of distance. A blind person operated on by Cheselden said that, as soon as he could see, colors appeared to him on a plane tangential to the orbit of the eye.
2. The idea of surface. Cheselden's experiment seems to suggest that sight does naturally provide us with some idea of surface; but this isn't conclusive, because the person born blind has – by his other senses – already formed an idea of surface, which influences the way he sees colors.

So no experiment has been conducted that would answer the question of whether sight naturally gives us the idea of extension.

Yet the empirical hypothesis is more likely. How else would the eye project the sensation of the perceived color into space? Even if it could do

72. Note in left margin refers to the "school of Müller" but is cut off and barely legible. Eds.

so on its own, the resulting notion of space would be quite rudimentary, and a great deal of experience would be required to arrive at the notion of space that we have today. And by analogy, the incapacity of sight to provide the third dimension makes it equally unlikely that it could recognize the other two. So we can say that, for the time being, the empirical hypothesis seems the strongest.

Many hypotheses have been advanced to explain how, little by little, we come to associate color and extension. Alexander Bain, for example, has shown how time and the muscular sense combine to give us knowledge of extension, and, to explain the association of the ideas of extension and color, he invented the theory of local signs.

TWELVE

External Perception. The Origin of the Idea of Externality

It's through external perception that the external world becomes known to us. But does this world really exist? This is the question we'll address in the next few lectures. It can be subdivided into two other questions:

1. Does anything exist outside the self?
2. If something does exist outside the self, is it as we perceive it?

Before answering these questions, there's another we have to answer first: Where do we get the idea of externality, or – as it's also called – of the nonself?

An idea can have only two kinds of origins. Either it's somehow given to the mind or it's constructed by it, a work of the mind resulting from some kind of intellectual labor.

Let's see if the idea of externality is constructed.

A number of philosophers – from different philosophical schools – have responded that it is. Cousin was of this opinion, as was Stuart Mill, whose theory on the matter was the best developed. According to Mill, the idea of externality is constructed in the following way: All we know about the external world comes through sensation, which is – by its very nature – subjective. When as adults we have a sensation of color, of course, we immediately conclude that a colored object exists. But how do we reach this conclusion? This is what must be explained. By itself, a sensation is purely affective and subjective. So how could it give us the idea of externality?

We arrive at this idea through a division of sensations – for example, I enter into a room: I have the perception of the door, then of a library, and then of a table. Each time I enter the room, I have these three sensations in the same order. And even when I don't actually experience them, I still know that I can experience them. So Mill calls these possible sensations, contrasting them with present or actual sensations whose order can't be known in advance.

These two kinds of sensation are very different – the second is fleeting, while the first is permanent. Possible sensations, which come about with great regularity, demand an explanation. According to Mill, this is what leads the self to imagine that their cause is distinct from the self. Since they're possible, he says, they continue to exist without my perceiving them. So they're not the same as the self, and the nonself – or the external world – consists of the causes of possible sensations.

But this theory alone doesn't completely explain the idea we have of the external world. The nonself does not consist of random sensations but of atoms, of substances with qualities that cause sensations. So the theory must be expanded. Possible sensations, Mill argues, are associated with one another in groups and appear to us as coexisting – a sensation of color, for example, together with a sensation of extension, another of resistance, another of taste. We call a thing imagined by the mind an "object," and the various possible sensations of this object, grouped together, are only its different qualities.

Such is the theory of Stuart Mill on the origin of the idea of externality.

But there are serious problems with Mill's theory. All sensations, without exception, are subjective. On the basis of sensations, therefore, we couldn't possibly form an objective idea. So the difference Mill establishes between possible and actual sensations isn't enough to show how the mind is able to form the idea of externality.

Neither is there an opposition between possible and actual sensations. Three sensations occur sequentially, in the same order, on separate occasions. Does the mind conclude that an external object is present? Not necessarily. For it might equally conclude that these sensations follow one another in this way because of some law of the mind, or that a certain number of subjective states are subject to an absolute determinism.

A general truth emerges from this refutation of Mill's theory. To be constructed, the idea of externality must have sensations as a foundation. But as sensations have no objective value, the idea of the external world – which is objective – can't be constructed. Since we do have this idea, it naturally follows that it's given.

The idea of externality is therefore given. But it might be given in several ways. Is it given in experience, already fully formed by one or several sensations? Or is it inherent in the nature of the mind itself? These are the only two ways in which the idea could be given.

Let's start by asking whether the idea of externality is given in experience. The perceptionists (philosophers who claim that it is) are divided into two camps. Some, like Hamilton, suggest that all sensations give us the idea of externality. Others, like Maine de Biran, argue that this is true only of muscular effort, that the sensation of resistance gives us the idea of the external world. The obstacle, according to Maine de Biran, could only be a nonself.

We can refute the first theory with the same arguments we used against Mill. Sensations, which are entirely subjective, can't give us the idea of objectivity. They are states of the modification of the self, and their cause could just as well be in the self as in the nonself.

The sensation of muscular effort is no exception to this rule. The obstacle that stops our movement might just as easily be in the self as outside, and we might feel a resistance when, in reality, there's nothing. [73]

If the idea of externality can't be constructed, and the essentially subjective nature of sensations means that it can't be given in experience, then the idea must be given outside of experience and derive from the very nature of the mind.

An idea that's inside us without having been deposited there by experience is called an a priori idea.

Now let's try to go still further and see how this a priori idea is given to us.

This happens because we have a more general idea – inseparable from the nature of our intelligence – called space. Space surrounds us and is thus distinct from the self. Until we've experienced sensation, space exists for us only potentially. But as soon as a sensation is experienced, we spontaneously objectify it and situate its cause in space. And this is how the idea of externality is born.

But if we form the idea of externality spontaneously, it's only through experience that – into this primitive chaos – we introduce the order that we conceive it to have. We do this by making an object of the cause of the possible sensations that are always experienced together. Therefore, although Mill's theory is false with respect to the origin of the idea of externality, it's true with respect to the ordering of sensations experienced and spontaneously objectified by the self.

73. Foucher; Taine, *Intelligence*, vol. 1. Lalande.

THIRTEEN

External Perception. On the Objectivity of the Idea of Externality. (1) Does the External World Exist?

As we now know where the idea of externality comes from, it seems that we're in a position to decide if this idea corresponds to real objects existing outside of us. The idea of externality is given to us in the idea of space. So the question might be asked as follows: Does the idea of space correspond to an objective reality? But we're not quite ready to answer this question, which amounts to asking if objects really exist in space. This can't be answered until we've decided that objects really exist, and this is what we're going to consider in this lecture. The question of the objectivity of the idea of space is actually part of another, more complicated question of knowing if the laws of the mind are also the laws of things, to which we won't turn for a while.

So in order to know if anything really exists outside of ourselves, we'll have to proceed in some other way. Using an inductive approach, let's imagine that we have a sensation and then try to determine its cause. If we decide that the cause lies within us, we'll conclude that there's no such thing as the nonself. But if we decide that the cause lies outside of us, we'll conclude that the external world does exist.

How do we determine the cause of a phenomenon? Logic can be our guide. Let's say there are two phenomena, A and B. If every time that A occurs, B also occurs, there's a very strong presumption that A is the cause of B. Inversely, if A occurs frequently without B occurring, there's a very strong presumption that A is not the cause of B. This presumption becomes a certainty if we establish that nothing has kept A from producing its effect.

Let's apply this principle to the matter at hand. I'm in a room. My self comprises memories, emotions, passions, sensations, etc. I designate these diverse states of consciousness A, B, and C. Suddenly, a sound D occurs. This is a new sensation. What's its cause?

It's not in the self.

But could it be that some obstacle is simply preventing A, B, and C from having their effect? If so, this obstacle would have to be either in the self or outside the self. The obstacle wasn't in the self, because the self was composed only of states of consciousness A, B, and C, and these states of consciousness persisted after D occurred.

So the obstacle could have come only from the outside. Whether the phenomenon D was produced by an external cause or held back for a certain time by such a cause, the demonstration still shows that there is something outside of us.

Here's another method that yields the same result.

If a phenomenon B occurs without being preceded by another phenomenon A, then A is not the cause of B.

Let's apply this principle. I enter a room. My self is composed of diverse states of consciousness A, B, C; I experience the sensation of this room that I designate D.

After a certain time, I return to the room, thinking that nothing has been changed. My self is then comprised of states of consciousness A1, B1, and C1. I enter the room and have sensation D.

Is the cause of D within me or is it outside of me?

It's not within me, because it would have to have been present in the first experience A, or B, or C. But none of these states of consciousness existed in the second experience in which D occurs. So none of them is the cause of D.

Therefore, the cause of D is external.

The two methods lead to the same result – the objectivity of the external world is demonstrated.

FOURTEEN

External Perception. On the Objectivity of the Idea of Externality. (2) On the Nature of the External World

We now know that the external world exists. But what is its nature? Is it as we perceive it to be? Or is it different? This is what we'll address in this lecture. We perceive the external world through our senses, so let's see if our sensations correspond to qualities that naturally inhere in matter.

The qualities of matter that are known to us through our senses can be divided into two distinct classes.

Not all objects have qualities of the first class, for we can conceive of objects independent of them. These are only forms of other properties of matter, and thus we call them secondary qualities – for example, heat, color, taste, odor, etc. Clearly there are objects that have neither taste nor odor, and we can imagine an object lacking color or heat. Science tells us that sound and color are only varieties of movement, and the same might be said for the other secondary qualities.

Qualities of the other class – primary qualities – have the opposite characteristics. All objects have such qualities. We can't conceive of an object independent of them. All secondary qualities can be reduced to these primary qualities, whereas they themselves are irreducible.

There are only two primary qualities – extension and movement. All bodies are extended and mobile, as we can't conceive of an object which would be unextended or immovable.

Without prejudging the nature of the external world, the distinction between these two classes of objects at least permits us to say what it isn't. Secondary qualities are merely appearances of the forms of primary qualities and differ from them only because of the intervention of the senses. As there's nothing more to matter than these primary qualities, we can offer the following provisional definition:

Matter is extension susceptible to motion.

So far, however, we haven't shown that these primary qualities are really those of objects themselves and not mere appearances. In short, we still have to determine what's objective about them.

We'll begin by showing that the very idea of extension is contradictory. We proceed on the following principle: A whole composed of parts can always be quantitatively measured, or at least could conceivably be so measured through means more powerful than those presently available. This is so because extension is continuous, and everything that's continuous can be divided into like parts.

But we can show not only that extension can't be divided into a finite number of parts but also that it can't be divided into an infinite number of parts.

First, extension can't be divided into a finite number of parts. No matter how many of these parts we count, each of them, too, will be extended and can be further divided indefinitely.

Second, extension can't be divided into an infinite number of parts because the notion of an infinite number is itself contradictory. By definition, a number is capable of being indefinitely increased or decreased. But infinity has the opposite characteristic – it's fixed. Infinity can't be increased or decreased. So the notion of an infinite number is meaningless.

Mathematicians, of course, frequently use the notion of infinity. But in the context of mathematics, infinity is just a symbol. It's said, for example, that a regular polygon with an infinite number of sides has a perimeter equal to its circumference. But all this means is that when we increase the number of sides of a polygon, the difference between its circumference and its perimeter decreases constantly and that this difference can be made as small as we like. It's this symbol – infinity – that allows us to apply the laws of the polygon to the circumference, those of the pyramid to the cone. But clearly it's nothing more than a symbol.

When we write that the series $\frac{1}{2} + (\frac{1}{9})^9 + (\frac{1}{7})^3 + (\frac{1}{2})^4 \cdots + (\frac{1}{2})^n \cdots$ approaches 1, we don't mean that the moment will come when the equation actually equals 1, only that the farther we extend the series, the more its difference from 1 decreases. All this leads us to conclude that there's no such thing as an infinite number, which means that extension can't be divided into an infinite number of parts.

But there's another possible way to divide extension – division into an indefinite number of parts. By definition, we can't count the number of these. But we've established that wholes composed of parts can be measured quantitatively and also that space is a whole composed of parts of space.

So:

On the one hand, it's impossible to quantitatively measure extension. On the other hand, extension is quantitatively measurable.

Obviously this is a contradiction. This means that the idea of extension should be rejected – it's nothing more than a deceptive appearance.

So objects aren't extended. But we know that they're divisible into unextended parts. Moreover, the number of these parts isn't infinite, for the notion of an infinite number is contradictory. So the number of parts has to be finite. Objects are thus divisible into a finite number of unextended and distinct parts.

Without verging into speculation about the nature of objects, we note at this juncture that physics and chemistry also recognize objects to be formed of a finite number of unextended parts that these sciences call atoms.

How should we understand these unextended elements of objects? As beings. The only way for us to conceive of them is by analogy with the only being we know – the self. And what are we? We're a force that's conscious of and moves itself: *vis sui consciea sui motria*. The force that we are also has sensibility and intelligence. Obviously, the beings we're talking about now don't have these latter two characteristics. Their distinguishing characteristic is activity.

We can imagine the elements of objects to be similar to what our soul would be if it lacked sensibility and intelligence – if it were, in short, an unconscious force. In fact, these beings are nothing more than the forces that limit and suppress the force that is the self. And it's because of these limitations that the self recognizes these beings to be similar to itself.

We now know the nature of objects. They're composed of a finite number of elementary forces.

Extension and movement are only appearances. We've shown this for extension. Because movement is only a change in extension, it too is shown to be merely an appearance once we've demonstrated that extension has no objective reality. The only real thing is force, forces similar to those that we are and that don't need extension in order to act. Entirely outside of extension, our will can act on our intelligence, and the same is true for the external world.

Let's look at the different theories about the external world. There are two major branches – idealism and realism. The first asserts that the external world has no objectivity, while the second argues that the external world really does exist. So our doctrine is a realist doctrine.

But there are different versions of realism.

We could imagine the external world to be formed of parts of extension in movement. This is called mechanism or dynamism and was the theory advanced by Descartes.

Alternatively, the external world can be thought of as composed of beings similar to ourselves; beings in whom, however, consciousness is almost completely extinguished. This kind of realism is called spiritualism.

According to this theory – which we accept – there's no break in the continuity of nature. From the highest mind all the way down to inorganic matter, all is spirit, all is force. It's only a question of the degree of consciousness.

As for extension, movement, the primary and secondary qualities – these are mere appearances, generated as a result of the deformation that things undergo when we perceive them through the intermediary of the senses.

There's no such thing as dead or inert properties. Everything in nature is animated and alive.

This doctrine was first proposed by Aristotle, but the greatest genius to have advanced it was Leibniz.

FIFTEEN

Consciousness. On the Conditions of Consciousness

Consciousness is the faculty by which internal phenomena become known to us. Let's examine the conditions of internal perception, just as we did those of external perception.

The first is that a modification of the self must occur. Every internal phenomenon is a form of knowledge, and for there to be knowledge, there must be something to know. This something is the psychic modification, the object of knowledge of consciousness, and the requirement that such an object exist corresponds to the first condition of external perception.

Second, this knowledge requires a subject – the self. The second condition of internal perception (which corresponds to the second condition of external perception) is thus the intervention of the self, which alone is capable of knowing. So internal perception has all the same conditions as external perception, except for the need for one of the senses to serve as an intermediary between subject and object.

It's been argued that some internal phenomena don't meet all the required conditions and thus can't be observed by consciousness. Leibniz, who first drew the attention of philosophers to this point, suggested that the internal world is composed of perceptions and apperceptions. We're fully conscious only of the latter. Leibniz's idea had significant implications and led to the formation of an entire doctrine whose most prominent representatives are Schopenhauer, author of *The World as Will and Representation*, and Hartmann, author of *The Philosophy of the Unconscious*.

Proponents of the theory of the unconscious base their claims on internal phenomena that seem to be the object of a very weak or nonexistent consciousness. Here are some examples.

When we walk on the seashore, we don't hear the individual sounds made by the collision of each molecule of water against others or against the beach. All we hear is the larger sound. But for this to occur, the self must have undergone a modification – the sum of all the individual modifications. This means that these individual modifications did occur, but we didn't perceive them, were not conscious of them.

Another case: Under the influence of habit, certain phenomena of which we're initially conscious become unconscious. This is so with the nervous movements called tics or with the miller who no longer hears the noise of his mill. But if the noise stops, he notices – proof that he perceives the sound without being conscious of it.

A great passion can lead to the same result. A wounded soldier, in the midst of combat, feels his wound only after the battle has ended. The pain is present and has been perceived, but unconsciously so. Similarly, an individual who falls prey to an obsession may see objects placed before his eyes but won't be conscious of this perception. The proof that a perception has really taken place is that, if a movement occurs, it's immediately perceived, and the subject is conscious of it.

It also sometimes happens that when we've consciously pushed our reflection in a certain direction, the movement of intelligence continues unconsciously. We search for a citation we can't find. We stop thinking of it consciously, but after a while the citation simply comes to mind. Unconscious work has taken place. The same thing happens when we spontaneously solve a problem that has previously confounded us.

Eduard von Hartmann has put together a compendium of all the facts that establish the existence of unconscious phenomena, arguing – among other things – that memory depends on the unconscious, because the psychic modification that becomes conscious at the moment of recollection existed unconsciously before. He's also argued that instinct is an example of an unconscious phenomenon. For if instinct were conscious, then animals would possess a sense of foresight infinitely more developed than that of human beings. To believe that bees consciously build the combs destined to receive their honey, we must believe that they understand geometry. The same might be said of the inexplicable instincts of most animals.

From this, Hartmann concludes that unconscious phenomena form the foundation of the self and that conscious phenomena are only the effects of their unconscious counterparts. The world of consciousness, in other words, has its roots in the world of the unconscious. Common sense, which situates the entire self in the world of consciousness, is only an illusion. We believe we have ends, goals, and personal wills, but we're only instruments of the unconscious. Here we see the pessimistic tendencies of Hartmann's system. To be happy, we must let ourselves be deceived. If we refuse and stay true to the nature of things, we must resign ourselves to unhappiness.

Leaving aside the sad moral and metaphysical consequences of Hartmann's doctrine, it's not difficult to show that his arguments lack any solid foundation. The examples he gives don't demonstrate that completely unconscious phenomena exist. Each could be explained by an extremely weak consciousness as easily as by none at all. Moreover, having left the conscious self, how would these phenomena reenter?

This refutation is supported by the facts. Sometimes when we reflect on slow mental work of which we weren't conscious at the time, we can remember when a psychic phenomenon occurred – for example, the citation or solution that the mind searches for unconsciously. Until it's found, the mind feels a certain tension or fatigue that it doesn't attribute to anything specific but that nevertheless shows some consciousness of this allegedly unconscious reflection.

And how are we to imagine an unconscious psychic phenomenon? A Latin adage tells us: *Intelligere nil aliud est quam sentire se intelligere* (To perceive is nothing else than to realize that one perceives). What would become of a psychic phenomenon that had left consciousness altogether? And once it had done so, how would it return? It's arbitrary to assume that one part of the soul is shielded from the gaze of consciousness, so we conclude – in opposition to Hartmann – that there's nothing absolutely unconscious in psychological life.

SIXTEEN

Consciousness. On the Origin of the Idea of the Self

All philosophers agree that consciousness gives us knowledge of psychological phenomena. But is this all it gives us?

We now know that consciousness also allows us to see a being – the self – whose existence we acknowledge constantly and to which all psychological phenomena are related. The pronoun "I" or "me," expressed or implied, is the subject of all our sentences. When I say, "It's hot," what I mean is, "I am experiencing a sensation of heat." "The external world exists" is a way of saying, "I hold that the external world exists." The self is thus the center around which all our states of consciousness converge, bringing unity to our inner life. But if this much is well established, we still have to determine whether the idea of the self is an invention, a construction of our mind, or given by consciousness itself. Here we come to a question analogous to that dealt with in our discussion of the origin of the idea of externality. So we'll use the same method here that we did there.

Every idea is either given or constructed.

Is the idea of the self constructed? The only materials that might be used to construct it are the various states of consciousness, and the method of construction would consist in extracting from them one or more characteristics that are somehow analogous to the idea of the self. This idea – like that of weight – could then be formed through generalization.

Of all the philosophers who've taken this approach, Taine has done so most systematically. He believes that the idea of the self is constructed as follows:

We divide our states of consciousness into two categories – the first consisting of states relating to something outside themselves (external perceptions or sensations) and the second of states that don't relate to anything outside themselves (emotions).

Perceptions are external. By contrast, the states of consciousness that fall into the second category share the property of being inside – which necessarily implies the idea of a container. This imaginary container is what we call the self.

This approach to the origin of the idea of the self rests on the purported identity of two ideas – the idea of the self and the idea of an inside. But is such an identification legitimate? Isn't the self rather a center, a point of convergence where all states of consciousness are centralized, rather than an enclosure that contains them? Let's think about it in geometric terms. To think about an inside, imagine what's enclosed in a sphere. The idea of the self is the center of this sphere. States of consciousness might then be thought of as spokes radiating out from the center yet still enclosed in the sphere and converging at the self. Here there are clearly important relationships between the sphere and its center, between the idea of an inside and that of the self – but the two aren't identical.

Let's go further. Taine assumes that states of consciousness are given outside the self. Is this possible? Since every state of consciousness is a form of knowledge, each requires both a subject and an object. Remove the subject and nothing remains. But with states of consciousness, the subject is necessarily the self – which Taine claims does not yet exist – so neither would the states of consciousness said to be its foundation.

This can be expressed another way. In his effort to show how external perception provides the foundation of all knowledge, Condillac brings up the idea of a statue on which he chisels all the senses, one by one. The first is the sense of smell. A rose is brought near the statue, Condillac says, and the statue perceives the odor of the rose. Yet the statue would be able to sense this odor only had it already been granted a sense of smell; and the statue would be able to sense the corresponding modification of itself only if it were self-conscious independent of this phenomenon. Otherwise it would be impossible for any sensation to occur.

The self is thus the indispensable antecedent of every state of consciousness. The so-called unconscious states of consciousness to which Taine makes reference simply don't exist.

To this, the positivists respond: "We don't at all assert the existence of unconscious states of consciousness. Each is conscious by itself, independent of the consciousness that, according to you, the self alone can give to it."

But by giving each of the states of consciousness its own special consciousness, the positivists only multiply the difficulties. Each state of consciousness would then have its own distinctive self, and the same question would still arise: How does each have an idea of the self?

So the idea of the self can't be constructed. It must be given. But how?

Here, the parallel with the case of external perception comes to an end, for the idea we seek is within us – is us. Between the idea of the self and us, there's no abyss like that which separates us from the external world. The idea of the self isn't deformed as it's presented to us. Through the eye of consciousness, we perceive it directly. The self becomes known to us simultaneously with the phenomenon of consciousness – the idea of the self is given in consciousness.

But does the self really exist? This question is analogous to the one we raised after showing how we're given the idea of externality. But here, experience itself is enough to prove that the self really exists. We see it, and we're unable to assume its nonexistence. In short, the very fact that we have the idea of the self proves that the self exists.

SEVENTEEN

Consciousness. On the Nature of the Self

We know that the self exists. But what is its nature? Here again, we run across a theory that we've already examined from another perspective. We want to ask if, as some philosophers claim, there's something in us besides the self, something distinct from the body – if somehow the inner world transcends that revealed to us by consciousness – if, in short, the soul is greater than the self.

Maine de Biran believed that it is, pointing to another reality beneath the self that serves as a substratum of conscious reality. By contrast with the active self, he gave the name "substance" to this other part of us. Cousin also believed there's something outside the self that escapes consciousness, whose existence is implied by reason alone.

But what we said about Hartmann and the *Philosophy of the Unconscious* refutes this theory.[74] Quite aside from the fact that there aren't any unconscious psychic facts, the concept of substance is vague, empty, and indeterminate. What's the nature of this unconscious being? By definition, it's not active, and if it were, it would give rise to phenomena that would be observable by consciousness. Since it's inactive, all it can do is serve as the foundation for the self's actions. The only role that Maine de Biran gives this unconscious being is to serve in support of the self. But as we can't even imagine such a being, the concept of substance is void of any precise meaning.

Outside of what consciousness makes available to us, there's simply nothing. The soul and the self are one and the same.

This established, let's look at the nature of the self.

74. See Lecture 15. Lalande.

It has three essential characteristics:

1. Unity. The self is one, indivisible, and can't be separated into parts. Consciousness itself tells us this, and reason confirms it – we must have the idea of unity. In principle this idea could come to us from within or without. But in fact it couldn't possibly come from outside, where everything is multiple and perceived by us as indefinitely divisible, so we must get it from the nature of the self alone.
2. Identity. Despite all the changes it undergoes, the self is – and senses itself to be – identical to itself. Here our reasoning is the same as for unity. In the external world, everything is in flux, and nothing remains the same for very long. So it could only be from ourselves that we derive the idea of identity. As we'll discuss later, the idea of identity is also one of the necessary conditions of memory.[75]
3. Causality. The self is a cause – we feel that we're responsible for our actions, as we can see them result from the exercise of our wills. We also know that we're but one among many causes. Where would we get this knowledge if not from knowledge of ourselves? In the external world, all we see are phenomena succeeding one another, not their causes. We say that movement causes heat, of course, but in reality all we see is movement preceding heat. It's only within us that we recognize a cause producing its effect. The idea of cause thus originates in the self.

A being that has unity, identity, and causality is what we call a person. It's obvious that for a being to be a person, it must first be one and identical. In addition, the being's actions must emanate from it and it alone. This is what distinguishes a person from a thing. The latter acts only if some shock makes it move. One of the essential characteristics of a person, by contrast, is that its actions are its own. All human beings are one and identical to the same degree; but we're not all equally the cause of our own actions. While it's true that no one completely lacks the power of causation, some human beings have more will than others. Some do nothing they haven't willed. Others are only instruments in the hands of other people or the things with which they come into contact. Everything they do results from an impulse from outside themselves, their actions merely echoing demands of the external world.

75. See Lecture 25. Lalande.

So not all selves are persons to the same degree. All are persons, but there are important differences that we must acknowledge.

Our study of consciousness is now complete. We've observed its conditions and its object. We've questioned the objectivity of the ideas with which it provides us. So now we're in a good position to answer the following question:

Is consciousness a distinct faculty?

Those who answer this question negatively base their view on the argument that it's very difficult to distinguish the object of consciousness from the objects of the other faculties, since the former comprises the states of consciousness of intelligence, memory, will, and sensibility. Since there's no idea we owe to consciousness alone – or so the argument goes – consciousness isn't a distinct faculty.

This would be true if consciousness merely revealed various phenomena to us. But we've seen that it also makes known to us the self as well as its attributes. In other words, there are ideas we get from consciousness alone, which thus has its own proper and distinct domain, granting us ideas we wouldn't have without it. So it is a distinct faculty.

What consciousness – together with external perception – provides is experience. For this reason, these two faculties are called experiential faculties. In the next lecture, we'll ask if experience alone can explain all our knowledge.

EIGHTEEN

Reason. The Definition of Reason

The two faculties we've just examined – external perception and consciousness – yield experience. But can experience alone explain all of our knowledge? Or do other faculties also play a role? We'll consider this now.

To this end, let's determine the characteristics of the judgments we owe to experience. If we then discover judgments that have entirely different characteristics, we'll conclude that another faculty exists within us.

The characteristic of judgments owed to experience is that they're contingent – the mind can conceive of the opposite judgment being made.

Let's take an example from external perception. It's almost universally recognized that bodies fall in a vertical line. Yet it's not hard to imagine that they might well fall in another direction. Epicurus, for example, believed that atoms follow an oblique path. So this judgment is contingent.

Let's take another example. I say: "Man is a being with sensory abilities." This is true, but we can certainly conceive of a being who would have all the other faculties of man while lacking this one. This judgment is also contingent.

In fact, all judgments derived from experience are contingent. How could it be otherwise? What would keep us from conceiving of the opposite judgment? Certainly not the nature of the mind, from which judgments formed under the influence of the facts remain independent.

But now consider another truth: "Every phenomenon has a cause." In this case, the opposite judgment is inconceivable. The judgment is thus called necessary. So this judgment has the opposite characteristic from that of judgments given by experience, and there must be a faculty capable of producing judgments of this kind. In fact, there is – the faculty of reason.

Sometimes these kinds of judgments are called universal rather than necessary. But this terminology isn't very helpful, as it's easy enough to find an experiential judgment to which there's universal agreement. If the human mind can't imagine the contradiction, of course, the judgment will perforce be universally accepted. Yet the possibility of universally accepted experiential judgments remains, so we adopt the alternate terminology and say: "Reason is the faculty that provides us with necessary truths."

We've just said that necessary judgments are those whose contradiction is inconceivable. We could put this differently and say that they're judgments the terms of which can't be separated.

But what's the origin of this impossibility? Does it stem from the fact that the two terms of the judgment always appear together in experience? This isn't enough, for this wouldn't make it impossible to conceive of the contradiction. But if this impossibility doesn't come from experience, there's only one other place it can come from. It must be inherent in the very nature of the mind.

If there are necessary truths, it's because there are judgments that the mind, by its nature, can't conceive. There's an antagonism between these judgments and the form of the mind (just as other judgments derive from this same nature).

Whatever derives from the nature of a being is called a law of the being. Necessary judgments are therefore nothing but the laws of our minds, and we can say: "Reason is the collection of the laws of the mind."

Since the mind has a distinctive nature and its own laws – and since the external world also has its nature and laws – things can be known by the self only if they're in harmony with the laws of our minds. Things known in this way constitute experience.

Another way of describing judgments that are necessary and derive from the nature of the mind is to say that they're given to us a priori. Sometimes these judgments are called "innate," but here we have to be careful not to interpret this to mean "existing before all experience." No ideas come to us already made, engraved in our minds prior to all experience. There is nothing before experience. Innateness understood in this way is meaningless.

From the onset of experience, however, the mind begins to act according to its laws, connecting phenomena to their causes. Necessary truths are to the mind what weight is to bodies – a property that's part of and expresses its very nature.

Some philosophers, however, have contested this understanding of reason. For them, necessary truths result from our more or less mysterious relationships with a supraexperiential world. This was the view taken by Plato. The νοῦς (mind), he says, simply reflects the supraexperiential world of ideas. Reason is therefore impersonal. The universality of necessary propositions derives from the fact that all minds are but a reflection of this ideal world, which he calls the intelligible sun. Without it, he claims, human reason would be extinguished.

Victor Cousin seems inclined toward this theory, and Bouillier, one of his disciples, has written a work in this vein entitled *Impersonal Reason*.

But as we understand it, reason is utterly personal. It depends on no external cause whatsoever and isn't a reflection of some higher realm. It's simply the expression of the very nature of each of us. The most illustrious philosopher to have taken this view was Kant.

NINETEEN

Reason. The Material of Reason. (1) Principles of Reason

We've seen that the principles of reason derive from the nature of the mind itself. This means that if we succeed in grasping the nature of the mind – its essence – we might deduce directly from it all the principles of reason. What's the essence of the mind? Briefly, the need for unity or simplicity. For the mind is simple and understands well only that which is also simple. We understand geometric figures best, because these are composed only of homogeneous space. The mind's need for simplicity is so great that when it examines any more concrete object – necessarily multiple and complex in nature – it has to conceive of it as though it were simple. The mind never renders these objects simply as geometric figures, of course, but it's compelled to introduce a certain unity and order. So we can say that the aim of the laws of the mind is precisely to introduce this order and unity. Does this order demanded by the mind really exist in things themselves? We won't try to answer this question now. But whatever the answer, such order is clearly required by the nature of the mind.

The principles of reason thus introduce order into our knowledge. But what are these principles? Without imagining that we can do so in an utterly deductive way, we'll try to identify them now.

What's given is multiple, and what the mind wants is to impose upon it some kind of order. To this end, all the terms of multiplicity given in experience must first receive a kind of external ordering – according to their nature, they must be placed in different contexts. There are two major types of experiential knowledge – external and internal. The context in which we place the first, knowledge given by the senses, is space. The context in which we place the second, knowledge given by consciousness, is time.

As soon as experience begins, therefore, the mind divides phenomena into two groups, placing one in space and the other in time. The mind conceives of psychological phenomena as durational [*durant*] and external phenomena as coexisting [*coexistant*].

From this we can derive two principles of reason – all states of consciousness occur in time and all phenomena given by sensation occur in space.

But this initial ordering, which is wholly external, isn't enough. The mind is compelled to conceive of a higher order among things, which it does by conceiving of the phenomena given by experience as modifications of some being or reality independent of intelligence – a reality called substance. From this comes the principle: "All phenomena are modifications of substance."

The mind thus places phenomena into groups and conceives of a being at their center. But what are the relationships among these phenomena?

They are causal. For the mind can't conceive of any phenomenon without assuming that another phenomenon is its condition. It conceives of all in terms of cause and effect. From this comes the principle: "Every phenomenon has a cause." Note, however, that we don't say: "Every effect has a cause." The truth of this is obvious, but that every phenomenon has a cause is less so. Yet under the influence of the principle of causality, we see the entire world as comprising immense series of phenomena in which each term is both cause and effect.

But this ordering still isn't enough for the mind. More specific relationships must be established among the various series, which occurs when the mind conceives of them as converging toward certain end points, toward their common aim. From this comes the principle: "Every phenomenon or series of phenomena has an end." This is the principle of finality, of conceiving of the world as comprising systems converging on the same center.

So there are five principles of reason by which we gain knowledge of what's given in experience (what Kant called, for this reason, the constitutive principles of experience). These are the principles of time, space, substance, causality, and finality.

Once constituted by means of these principles, however, our knowledge functions according to laws of its own. For the elements of knowledge also have definite relationships among themselves, which gives us the new principle of identity and contradiction (what Kant called the regulative principle of knowledge). This principle is as follows: "All that is, is; a thing can't be, at the same time and from the same perspective, itself and its opposite." This law governs all of our knowledge.

Kant was not the first to recognize the importance of these principles, for his constitutive principles had already been subsumed under Leibniz's notion of sufficient reason. Leibniz also introduced the idea of identity. But unlike Kant, he didn't believe that time and space are given a priori. The first of the two principles that form the basis for his system is: "Everything that is has a reason for being."

Be that as it may, what we've shown is that there are two different kinds of principles of reason – those governing the acquisition of knowledge and those governing knowledge that has been acquired. The first are the laws of reasoning, and the second the foundations of logic.

TWENTY

Reason. The Material of Reason (2) Rational or First Ideas

To this point in the course, we've described reason as the faculty that, from the onset of and without any help from experience, is able to combine two given ideas. Now it's time to ask where we get these ideas. All ideas have the same subject – a phenomenon. This was demonstrated by the earlier definitions, but it might have been anticipated a priori by the following reasoning. Necessary propositions state the conditions to which experience is subject. This means that every necessary proposition has to contain two terms – the part of experience with which the proposition is concerned and its conditions. Hence, all rational judgments have the following form: "Phenomena of such and such a kind are subject to such and such a condition."

Of the two ideas that make up a rational judgment, therefore, one has an origin that we already know – experience. But whence comes the other? Its origin must be outside of experience, for otherwise it couldn't be related to experience. So these are a priori ideas (also called rational or first ideas). More specifically, they're the ideas of time, space, substance, cause, and end. Explaining their presence in the mind, Kant conceived of them as "determined forms," as molds whose forms are taken on by phenomena as they are perceived. The mind simply takes note of this process and, when it has done so a certain number of times, concludes that: "All external phenomena are subsumed under the concept of space." We then derive the principle that: "All external phenomena are situated in space." Kant actually reserved the word "forms" for time and space alone, which he called the "a priori forms of sensibility," and used the terms "a priori concepts" (or "categories of understanding") for the other rational ideas.

Beginning with the related notions of time and space, let's examine each of the rational ideas. Some philosophers – Herbert Spencer, for example – deny that these have an a priori origin, claiming instead that their origin is empirical. According to Spencer, when experience begins, we still lack the idea of time but possess states of consciousness existing in some positional relationship with one another. Some come before, others after. Indeed, all states of consciousness are in such positional relationships, which leads us to conceive of them as successive. In this way, Spencer argues, we form the idea of time.

For Spencer, the idea of space is derived from that of time. The characteristic quality of space is coexistence. Where do we get this idea of coexistence? It happens as follows. I touch a point A. Continuing the movement, I next touch a point B, then a third point C. When I get to C, I reverse the movement, retouching B and then A. In so doing, I have each of the same sensations that I did the first time around, but now their order is reversed. From this exercise it becomes clear that when I was at B, C and A still existed, because I was still able to have the sensation of them when I touched them again. From this I learn that A, B, and C coexist. The idea of coexistence – as well as that of space, which derives from it – thus originates in the possibility of reversing the order of a series of states of consciousness.

But there's a problem with this theory. If the mind didn't already have the idea of time, it couldn't conceive of states of consciousness being situated before and after one another. So using this approach to explain the origin of the idea of duration creates a vicious circle. It just won't work.

As for the construction of the idea of space, there's no proof at all that when I'm at point C, B and A haven't disappeared. And in fact there are certain states of consciousness whose order can be reversed without implying their coexistence. When I hear someone playing a musical scale, for example, I don't conclude that the notes that have been played coexist.

So the origin of these ideas is a priori.

Thinking about things in this way also helps us understand why geometric figures are a priori. Some people claim that they're only generalizations and abstractions, formed by taking the figures found in experience and abstracting just their extension. How do we form the idea of a triangle? According to this theory, we do so by observing many triangles in nature and from these abstracting an ideal triangle.

But this theory runs aground, for a generalization is nothing more than generalized particulars. There's nothing more in the idea of humanity than there is in any particular man. So if geometric figures were simple generalizations, they'd have only the characteristics shared by real triangles. But in fact they have an additional characteristic – perfection, which can't be found in the real world, where there are no perfect triangles or circles. So the characteristic of perfection – a key feature of geometric figures – can't come from generalization.

Instead, their origin lies in the fact that, a priori, the mind already has the ideas of space, of a point within space, and of the upper and lower boundaries of extension. The idea of geometric figures comes about from the movement of this point in space. Strictly speaking, therefore, geometric figures aren't given a priori but are constructed by the activity of the mind using the a priori idea of space. We're the ones who construct these objects, which is why the mathematical sciences seem so clear to us (and why we like to define things in mathematical terms).

Now let's turn to the ideas of substance, finality, and causality. Maine de Biran and Cousin claim that these ideas come from consciousness, and we've also argued that consciousness gives us the idea of causality. For Maine de Biran, the principle of causality comes about as we generalize from what we discover through internal observation, and the same is true for the ideas of substance and finality. For Cousin, by contrast, the principle of causality is indeed a priori, but the idea of causality is given to us experientially. But how could the principle be a priori when none of the ideas associated with it is?

We can resolve this difficulty by recognizing that these three ideas, as they're given by experience – and the same three ideas, as they're given by reason – aren't identical. Let's begin with substance. Reason compels us to relate phenomena to something other than themselves. But it can't tell us what this something is. Experience must intervene, giving us the concrete representation of the idea of substance.

As for the principle of causality, reason indeed gives us the idea of cause. We conceive of a cause as the necessary antecedent to a phenomenon. But this results only from an internal experience we have that makes us see how the cause that we are produces its effects.

We turn next to finality; the idea of an end that reason gives us is that of the point at which several series of phenomena converge. This idea is totally abstract, and, for us to understand it concretely, experience must show us intelligence deliberating over some end to be achieved. If not, we'd conclude that things move toward their ends by themselves – the hypothesis of immanent finality. Or if we didn't accept the notion of immanent finality in things, we'd have to assume that there exists, outside of the universe, an intelligence analogous to our own, disposing of things according to its own ends.

In sum, the conditions of experience – in an abstract and general way – are conveyed to us by reason, while experience enables us to conceive of these conditions more concretely.

According to some philosophers, however, reason also gives us three additional ideas – the absolute, the infinite, and the perfect. Plato saw these as constituting the foundation of human knowledge. To understand what's relative, we must be able to relate it to the absolute. To understand what's finite, we must be able to relate it to the infinite. And to understand what's imperfect, we must be able to relate it to the perfect. These philosophers believe that reason is, by nature, impersonal.

But we deny that these ideas are a priori.

To explain why, we'll first note that all these ideas can be reduced to that of the absolute – that which is complete, exists in itself and by itself, and needn't be related to anything other than itself. Clearly, the infinite is the absolute in quantity. To say that something is infinite is to say that it's without limits and that we needn't relate it to something that limits it in order to understand it. Likewise, perfection is the absolute in quality. When we speak of something that's more or less perfect, we can mark off the various degrees of perfection only in relation to something that's absolutely perfect – while perfection itself needn't be related to anything else. The absolute, the infinite, the perfect – these three words come down to the same thing. The last two are merely different forms of the first.

The idea of the absolute isn't given a priori – on the contrary, there's an antagonism between it and the nature of the mind. It's impossible for us to understand anything except in relation to something else. Knowledge requires at least two ideas, as the general formula of the principles of reason tells us: "Phenomena of such and such a kind are subject to such and such a condition." To think, in other words, we have to relate things to some condition; but the absolute neither has conditions nor exists in relation to anything else.

Because of this, we can't think about the absolute without making it relative, at least to time and space. If we think of it as a cause, we must necessarily and simultaneously think of it as an effect. We might say that the absolute is outside of time, space, and causality, but – as such – it's impossible for us to think about. To think, an English philosopher has said, is to condition. All knowledge is relative. So it's impossible for the human mind to think of the absolute.

We don't mean by this to deny the existence of the absolute. This is simply a question we're not going to deal with now. Yet clearly there's a presumption in favor of its existence, for the history of philosophy shows that all philosophers have tried to explain it. To be sure, not all of them understand it in the same way, often insisting that it can't be defined. But all, upon reaching a certain point in their investigations – even when they refuse to consider it – are obliged to admit the existence of something outside of what's relative. Spencer calls this the unknowable, Littré the endless sea on the shores of which man is forced to stop, having neither the boat nor the sail to attempt a crossing. What is this ideal so long pursued by human thought? We'll take up this question in our discussion of metaphysics.

TWENTY ONE

Reason. Empiricism

One philosophical doctrine – which historically has gone by various names – denies the existence of reason and recognizes only consciousness and external perception. A version of this doctrine, called sensualism, derives everything from sensation. This theory, which was advanced by Democritus and later by Epicurus and the Stoics, explains knowledge as a function of idea-images. Working from the assumption that the only action is that of like producing like, the sensualists hold that the soul, like the body, is material. Nevertheless, the soul remains distinct from the "atoms" that bodies in space throw off from themselves. These atoms, or εἴδωλα (images), are like condensed images of the bodies, and as they strike us the images become imprinted on the soul, leaving impressions representing the bodies from which they emanated. These impressions are ideas.

Over the years, the crudeness of this theory was gradually recognized. To improve it, the notion of consciousness was added to external perception, so that knowledge might be derived from experience alone. This doctrine, initially formulated by Locke, is called empiricism. According to the empiricists, the mind prior to experience is like a wax tablet on which nothing has yet been written – a *tabula rasa*, or blank slate.

More recently, an even stronger version of empiricism has been developed in England. Because it grants an important role to the association of ideas, this version is called associationism. Dugald Stewart was the first to notice the philosophical significance of the association of ideas, and, since then, many others have joined him. "The law of the association of ideas," John Stuart Mill has even said, "is to the mind what the law of gravitation is to bodies."

There's an important difference between the associationists and their empiricist predecessors. The associationists recognize that the mind has its own proper activity – that of coming to grips with experiential facts. By so doing, they also recognize that the mind has the capacity to go beyond what's simply given to it – something the older empiricists didn't accept. Let's examine this version of empiricism, which is epitomized in Mill's *Philosophy of Hamilton* and *Logic*.

As we've seen, rational judgments are necessary judgments – they comprise two inseparable terms. Mill explains the impossibility of separating these terms through the association of ideas and habit.

Mill begins by arguing that this impossibility is only actual. Nothing shows that rational judgments have always been necessary judgments. In fact, many judgments that appear necessary to us didn't seem that way in the past. Pascal didn't believe in the law of gravitation, for example, and many things for which the evidence is now compelling seemed absurd to our parents! Mill thus claims that we shouldn't assume that the two terms of a rational judgment are united eternally or necessarily, for their connection might be only local and provisional.

Having thus called into question the necessity of rational judgments, Mill then traces them to the association of ideas and to habit. A law of psychology holds that, once we've associated two ideas in a certain way, we tend to reproduce them in the same order – a tendency whose force increases with the frequency of the association in our experience. When there are no exceptions to this order, the association of ideas becomes so strong as to be indissoluble, and the judgment formed on the basis of it – derived from an inseparable association of ideas – is described as necessary.

Because all discussions of reason center on the principle of causality, we'll examine Mill's explanation of how the mind, in two steps, forms this principle:

1. Phenomenon A and phenomenon B occur in the same order several times, so an observer develops a tendency, after A, to recall B. If always, without exception, A precedes B, then the mind will no longer be able to think of A without thinking of B and without believing that A always precedes B.

2. The mind observes two other phenomena, C and D, and – seeing the same connection between them – concludes that C precedes D. Passing to the next pair of phenomena, the mind comes to the same conclusion.

As a result of this process, all phenomena seem to form inseparable pairs, each having an antecedent from which it can't be separated, without which it never exists. To this invariable antecedent, Mill argues, we simply give the name cause, and the consequence is the effect. To say that every phenomenon has an invariable antecedent, therefore, is to say that every phenomenon has a cause.

But there are problems with Mill's theory. He begins by casting doubt on the necessary character of rational judgments, asking us to admit that we accept as true judgments that, at other times in history, seemed absurd. But absurd isn't the same as inconceivable, and the characteristic of rational judgments is precisely that their opposite can't be conceived. There aren't any examples of inconceivable judgments becoming conceivable, or vice versa. So in fact Mill hasn't called into question the necessity of rational principles at all.

As for the second step of Mill's argument – of course, we completely agree that the mind has a tendency to associate ideas that repeatedly occur together. But there's a difference between such a tendency and the absolute impossibility of separating the terms of a judgment. There certainly are ideas that we always associate with one another, but even these we could, if we wanted to, imagine apart. Night always follows day, but we don't see day as the cause of night, and it's not at all impossible to conceive of a continual day or a permanent night. Mansel has refuted Mill quite well by providing examples of this kind. "We can imagine," Mansel says, "the same stone sinking in water ninety-nine times, and floating on the hundredth, although experience only shows us the former. Experience always shows a man's head on a man's shoulders and a horse's head on a horse's body. But it's not impossible to imagine a centaur." So experience never constrains our freedom of thought.

Let's apply these objections to the origin of the principle of causality, beginning with Mill's first step. From the fact that A has always preceded B, we can't conclude that A will always precede B. When A presents itself to the mind, the mind will have a tendency also to think of B, but this tendency isn't a necessity.

Consider the second step. The mind observes that a certain number of phenomena are preceded by invariable antecedents. But how could this observation be generalizable to all observable phenomena – future as well as past and present? Whatever use we might make of the association of ideas, it doesn't permit us to cross the abyss that separates the past from the future.

We can put this another way by noting that Mill's two steps of reasoning can be reduced to the following syllogism:

1. A regular succession of phenomena is noticed a certain number of times.
2. What's been noticed a certain number of times is true of all analogous cases.
3. So the noticed succession is the same in all cases.

The problem with the syllogism, of course, is that the minor premise remains unproven – there being no foundation in experience for the assumption that what's true for all cases that have been observed is also true for all analogous cases that have not. In fact, we do make this assumption, on the basis of the principle of causality. We're able to see relationships of succession as universal only because we already know that all phenomena come in inseparable pairs. In other words, we do so only because we know already that phenomena are subject to an inflexible order of succession – to the law of causality. So the only way Mill would be able to prove his point would be by first postulating, in all its generality, the principle of causality. But to do so would contradict his theory.

So experience alone isn't enough to explain our rational judgments. But we might have foreseen this conclusion because – in a different context – we've already refuted empiricism, which seeks to reduce our most diverse states of consciousness to a single form. This artificial reduction effaces the very real differences between them, and the strongest versions of empiricism are those that most artfully disguise this diversity. In the end, however, what is different remains different. Earlier we noted that we can't construct anything objective on the basis of subjective sensations – the idea of substance on the basis of phenomena. Similarly, we now see that we can't construct necessity on the basis of contingency, for – however many contingent truths we observe – their nature doesn't change. In experience, we can't find that which is the very condition of experience.

TWENTY TWO

Reason. Evolutionism. The Theory of Heredity

By refuting empiricism, the preceding lecture established that individual experience alone can't explain rational judgments. But recently a new version of empiricism has appeared – one that escapes the objections we've just made. According to this new doctrine, rational judgments are innate but derive from the experience of the species. The first ideas attributed to reason aren't constructed *de novo* in the mind of each human being but – together with their derivative judgments – are there already formed. Their presence, however, can be explained as a kind of trust, made up of the accumulated experience of the species. Recognizing that many things are transmitted by heredity from ancestors to their descendants, this doctrine explains all of knowledge in this way. Reason thus might be defined as the totality of hereditary knowledge.

This theory of the origins of reason is part of the broader hereditary theory, which itself is but one chapter of the famous doctrine that follows from Darwin's hypothesis – evolutionism. The greatest philosophical champion of this doctrine is Herbert Spencer, who extended it from its original domain – natural history – to philosophy. The general exposition of his system is contained in his *First Principles*.

To better judge the value of hereditary theory as applied to the origins of reason, let's examine the fundamental principles of evolutionism.

The evolutionist (or transformist) theory replaces that of special creation – an ancient and widely accepted doctrine holding that each genus (and, within each genus, each species) had been specially created separately, that the Creative Force intervened several times to form the universe. For this reason, impassable lines of demarcation were thought to exist between the worlds thus created. Evolutionism calls this doctrine into question, arguing that the belief that the first cause intervened several different times has no scientific foundation. Rather than gaps between the various species, the evolutionary hypothesis sees a unity that connects species together in a continuous line, each considered as the development from a lower species and as a point of departure from whence a higher species raises itself.

According to the doctrine of special creation, the world is composed of elements harmoniously combined by the Creative Force. For the evolutionists, however, all such elements must be considered the result of evolution, of the transformation of a first being. Spencer argues that this transformation occurs according to a fixed rhythm, which he tries to measure, because beings must necessarily adapt to their environments.

To survive, Spencer says, every being must adapt itself to its environment, and because this environment is always changing, these beings change as well, producing the transformations just mentioned.

But not all beings undergo these modifications. How, then, do they become fixed in a species? It happens as follows. Precisely because these modifications are advantageous, they render those who have undergone them superior to those who haven't. If the modification is absolutely crucial for survival, those who haven't undergone it will die off. If it's merely advantageous, those same beings will be at a disadvantage relative to those favored. This kind of choice between individuals – some called to live, to be superior to others, elected at random, so to speak – is what the evolutionist theory calls selection.

The result of selection is that only those beings adapted to their environment survive. Once this happens, heredity intervenes, fixing the modification and making it a characteristic of the species as a whole.

The principles of evolutionism can thus be restated as follows: All beings develop out of others, and all ultimately derive from a single primordial one. The need to adapt to the environment leads to the modification and perfection of some organisms, and selection does away with the others. Finally, heredity fixes these modifications and makes them an attribute of the species.

Now that we know the general principles of evolutionism, let's look at its application to the theory of reason.

Transformism explains reason as it explains everything else, as a well-developed form of instinct, while instinct itself is simply a sophisticated reflex action. Like Mill, therefore, the evolutionists want to minimize the differences between the various forms of our psychological activity. The difference between them and the empiricists, as already noted, is that they trace the formation of rational ideas not to individual experience but to the experience of the species. Spencer does admit that knowledge includes things not given by experience alone, recognizing as we do that knowledge comprises two elements — the multiplicity given by experience and the activity of the mind. For thought to occur, there must be a continuous differentiation of states of consciousness. At the same time, there must be some order imposed on this multiplicity, so these diverse states of consciousness somehow have to be "integrated" (Spencer's expression).

Reason is the faculty that does this unifying and integrating, and Spencer shows how it's formed by evolutionary processes. To adapt to its environment, he explains, the nervous system over time becomes more and more complex and centralized. At first, all that exists is a confused succession of decentralized states of consciousness that produce reflex actions. As the nervous system develops, however, intelligence grows and becomes more refined. These modifications are then fixed by heredity, and as a result what's been learned though previous experience is passed on. Through this process, reason — or the faculty of integration — comes to seem innate in the individual.

We'll begin our critique by repeating what we said earlier about associationism, for evolutionism also has a tendency to consider all differences as merely apparent and as disguising a permanent identity. Beings that seem to us so diverse, phenomena we perceive as so different — evolutionism seeks to reduce all to one.

Yet if there's one idea that stands out from this entire course, it's that the best method is to look for differences and respect them. Of course, the mind finds great satisfaction in bringing unity to things. Multiplicity goes against its nature, and there's nothing it finds more displeasing. But there's no proof that objects have the unity that evolutionism or associationism claims for them. On the contrary, everything we know leads us to believe that multiplicity and diversity are the nature of the world. For now, however, we'll be satisfied with having simply mentioned — but not demonstrated — this idea.

We'll encounter the doctrine of evolutionism again when we discuss metaphysics, and it will then be examined in greater detail. What we must do now is evaluate the theory of heredity as applied to the formation of reason and rational ideas.

Look at the objections to which this theory is vulnerable:

First, it's no more than a hypothesis — one impossible to verify experimentally. For such a demonstration to be possible, we'd have to find people who are lacking one or more of the rational principles, but we have no evidence that such people exist. Spencer, who has extensive knowledge of the intellectual development of uncivilized peoples, can't find enough evidence for even a peremptory demonstration. However uncivilized the peoples, none lacks rational principles or possesses them to a lesser degree. To be sure, the speculations of these people are childlike. They apply necessary truths in a naïve way inconsistent with what we know from science. They understand causality, for example, quite differently than do our scholars and scientists. But this childlike quality itself demonstrates that the mind's search for causes – whether done well or poorly, seriously or in a childlike manner – occurs ineluctably, of absolute necessity.

But the impossibility of experimental verification isn't enough to reject a doctrine, and the theory of heredity faces a stronger objection.

All empiricists consider the mind prior to experience as a *tabula rasa*, as without a determinate nature of its own. This is true for empiricists who believe that the mind exists substantially as well as for those who hold it to be only a collection of phenomena. Both maintain that the source of all knowledge lies in experience. This being so, the mind prior to experience is said to have no laws of its own – no determinate nature – for such laws express the very nature of the being. But everything that is is defined. The indeterminate doesn't exist, so empiricism arrives at an unacceptable conclusion – that the mind has a real existence only at the moment when experience begins.

Evolutionism can't escape this criticism any more than can ordinary empiricism or associationism. The latter two systems place this indeterminate, unintelligible being at the origin of the mind of each individual, while evolutionism pushes it back to the origin of the species. Yet to push back a difficulty isn't to resolve it. The objection remains in full force.

But there's more. Without believing that rational principles are innate, we can't imagine the mind prior to experience; but even if such a mind could exist, it couldn't ever acquire knowledge, for it would be incapable of forming rational judgments. Knowledge – as Spencer recognizes – requires that the multiplicity given in experience be integrated within the mind. In any mind lacking this integrative faculty, thought is an impossibility. Yet for there to be rational judgments, there must already be thought – a vicious circle.

Evolutionism doesn't resolve this difficulty. The mind could never have been a *tabula rasa*, now or centuries ago. It's always had its own nature and, as the expression of this, its own laws – not to mention reason, which is the totality of these laws. There's something innate in the mind – itself, its nature. The formula of knowledge was given by Leibniz: *Nihil est in intellectu quod non prius fuerit in sensu – nisi ipse intellectus*. There are two sources of knowledge: experience (*quod prius fuit in sensu* [that which was first in sensation]) and reason (*ipse intellectus* [intellect itself]). Since reason can't be derived from experience, rational ideas and principles must be innate within us.

TWENTY THREE

Reason. On the Objectivity of Rational Principles

Earlier, when we discussed the nature of the external world, we didn't have the necessary foundation to ask if rational principles express the laws of this world in the same way that they express the laws of the mind. Now we'll try to solve this problem. By necessity, the mind sees all things under the form of rational judgments. But are things themselves also subject to such judgments? Do the laws of the mind have objective value? We'll examine them and find out.

For Kant, rational principles have only a subjective value. As we've already seen, he distinguishes between the a priori forms of sensibility [76] and the categories of understanding (of which the most important is the rational principle of causality). Kant views both kinds of principles as equally subjective – as the forms under which the mind must conceive all things, thereby denaturing them. The sensory multiplicity that experience provides is confused and disordered, so we impose on it an artificial order that enables us to understand – at the cost of completely transforming the material of experience. So we ourselves construct the world that we know. Kant calls this the phenomenal world τῶν φαινομένων (of manifest things) – the world of things as they appear, which itself has no reality.

Kant doesn't deny that things exist outside the mind, of course, insisting only that we can't know them in themselves. For to know them, we must apply to them the forms of the mind – thereby distorting them. The most we can do is conceive the existence of these objects. Taken together, they make up a world that serves as a kind of substratum, a

---

76. For Kant, as mentioned earlier, sensibility means experience. See Lecture 20. Lalande.

springboard from which the mind leaps in order to construct the phenomenal world. Kant calls this the noumenal world – the world we conceive of existing by reason alone τῶν νοουμενων (noumena).

All reality – inside the mind as well as out – is subject to this division. For self-knowledge, we must apply the laws of the mind to ourselves, so that each of us has two selves: a noumenal self that exists but that we don't and can't perceive and a phenomenal self that we perceive but that doesn't exist.

Because this doctrine implies that external objects exist, but only in a transcendental world – one that transcends the limits of intelligence – Kant called it transcendental idealism.

We agree with Kant that the mind has its own proper nature – one consequence of which is that it will leave, in knowledge, some trace of its activity. But does such a trace completely obscure the real nature of objects? Knowledge involves a coming together of object and subject, and it's always possible to find in knowledge elements of both. For the empiricists, the objective world of things acting upon the mind is the source of all knowledge. For Kant, the opposite is true – knowledge involves the mind acting upon things. But we consider both theories too extreme. Of the two, empiricism is the less logical, for it doesn't recognize that the mind has its own determinante nature. But while we agree with Kant that the mind is something definite whose forms are immutable, and also that there exist objects whose nature is no less determined than that of the mind, we think the natural conclusion is that knowledge is a synthesis of these two constitutive elements. This is why transcendental idealism seems to us problematic. We don't see why there should be an antinomy rather than a harmony between the mind and things. The hypotheses of both the empiricists and Kant are unwarranted.

It's true that Kant – in that part of his *Critique of Pure Reason* called the "transcendental dialectic" – introduced what he considered an incontrovertible argument concerning the "antinomies." All speculation on the world, Kant says, ends in antinomies or contradictions. For example, we can demonstrate that "the world is limited in time and space" and also that "the world is infinite in time and space." Kant identified four such antinomies, each with a thesis and an antithesis. These contradictions can be explained, he argued, only if we acknowledge that the thesis relates to the noumenal world and the antithesis to its phenomenal counterpart. Yet if we were to reject the distinction between these two worlds, then these antinomies – in which reason becomes lost – couldn't be explained. So the only way to save the principle of contradiction is to accept the premise of transcendental idealism.

But this argument is valid only if we accept that the thesis and the antithesis of each antinomy have an equal logical value – and they don't. In each of the alleged antinomies, there's one proposition that's true and another that's false. This means that there is, in fact, no contradiction, and the Kantian argument falls. In the thesis of one of his antinomies, for example, Kant suggests that every complex substance is also composed of simple parts, and in the antithesis, that no complex subtance is composed of simple parts. In our discussion of the nature of the external world, however, we already showed that the antithesis is false and that only the thesis is true.[77] But even if the antinomy couldn't be resolved, this still wouldn't be proof of an absolute antagonism between what is and what we know.

Since none of these efforts has been able to establish whether the rational principles are either absolutely subjective or absolutely objective, we'll have to investigate for ourselves what part of knowledge comes from the mind and what part from things themselves.

For this investigation, we'll first need some criterion, an objective principle that will allow us to judge the objectivity of other principles. We'll use that of contradiction.

Clearly, this principle has objective value. Since it's not one of the constitutive principles of experience and therefore is not responsible for the construction of knowledge, there's no reason to doubt its objectivity; and more direct proof can be found when we examine its role in scientific calculation. Imagine, for example, an astronomer observing some phenomenon and through calculations (where he relies entirely on the principle of identity) concluding that this phenomenon will occur again at a certain point in time. As predicted, the phenomenon occurs. Things in the external world have followed the same course as the mind guided by the principle of contradiction. So the principle is objective.

Using this criterion, let's take another look at knowledge. We will argue that there's a contradiction at the heart of two notions – that of the infinitely great and of the infinitely small – which together we'll call continuity. What we want to argue is that the notion of continuity has only subjective value.

Earlier we discussed some of the contradictions inherent in this notion. All things in the world, including time and space, are

---

77. See Lecture 14. Lalande.

discontinuous. This is certainly true for time, for it's composed of states of consciousness that are distinct and juxtaposed to one another. Were we, through a thought experiment, to remove these states of consciousness, we'd immediately see that time is composed of successive and discontinuous moments. Similarly, once we assume that extension is composed of discontinuous elements, we can imagine it under the form of a whole of discontinuous points, which would represent the sites of action of the elementary forces we described earlier.[78]

Causality is also discontinuous – an effect is not the continuous development of a cause. Between cause and effect there are definite solutions of continuity. Cause and effect together form an order, of course, and are harmoniously coordinated; but this order itself supposes a real distinction between them. It's therefore an aesthetic, not a mathematical, order. Here again the notion of continuity is shown to have only subjective value.

The same result obtains when we consider infinity in size. A whole composed of a number of real and finite parts is real only if the number of these parts is finite. Time and space, the series of causes and effects, are finite. Everything that is is defined, and what is defined is finite. The purely subjective notion of infinity in size forces us into an infinite regress, but in the real world things are not indefinite but finite.

Beyond being finite, they're also subject to the principles of causality, finality, time, and space.

78. See Lecture 14. Lalande.

TWENTY FOUR

Faculties of Conception. On the Association of Ideas

The association of ideas is the faculty that connects our ideas to one another. Nothing in the world is isolated, and so it is with our ideas. But this isn't to say that the association of ideas ever acts by chance. There's always a reason why two ideas seem to call out for one another. Here people often mention a story told by Hobbes. In the midst of a conversation about Charles I, someone asks about the value of the Roman *denier* under Tiberius.

The association of ideas guarantees the continuity of our intellectual life. Because ideas are associated with one another, the life of the mind is continuous – one idea calling for another, and so on indefinitely. Even when the activity of the mind is suspended, it continues to connect ideas unconsciously. In dreams, for example, the self no longer regulates the succession of ideas, but this succession continues unabated. Neither does all sensory communication with the outside world cease during sleep, for while the nervous system is at rest, it still transmits communications from the outside. These bring ideas – more or less conscious – into the soul, where they are mixed into the stream of other ideas.

In fact, the association of ideas continues even when we have blackouts, so there's no gap in the life of the mind. Although we don't have any experimental proof of this, it's incomprehensible that mental activity might cease only to start again a moment later.

Leibniz said that the soul always finds expression in the body, and we'd argue that the continuity of sensation and the association of ideas ensures the continuity of thought.

Associations of ideas are often divided into two major categories – rational and accidental. The first result from a rational relationship, whose principal types are:

1. The idea of a cause calls for the idea of an effect, and vice versa.
2. The idea of a premise calls for the idea of a consequence, and vice versa.
3. The idea of a means calls for the idea of an end, and vice versa.
4. The idea of a genus calls for the idea of a species, and vice versa.

Since we're unconscious of any third idea connecting the other two, however, these are less true associations than almost instantaneous reasonings. When I reflect on the idea of human mortality, for example, I think to myself that Paul is mortal – but what I'm really doing is drawing an instantaneous syllogism. So in these cases we aren't dealing with a real affinity of ideas acting on its own. True associations of ideas are those we call accidental. The principal types are:

1. The idea of two similar things that call for one another.
2. The idea of two different things that call for one another.
3. Two states of consciousness that occur at the same time tend to be reproduced at the same time.
4. Ideas of two objects that are contiguous in space call for one another.
5. Finally, signs evoke the idea of the thing signified, and vice versa.

Some philosophers have tried to reduce all these associations to a single type. But the association of ideas by resemblance is quite different from that by contiguity. When we associate two ideas because they resemble one another, we feel strongly that it's the resemblance alone that produces the association. This means we should recognize at least two types of associations of ideas – association by contiguity and that by resemblance.

What's the role of this faculty in the life of the mind?

Ideas are associated either by logic or by affinity, and the affinity that some ideas have for one another can be very great – even without the intervention of reason. In fact, the power of the association of ideas is such that one theory describes it as the master faculty of the mind. We won't consider this theory in any detail here, as we've already refuted it. Still, there's no doubt that the association of ideas sometimes produces the same effects as the logical and rational association of ideas.

From the association of ideas, superstitions and prejudices – all of them illogical – arise. So there's good reason to keep close watch on this faculty. The habit of associating certain ideas produces certain manners or inclinations, thus greatly contributing to the formation of our character.

Although the association of ideas isn't – as Mill would have it – the source of all knowledge, it's still an important faculty with which we should become familiar.

TWENTY FIVE

Faculties of Conception. Memory

Memory is the faculty whereby a past state of consciousness is reproduced within us so that we recognize it as past. A memory must fulfill both of these conditions.

This definition shows that there's something inexact about the expression "I remember such and such a thing." Strictly speaking, we remember not things but only the states of consciousness in which they first appeared. This is what Royer-Collard means when he says that, in fact, we only remember ourselves.

Memory can take different forms. Sometimes it's quick, so that seeing something once is enough to remember it, and sometimes it's easy, so we can recall things without difficulty. Sometimes it's exact, recalling things with precision, and sometimes it's tenacious, retaining a state of consciousness for an extended period of time.

It's rare to find all these qualities together in the same individual. But memory can be classified still further. We have memories, for example, of verses, colors, sounds, numbers, and so on. The general character of a man's mind often can be deduced from the type of memory he has.

Means for improving memory have often been sought, and together these efforts compose mnemonics. Although poorly developed, this science has come across some useful principles that might have been deduced from the definition of memory itself. The more of ourselves we include in a memory, the easier it is for us to remember it, for states of consciousness in which we're active are easier to retain or reproduce than others. This principle is behind every rational approach to mnemonics.

Three means can be used to arouse the necessary activity:

1. Repetition – if we are forced to pay attention to the same idea several times, it becomes more firmly set in our minds.
2. Emotion – emotional arousal provides energy that helps us to remember.
3. Attention – by ordering our memories, we enhance our attention and thus remember things better.

Now let's move on to the more general study of memory. Each memory has three phases:

1. In reproduction or recall, a past state of consciousness is produced. Memory could stop here. We might fail to recognize the past state of consciousness as past. Reduced to this, memory is reminiscence, which plays a very important role in life. How many ideas that we believe original turn out to be mere reminiscences of our childhood!
2. The state of consciousness appears to us as past. We recognize it as a memory, as something not occurring for the first time. At this second phase, again, memory might stop.
3. The memory is completed when we identify the precise moment in the past when the state of consciousness first occurred.

A memory in its complete form includes all three phases.

But if this is what memory is, it still remains to be explained. To this end, let's examine each of the three phases again.

First, consider reproduction. For a past state of consciousness to be reproduced, it must have somehow been stored within us. But how and where?

Several philosophers, including Descartes, have answered that states of consciousness are stored in the body. Taine recently offered the best formulation of this explanation. Whatever we think of the hypothesis that the soul is immaterial, it's clear that modifications of the soul are always accompanied by physiological changes and that these changes to the body persist long after the cause that brought them about has disappeared. When the physiological change is reproduced, Taine argues, so too is the psychic modification, and this is how the reproduction of past states of consciousness comes about. But this doesn't account for the second phase of memory. How do we recognize the phenomenon as one we've already experienced? Taine's answer is that reproduced states of consciousness tend to impose themselves on the self as a perception. But they differ from our present perceptions, and since we can't locate the state of consciousness anywhere in the present, we identify it as past.

But while this response explains why we don't see the state of consciousness as occurring in the present, it doesn't explain why we link it to the past rather than the future. The physiological explanation of memory doesn't resolve all the difficulties, so we would argue that the place where states of consciousness are retained is, instead, the self. This means that the condition of reproduction is continuity of the self.

Under what conditions do we recognize a phenomenon as past? Every memory can be expressed in the following terms: "I remember that I've seen such and such thing." The "I" who remembers isn't the same as the "I" who has seen. Nevertheless, for there to be a memory, these two selves must be one. So every memory involves a synthesis between present and past. To have a memory, it's essential that the self be identical.

The association of ideas completes memory. The state of consciousness that couldn't be located in the present comes to be associated with the states of consciousness with which it first occurred, locating the memory in the past.

Together with the association of ideas, memory plays the same role in intelligence that habit plays in activity. There are two characteristics of habit – it's a faculty of preservation, and it tends to reproduce itself. Similarly, memory serves as a faculty of preservation for intelligence. But memories also reproduce themselves. The latter characteristic – which also resembles that of habit – most likely is produced by the association of ideas.

Forgetfulness, by contrast, results from the disappearance of one of the two causes of memory – either the affinity that ties the ideas together diminishes for lack of exercise or the state of consciousness simply fails to become stored in the self. Little by little the psychological modification is worn away, to the point of being almost nothing.

Memory has been much maligned and is often seen as a characteristic feature of second-rate minds. To be sure, it isn't a creative faculty and doesn't yield anything original or personal. But memory does furnish us with the elements necessary to creativity, providing us with the materials that form the basis for our intellectual life. A man with a well-developed memory will never repeat himself, but, more important, a mind without memory is condemned to waste itself in ineffectuality. For without memory, the materials necessary to bring about what's otherwise within our power would be lacking.

Faculties of Conception. Imagination

According to a current theory, imagination is the faculty that enables us to see objects in their concrete form. While imagining things, therefore, the mind is sometimes led to wonder if it's in the presence of a real object or just a conception. This distinguishes imagination from understanding – the latter generalizes, eliminating all that's particular and unique about an object, where the former leaves its object with its personal characteristics, granting a new life and a new depth to its individuality.

This applies to the three forms of imagination – reproduction, combination, and creation. Let's study each of these three forms in turn, noting their differences.

1. Imaginative Memory. Memory weakens past states of consciousness as it reproduces them because it abstracts, remembering primarily that which is general. For this reason, a man who has memory but lacks imagination will tend to forget everything that's unique about a state of consciousness. Imaginative memory, however, reproduces previously perceived objects under forms as concrete as those provided by perception. The resemblance can be so vivid that the mind may be fooled.

But imaginative memory goes no further than this, reproducing faithfully only what's been previously experienced. It's not passive – no faculty is – but it creates nothing new, merely repeating our past life and primarily reproducing sensations. Now, it's often been asked if imaginative memory reproduces all sensations or only some. Clearly, it's most active when it comes to visual sensations, but it reproduces sensations of sound just as well. Most people can't reproduce lower sensations with their original intensity, but it isn't impossible – gourmets, for example, can recall sensations of taste without any difficulty. But the reproduction of these sensations is always less vivid than others. This difference reminds us that, above all, we recall those states of consciousness in which we've invested the most activity, to which we've given the most effort. We're simply much less active with regard to sensations of taste and odor, so it's harder for us to remember them. And this also explains how it's possible for some people to develop this aspect of their imagination. They invest a greater amount of activity in this direction.

2. Imagination as a faculty of combination. Under this form, which is intermediate between the other two, imagination generates no material of its own but rather combines the materials furnished by memory, enabling us to imagine things we've never actually seen. This faculty of combination isn't always under our control, for images sometimes combine with one another in an order different from that in which they were originally experienced – in reverie, for example, when it has a certain degree of intensity, and in madness, where images are often active and combine with each other against our will.

This kind of imagination plays a role in the arts, where it's called fantasy. A work of fantasy is based on a succession of lively images that come together without any rational connection, thus lacking that creativity, properly so called, which is the ideal of art.

3. Creative Imagination. The name of this faculty should be enough to define it – it goes well beyond what we've experienced in the past by adding new materials to consciousness. It's true that a great author will borrow certain elements from his memory, but it's his creative imagination that develops them into something new. When Newton formulated his hypothesis of gravitation, for example, he was influenced by Kepler's laws. But there were important differences between the hypotheses of the two men, and these stemmed from the intervention of Newton's creative imagination. It's the same with scholars who formulate a hypothesis for the very first time. A creative imagination is the *sine qua non* of the inventor.

What does imagination add to the preexisting materials? In a word, unity. What the artist brings together in his work is, in the real world, scattered about. It's the artist who unifies these elements. Observation furnishes him with the materials for his work, but its form comes from the artist, and this form is its unity. In fact, all the elements furnished by observation – not only in art but also in great scientific hypotheses – must somehow be organized, and this organization is the work of imagination.

Like many people, for example, Galileo observed the oscillations of a pendant, noting that they were isochronic. But it took the imagination of Galileo to dream that a general law could be formulated on the basis of this observation.

In short – given multiplicity, imagination reduces it to unity. So the creative imagination is the synthetic faculty par excellence.

Is the creative imagination a mélange of reproductive and intentional imagination – the former providing multiplicity, the latter unity? If so, the only features that could be attributed to creative imagination would be those in which general elements dominate to the exclusion of their individual counterparts. But this would mean that a substantial part of modern literature could no longer be called art, for it reveals the particular rather than the general. Whatever we think of this literature, it can't be excluded from the realm of art.

Nor is the unity of understanding the same as the unity of imagination. The latter is a unity of individualities that is quite different from the more generic unity of understanding – the difference between the unity of a dramatic personage and that of a category of natural history.

Now, if imagination is a synthetic faculty, it owes this property to passion, which is the main source of unity – for it's passion that unifies the images provided by imaginative memory. Passion and reason must therefore be allowed to coexist. At the same time, while passion is a necessary ingredient of imagination, it can be productive only when brought together with understanding.

Let's consider now the utility of imagination.

In the seventeenth century, imagination was denounced by philosophers like Pascal and Malebranche. For them, imagination meant imagination run wild, and it was seen as the source of all error. Cartesianism, too, looked down upon imagination, viewing it as an inferior quality, little more than a tendency of animal minds. This is why Cartesianism grants so little importance to imagination. But what we've just said shows how false these accusations are. Like all our faculties, of course, imagination is subject to error, but it doesn't deceive us any more than do the other faculties. Its conceptions shouldn't be accepted automatically – they have to be verified through understanding, and when we discuss logic, we'll examine the procedures used to correct for errors of imagination. But – this reservation made (and it's one worth making for all our faculties) – we still have to recognize that imagination is one of the most important sources of knowledge. Reason is sufficient in mathematics and abstract science; but when it comes to the study of concrete things, imagination is indispensable. The only way we know reality is by guessing at it, and imagination is the only faculty that allows us to guess. But the role played by this faculty in the sciences is even greater. Perhaps every law in the concrete sciences derives from a hypothesis, which is an act of imagination. So, despite what some have claimed, imagination isn't just a pleasant faculty, and there's no reason to mistrust it.

We might even say that imagination is the only faculty that truly augments our knowledge, that we owe to imagination everything new that enters the mind. Without it, the mind would be forever condemned to merely develop the consequences of ideas it already has, while reality – multiple and complex – would elude it.

TWENTY SEVEN

Faculties of Conception. Sleep. Dreams. Madness

Now we'll examine certain states – simultaneously physiological and psychological – connected to the three faculties of conception. Their common trait is that images become so vivid within them that they are mistaken for perceptions.

Consider dreaming, the most common of these states. The physiological conditions of dreaming are poorly understood, so we'll leave these aside and simply try to understand the relationship between dreams and psychic activity. Some philosophers claim that, during sleep, all thought ceases. We've already touched on this in our discussion of the association of ideas, where we decided that the chain of ideas is uninterrupted and that – even during sleep – we have sensations that give us ideas. We also argued that the self is entirely conscious, so that – if thought were to cease – consciousness would vanish and the self would cease to act or exist. But how could the self be reborn again and again after having been destroyed in this way? The answer is that it couldn't. So even in sleep, the soul never entirely sleeps and is never destroyed. In fact, according to Jouffroy, there is no psychological sleep, for the soul never sleeps at all. Neither is sleep, according to him, a purely physical phenomenon. For support, he cites our "indifference to habitual sounds" during sleep as well as the capacity some have for dreaming at will. These facts can be explained only if the self never sleeps in any absolute sense. We know that one of the important causes of sleep is a numbing of the senses, which breaks off communication with the outside world. But it's unlikely that this is the only cause. Experience seems to establish that sleep involves a certain numbing of the soul, although the body is never completely numbed. So sleep is produced by a relaxation neither of psychological nor of physiological life alone but of both.

The psychic relaxation of sleep seems to involve a resting of the will. All-powerful and constantly active in waking life, during sleep this faculty rests, retiring from its vigilance. The will lightens our other faculties of the yoke that weighs on them, granting them free rein, removing their constraints. The result is dreaming, a function of the attraction that ideas have for one another. When the strength of these attractions is no longer resisted by the will, we become prey to our memories. This explains why, if the will isn't completely asleep, neither the sleep nor the dream will seem whole. The ability to wake up at a desired hour is a result of this half-wakefulness of the will.

When Descartes presented his method of doubt, he observed that there's no logical reason for distinguishing wakefulness from sleep. Leibniz's response was that the distinction turns on the fact that, while we're awake, our ideas are tied together, but not when we sleep. During our waking hours, memories and sensations are very much at odds, but during sleep they're not, as all that exist are conceptions.

Madness should be seen as simply an uninterrupted dream – as well as an unhealthy state marked by the absence of will and the omnipotence of ideas, which associate with one another as they wish.

Madness, for its part, has two different forms – local, in which only one part of the mind is affected (called monomania), and general or total madness (mania).

In the first case, only one point of the mind is attacked, with the rest remaining sound. Insisting that this sort of madness is extremely common, Lélut sees monomania in Socrates's demon and in Pascal's amulet.

One of the more specific forms of madness is hallucination, an unhealthy state in which, even during waking hours, conceptions are confused with perceptions. When the mind falls victim to a hallucination, it sometimes recognizes it for what it is but is nevertheless unable to shake it off. The senses, which normally take their cue from external perception, do so here from its internal counterpart, and the resulting sensation appears real even if its object is not.

The resemblance between perception and hallucination is such that Taine regarded the latter as the normal form of knowledge. Some hallucinations, he argued, are rejected as false because they contradict one another, while others – true hallucinations – are those that correspond to perceptions.

But the following objection can be made to this theory:

All hallucinations involve memories that are extremely intense. Yet they are memories, merely repeating a previously experienced interior state. This means that hallucination is a reproductive phenomenon, and it makes no sense to regard what's only a copy as a model. True hallucination shouldn't be confused with ordinary perception.

This study of pathological states of mind and body leads to an important conclusion. The cause of dreams and madness lies in the natural affinity that ideas have for one another. This affinity renders a great service, for without it memory and imagination would be impossible. When we stop watching and let it do as it pleases, however, the result is mental illness, in which will and personality are destroyed. This affinity – and our inability to control it – also undermines the continuity of our ideas. To avoid being its victims, we must always keep a close eye on it.

TWENTY EIGHT

Complex Operations of the Mind. Attention. Comparison. Abstraction

So far, we've examined the three faculties of perception and the three faculties of conception. Next we must examine attention, comparison, abstraction, generalization, judgment, and reasoning.

Attention is the faculty that allows the mind to concentrate on a particular object. Condillac argued that attention is but another word for an intense sensation, but this confuses the conditions of the phenomenon with the phenomenon itself. We often ignore an object unless it is striking, of course, but sensations are effects that the mind passively receives from things, while attention is by nature fundamentally active. So we shouldn't confuse the two. Moreover, strong sensations often result from the application of attention. When an object strikes us, we pay attention to it, and the sensation grows stronger and stronger. For these reasons, Condillac's theory is unacceptable.

What most distinguishes attention is that it's the work of our will. Attention takes two forms. In the first, it's the object that attracts the mind, the will intervening hardly at all, while in the second, attention is wholly voluntary as we direct our mind toward the object. In the first form, where attention is barely voluntary, the mind doesn't exercise much control. It's the spectacle of the object that commands our attention and keeps us from turning away. Obsession – a variety of attention in which the mind has difficulty shaking itself loose – is precisely the same phenomenon as it occurs in our inner life.

The two forms of attention are so different that we might ask if they should be considered two distinct phenomena. Perhaps we should reserve the term attention for voluntary attention and call the other phenomenon distraction. Indeed, another way of thinking about distraction is to describe it as untimely attention.

What role does attention play in life? In fact, it's one of the mind's most fertile faculties. Applied to facts or ideas, there's no telling what the results will be. The two truly productive faculties are attention and imagination. Attention is the faculty of the thinker, just as imagination is that of the inventor. Buffon went so far as to say that genius is only great patience – the patience to allow imagination and attention to do their work over a long period of time.

Comparison is an operation that brings two ideas together and establishes between them a relationship of similarity or dissimilarity. Because ideas compared in this way have already been the object of attention, Condillac said that comparison is a kind of double attention. But we'd argue that comparison is a unique, irreducible phenomenon whose very definition implies the ability to think of two things simultaneously. While paying attention to one object, we perceive another. So where attention involves concentrating on one particular object, comparative judgments assume the simultaneous presence, in the mind, of subject and attribute.

We previously noted that memory is possible only if the self remains identical over time, and the same is true of comparison. Comparing two terms requires that we relate them to a term held in common.

Abstraction is the faculty by which we separate from a whole an element that doesn't exist outside it (for example, when we separate, from the idea of this table, the idea of its color or extension). There are two kinds of abstract ideas – particular abstract ideas involve ideas specific to a particular object, while their general counterparts involve isolating an element common to several objects (for example, extension is a property of multiple objects).

TWENTY NINE

Complex Operations of the Mind. Generalization. Judgment. Reasoning

A general idea is one that concerns multiple objects, and generalization is the means by which such ideas are obtained.

Generalization involves the convergence of two processes – comparison and abstraction. We compare several objects to see what they have in common, and then we abstract. The common qualities form the basis for the general idea – for example, we might compare different men to see what they have in common and, from this, abstract and formulate the general idea that all men have these qualities (sensory abilities, intelligence, activity, etc.).

What's the value of such ideas? In the Middle Ages, some philosophers – called realists – maintained that general ideas correspond to real things, while others insisted that general ideas are entirely subjective and that the term "general" is merely a *flatus vocis* – it doesn't refer to anything real or concrete. But for language, they believed, there wouldn't be any general ideas at all – a position known as nominalism.

Condillac and Taine were among the proponents of nominalism, while realism dates back to antiquity. Platonic ideas aren't general types in any strict sense, but they were conceived as applying to all individuals and thus can be considered, at least in part, as substantive types. Plato, in short, was a realist.

But experience alone shows the absurdity of realism. There's no such thing as a general type in itself. The resemblances that exist between particular objects are entirely a function of their common source.

Yet neither can we accept pure nominalism. When we think of a general idea, we're really thinking of something more than just a word. General ideas are always expressed in language, of course, but a word is only a sign – and a sign is only intelligible if we already understand what's being signified.

So pure nominalism, like pure realism, runs counter to the facts. Between the two, however, lies conceptualism, the doctrine of Abelard that general ideas are neither words nor substances but exist in our minds and thus have a subjective existence. General ideas also exist substantively in each individual object – by the very fact that the individual object belongs to the class, the class is realized in the individual. So general ideas are more than just words.

Which came first, particular or general ideas? The philologist Max Müller argued that the roots of language are found in common names and that, for this reason, general ideas lay at the origins of thought. Müller didn't ask if the mind, at the beginning of experience, already possessed complete general ideas; rather, he was concerned with whether particular objects were initially thought of as individual or as belonging to types and classes. His argument is quite controversial, and most grammarians don't accept it. But even if correct, it still wouldn't show that general ideas were the first formed – only that general ideas are the first expressed. Thought precedes language, so Müller's observation is beside the point.

In fact, it's difficult to imagine how thought could possibly begin with general ideas, for experience provides us only with ideas of particular objects. How could we come to see the class realized in the individual? This simply can't be explained.

So our position is not only that particular ideas came first – and that we thought of them as particular – but also that such ideas were the first expressed.

All that's required to show the role of generalization in knowledge is to point out, as we did earlier, how well science satisfies our need to understand. Generalization reduces the multiplicity of particular objects to the unity of the class, a procedure that's greatly satisfying to the mind. This alone allows the mind to understand reality – composed as it is of many different things that wouldn't otherwise be unified.

A judgment is the operation by which the mind affirms that one idea (called an attribute or predicate) somehow relates to another idea (called a subject) – for example, man (subject) is mortal (attribute).

How do judgments work? In the example just given, the class of men is included in the class of mortal beings – the subject is included in the attribute. From this, it follows that the attribute always has to be greater than the subject – something Kant expressed by saying that we subsume the subject under the attribute.

But this is only one way of looking at judgments. From another perspective, the attribute is included in the subject – mortality, for example, is a quality included within the larger concept of man. In the first case, we engaged in a numerical comparison of the individuals designated by the subject and attribute, while, in the second case, we examined not individuals but their characteristics.

Judgments of the first sort are made from the perspective of extension, those of the second from that of comprehension.

All this seems to suggest that every judgment involves the comparison of two ideas. But Cousin distinguished two kinds of judgments – the first formed through comparison, the second formed immediately without the mind having examined the two ideas compared. As an example of the latter, Cousin proposed the judgment "I am." Suppose we separate the two terms of the judgment. Cousin suggested that the idea of the self – separated from the idea of existence – is no more than the idea of a possible self. Joined together, these two terms imply the judgment "I might be," not "I am" – suggesting that the latter isn't formed through comparison.

But separating the idea of the self from the idea of existence yields not a judgment about a possible self but rather a conception of the self as outside all relation with existence, as nothing more than a collection of properties. Noting that these properties belong together, we then establish a relationship between the notion of a collection and that of existence. We affirm that the notion of a collection is subsumed under that of existence. And from there we form the judgment "I am."

Judgments can be classified in various ways. It's common to distinguish between particular and universal judgments – the latter affirm that the attribute pertains to the entire subject while the former affirm that the attribute pertains to only one part of it. Another distinction is sometimes made between positive and negative judgments. But the most important is Kant's distinction between analytic and synthetic judgments. The former are those in which the attribute is included in the subject, so that when we think of the subject, we immediately think of the attribute. In analytic judgments, therefore, the attribute can be deduced from the subject (for example, $2 + 2 = 4$). In synthetic judgments, by contrast, the attribute is added to the subject (for example, all bodies fall vertically). Here the property of falling vertically goes beyond what's included in the subject.

All principles of reason involve synthetic judgments. This means that the question raised earlier when we were discussing the theory of reason can be posed in the following form: "Are there synthetic, a priori judgments, and, if so, how is this possible?" But this is a question we already answered by showing that the mind – by its very nature – requires such judgments.

In reasoning, the mind brings together two previous judgments to form a new one. The two forms of reasoning are induction and deduction, each of which we'll discuss later in our treatment of logic.

THIRTY

The Object and Method of Aesthetics

In the next few lectures, we'll turn our attention to psychic phenomena relating to beauty, in which sensibility and intelligence are both at play. The science that studies these phenomena is called aesthetics, from the Greek term αἴσθησις (sense perception), or sensation. Departing from its usual meaning, Kant also used the word to refer to that part of philosophy that deals with interior and exterior experience.

The goal of aesthetics isn't to give those who lack it a feeling and taste for beauty. Nor does it try to establish the rules to which artists should conform. Its goal, instead, is to define beauty, which it does first in an abstract and general way, then moving on to the study of the beaux arts, the concrete forms beauty can take.

So aesthetics tries to solve two problems – abstract beauty as well as its concrete counterpart.

What is beauty? It's extremely difficult to give a completely satisfying answer to this question. A number of contradictory solutions have been proposed, but most confuse beauty with some other idea. So we'll begin by trying to distinguish beauty from what it's not. From this negative definition, we'll then search out beauty's positive defining characteristics.

It was once common to define the beautiful as what's useful. Socrates, for example, saw beauty in every useful object. But this definition misunderstands one of the essential characteristics of beauty, which evokes no instrumental feelings within us. We don't care whether a beautiful object is useful or not. The realm of beauty strikes us as completely distinct from that of utility, so that one of the characteristics of beauty is precisely its lack of utility. Kant thus observed that when we conceive of an object as useful, its aesthetic value is actually diminished, which shows that these two notions are profoundly different. But whatever we make of such theoretical considerations, the fact is that we frequently encounter useful objects that aren't beautiful.

A second definition confuses the beautiful with the agreeable. Beauty is always agreeable, of course, but what's agreeable isn't always beautiful. The pleasure given to us by beauty is of a quite specific kind. A good meal is agreeable but leaves no aesthetic impression.

Third, beauty isn't the same as goodness, for many beautiful things aren't good. Imagine an immoral man with the most detestable passions and the greatest vices. Provided that these vices aren't commonplace, that his criminal enterprises show great energy, that his passions are powerful, and that his activity, condemned by morality, is nevertheless great and violent – this man will, in his own way, be beautiful. Inversely, many things are good but not beautiful, and though great acts of virtue might have aesthetic value, this isn't the case with ordinary integrity and bourgeois virtue, which aren't lacking in merit from a moral point of view. Finally, things that are simply morally indifferent can be beautiful or ugly. There's neither vice nor virtue in a great landscape or a still life, for example, yet they provide the material for a work of art.

Fourth, beauty shouldn't be confused with truth. Great scientific theories, to be sure, are often beautiful. But this beauty doesn't stem from the precision of their reasoning, for much reasoning that is precise – and, as a consequence, true – isn't beautiful at all. And surely we can imagine a great hypothesis – Descartes' famous theory of vortices, for example – which is false but beautiful nonetheless.

Others have said that beauty is perfection. But the word "perfection" can be understood in different ways. We call something "perfect," for example, if it achieves the very end for which it was made. So if beauty and perfection were equivalent, beauty would consist of an adaptation of means to ends. Here the idea of perfection isn't much different from the idea of utility, for a perfect thing is one that fulfills its office. But many forms of beauty can't be reduced to perfection thus understood. In the sublime, for example, there's not a harmonious adaptation between means and ends but rather a tension between form and foundation. The sublime is a form of beauty that can find no adequate expression, involving a rupture of that equilibrium by which we've defined perfection. Defining beauty as order, we have the same problem. For "order" is an exact agreement among the parts of a whole. But this certainly doesn't characterize the sublime, in which passion – and with it incoherence and disorder – dominates. The notion of beauty as order might work for classical literature, where perfect harmony reigns, but it doesn't apply to ancient or contemporary literature, with their interest in the passions.

Sometimes, however, the word "perfection" is used in the larger sense of "absolute perfection" – not of a thing but in itself. Quite beyond the various relative perfections, which can't be conceived except in relation to this or that quality, there's a supreme perfection that's been seen as identical to beauty. Here beauty is absolute perfection, incarnate in a material form. But this is contradictory. No simple idea can contain all perfections within it, and thus the concept is meaningless. Beauty must have a determinate nature, or else it couldn't be represented; but if this perfection could in some way be determined – related to some specific quality, as general as may be – then it would be a relative, and not an absolute, perfection.

While it's very close to what's useful, agreeable, good, true, and perfect, therefore, beauty shouldn't be confused with any of these.

So let's search for its proper nature – by studying the various ways it's revealed to us and its resulting effects. Once we've ascertained these effects, we'll try to determine their cause.

First, how is beauty revealed to us? It's always through the medium of sensation. Whether distinct from this medium or not, beauty must appear under this form and, in order to reach us, also be perceived by the senses or conceived by the imagination.

But what is beauty in itself? This is impossible to say until we've analyzed its effects.

The first effect of aesthetic emotion is pleasure. Beautiful things leave us with agreeable sensations. The second effect seems to contradict the first, for while what's agreeable generally evokes our egoism (everything agreeable being somehow useful to us), aesthetic pleasure is always disinterested. When we experience this kind of pleasure, we completely abandon ourselves to the joy it brings us, not considering whether the object might or might not be useful. We don't engage in any calculation, nor do we try to keep for ourselves the privilege of the pleasure we experience. Aesthetic pleasure doesn't lead to the desire to possess, for ourselves alone, the object that produced it. Our love of beauty is satisfied simply by seeing beautiful things. We don't seek to own the objects that charm us. Although the art lover may collect paintings, it's not aesthetic sentiment that leads him to do so. He's driven not by the love of art but by the glory of possession.

Here are two other essential characteristics of beauty:

Aesthetic pleasure is simultaneously universal and individual. It's universal in the sense that, when I feel an aesthetic sensation, I assume that everyone in the same situation would feel the same thing. We might debate what constitutes good taste, but, as La Bruyère says, this doesn't change the fact that there are such things as good and bad taste. Enlightened people tend to call beautiful those objects that contain the same qualities. But from another point of view, taste is individual. What I find beautiful isn't necessarily – and to the same degree – judged beautiful by another. Exercising our judgment on the same work, we might disagree on its merit. Examples of this kind abound. It's often been said that the ideal beauty of one epoch isn't that of another. In the seventeenth century, beauty was to be found in order and regularity; by contrast, our own age tends to find beauty in great movements of passion. The century of Louis XIV loved exact proportion in everything, while what we love in works of art is richness and complexity.

So in judgments of beauty, there's simultaneously great variety and an obvious universality. Later we'll explain how this can be so.

THIRTY ONE

What Is Beauty?

Now that we've examined the effects of beauty, or aesthetic emotion, we'll try to find its cause. In other words, we'll try to deduce from the various qualities of aesthetic pleasure the qualities that its object – beauty – must have.

The first thing we know is that self-interest plays no role in aesthetic emotion. We can only be truly disinterested in an object if it has no concrete reality, for anything that really exists always has a certain utility – if only that of being agreeable. When we see such an object, it immediately inspires an ulterior motive – we want to keep it for ourselves. Yet beauty generates no such motive, so beauty can't be real. Indeed, it's nothing but a concept, an ideal formed by the mind.

We've also said that aesthetic emotion is pleasurable. Pleasure is produced by the effect, on our minds, of an object that conforms to its nature (pain results in the opposite case). The only thing we know is ourselves, and we judge all objects according to their relationships with us. So if aesthetic emotion is pleasurable, it must be that beauty conforms to our nature.

In beauty, therefore, there must be something of human nature. This is what Saint-Marc Girardin quite rightly acknowledged in his course on dramatic literature. What we look for in art is something of ourselves. A landscape isn't beautiful in itself. What gives it beauty, what renders it capable of becoming an object of aesthetic emotion, are the feelings the landscape awakens within us. Take away man and you take away beauty.

If beauty conforms with our nature, then to understand beauty we need only examine ourselves. We're essentially composed of three faculties, and each of these can be considered from two different perspectives.

In sensibility, we have on the one side multiplicity (inclinations and emotions) and on the other side unity (passion). In intelligence, sensations – various states of consciousness, all the material of knowledge – provide us with multiplicity, while reason brings them to unity. Finally, activity is composed of a mass of actions and instincts – multiplicity. The self intervenes in this chaos through the will, directs our activity, and imposes unity.

The multiplicity of experience reduced to unity by the self – such is the formula of all knowledge. The closer we come to completely unifying this multiplicity, the greater the intellectual pleasure.

Beauty must somehow conform to this formula. Yet beauty is also ideal – we might even say it's the idealization of unity and multiplicity.

For multiplicity to be ideal, it must be as complex as possible. For unity to be ideal, it must be as strong and coherent as possible, capturing multiplicity without allowing anything to escape yet without attenuating its complexity. From the perfect harmony of these two terms, beauty is born.

Unfortunately, this harmony too is entirely ideal and in practice can scarcely exist. In works of art, one of these two characteristics is usually sacrificed to the advantage of the other. This explains how aesthetic emotion can be universal and individual at the same time. It's universal because it unifies multiplicity and in so doing satisfies the two conditions we've already laid out; but it's also individual – first, because some prefer unity to multiplicity, while others prefer the opposite, and second, because there are differences of sensibility and personal disposition among those who assess the beauty of any concrete object.

Our conclusions can be expressed in the following terms: Unity is the concentration of all elements of a whole toward a single end and is perfect if none of these elements diverges from the common goal. Such unity is characterized by strength. Multiplicity, by contrast, is richness, variety, and complexity. So beauty can be defined as a harmonious balance between strength and richness. This balance can't ever be perfect, for sometimes richness works to the detriment of strength, while at other times strength works to the disadvantage of richness. Depending on his inclinations, an individual may prefer one combination over others.

For example, the work of Corneille, like the art of ancient Greece and that of the entire seventeenth century, shows a great deal of strength. But the trade-off is a loss of richness – Corneille's characters have strong sentiments but not much variety. By contrast, the romantic art preferred today consists almost entirely of diversity and richness. But its unity is lacking – there's more variety but less strength.

In short, the essence of beauty is power, expressed sometimes in breadth, with much richness and little unity, and sometimes in depth, with great unity and little variety. An impartial mind, however, will see an equivalent aesthetic value in these two forms.

But beauty shouldn't be defined solely from an ideal perspective. It's not degraded when it takes on a concrete form. After all, beauty exists only insofar as it's revealed to us – this is the very condition of its existence. Real beauty is strength and richness clothed in a concrete form, approaching as much as possible the perfect harmony that is its ideal.

THIRTY TWO

Prettiness and the Sublime. Art

In this lecture, we'll try to define two terms related to the idea of beauty – the sublime and prettiness.

For Kant, the sublime was a quite specific notion, bearing no resemblance to beauty. As he saw it, beauty always shows itself in a concrete form, while the sublime conveys the impression of being limitless. Beyond their nature, however, the beautiful and the sublime also differ in the emotions they evoke. The beautiful evokes a calm, tranquil pleasure, while the pleasure of the sublime is tinged with sadness. According to Kant, contemplating the sublime inspires a slight sorrow, a sort of aspiration toward infinity that the mind can't completely embrace. This is the source of our discomfort, however agreeable it might also be. And because our effort to embrace the sublime necessarily fails, it becomes elevated in our eyes, yielding a higher form of satisfaction. In his *Critique of Judgment*, therefore, Kant saw the idea of the sublime as quite distinct from that of beauty.

But if Kant's theory were true, the sublime could never exist in any well-defined thing – in classical literature, for example. But what could be more precise than the "*Qu'il mourût!*" of Horace? Yet isn't this a good example of the sublime?

So we don't agree with Kant that there's an abyss between beauty and the sublime. The sublime is simply the highest expression of beauty – beauty raised to its greatest intensity. And because beauty can take two different forms, the same must be true of the sublime. So we distinguish between the sublime in strength and the sublime in richness. The verses of Corneille, so simple and strong, are sublime, but so is an immense plain that offers the eyes an incredibly varied spectacle. The term "sublime" should be applied to everything that deserves it – Faust no less than Rodrigue.

Where the sublime is the highest expression of beauty, prettiness is the lowest. The normal condition of art is beauty – prettiness is art's whimsy, the sublime its happy accident.

What characterizes prettiness is a specific balance between the two elements of beauty – unity and variety. Things that are pretty privilege variety over strength. For this reason, we can say that prettiness is facile.

Like beauty and the sublime, prettiness exists only when it takes concrete form. The task of art is to render the aesthetic ideal concrete, and thus art is the antithesis of theory – theory is speculative, while art is a means to apply those truths established by speculation. When art eschews speculation altogether and concerns itself with beauty alone, it's called the beaux arts – to which we'll now turn.

First, art is like a language, expressing beauty by using things as signs, discovering in sensory reality the forms with which the aesthetic ideal might be expressed. Matter in itself has no aesthetic value, just as words in themselves have no meaning. Matter acquires aesthetic value only when it becomes the material of art, which the artist uses to express – in sensory form – his conception of the ideal.

It's often been said that there are two main styles of art – idealism and realism. Idealism tries to make us forget reality, to come as close as possible to the ideal, to downplay the difference between men and things, and to portray both out of their natural proportions. Realism, by contrast, reduces art to a photographic reproduction of nature. Putting aside dreams and imagination, the realist simply copies what he sees. His goal is to depict things exactly as nature has made them, to show reality as it really is.

But is realism really art? It seems to us that it's not. The purpose of art is to express beauty, while the purpose of science – not art – is to teach us about reality. Art should take us away from the pettiness of real life, setting us on an ideal plane – that's very much a part of who we are anyway – where everything is elevated and larger than life. This is art's true purpose. Realism sees itself as a science of observation, a history of the present; but if it makes no room for the ideal, it's not art.

Idealism must of course begin with what's real, observing the true nature of reality in order to idealize it. But it's the second part of this task that makes it art.

To this theory of art, we'll now add a classification of the beaux arts. The different beaux arts express beauty in different ways, which will be the basis for our classification.

Beauty can be expressed through two kinds of sensory forms – visual, which permits us to see, and aural, which permits us to hear. These are the two aesthetic senses.

This classification already yields three categories – the arts addressed to seeing, to hearing, and simultaneously to both.

We might further classify the arts included in each of these categories according to their capacity to express beauty. In the case of sound, for example, poetry is obviously better able to express the aesthetic ideal than music; and similarly, in the visual arts, painting [*couleur*] is better able to express beauty than sculpture or architecture.

From this, we can divide the beaux arts into three groups:

1. Those which pertain to hearing – music and poetry.
2. Those which pertain to both hearing and seeing – dramatic and oratorical art.
3. Those which pertain to seeing – architecture, sculpture, and painting.

Such is the classification of the beaux arts.

THIRTY THREE

On Activity in General. Instinct

Activity is the faculty by which we act in the world, and it has three different forms – will (activity that's voluntary), instinct (activity that's never been voluntary), and habit (activity that was once voluntary but is no longer). We'll begin with instinct.

What distinguishes the actions caused by instinct is that they're not determined by prior experience. Instinct plays an especially important role in the lives of animals, which are, in fact, little more than the playing out of a series of instincts. But instinct also plays a more limited role in the lives of children, one that diminishes as they grow older. It's instinct that drives the child to its mother's breast, for example, to do what it must to draw sustenance. In adults, however, instinct plays a smaller role, and even the instinct of self-preservation diminishes in significance.

Here are the principal characteristics of instinctive activity:

1. Unconsciousness. When they act instinctively, animals are conscious of the movements they engage in but not of the ends they serve. Were this not the case, we'd have to grant them greater foresight than we ourselves possess. An animal might eat by instinct but not with the express purpose of survival.

2. Perfection. Instincts are perfect – their means are perfectly tailored to the ends they're designed to achieve. This perfection exists from the first day of the being's life and isn't a function of education or experience.

3. Immutability. Instincts are immutable – the same today as they've always been (bees, for example, make their honey as they always have). Yet this immutability isn't absolute, for the influence of man or

environment can change instinct (the instincts of animals, for example, can be altered through domestication).

4. Specialization. Instincts are specialized and can't generate an endless variety of actions. Each action has a specific aim, and the same actions are always used to achieve it.

5. Generality. Instincts are common to all members of a species. All spiders of the same species, for example, weave their webs in the same way.

Some philosophers have argued that instincts are purely physiological, that instinctive movements are merely reflex actions resulting from physiological rather than psychological laws. Descartes held such a view – that instincts aren't psychological facts, that all physiological movements are mechanical, and that animals are but machines.

But this theory can be refuted by showing the absurdities to which it leads. One version of the theory has also been disproven by modern science. We know that animals, or at least the higher animals, have intelligence and can organize themselves socially. Finally, the theory of physiological instinct is contradicted by the fact that two identical organisms can have different instincts.

What ultimately demonstrates the problems facing this thesis, however, is that over time we can gain conscious mastery over our instincts, so that they are transformed into voluntary movements. If instincts can become voluntary, they can't be completely physiological.

So instincts can't be reduced to mere mechanisms, because instinct is a psychological – not a physiological – phenomenon.

Condillac sought to explain instinct by reducing it to habit. For him, an instinct is an experience that has gradually become habitual and thus instinctual.

But everyday experience shows that this theory is false. It's easy enough to find examples of animals engaging in instinctive actions that have no basis in experience and that experience can't explain. Certain animals can distinguish between safe and poisonous plants, for example, and to learn this from experience would have cost them their lives.

A far more significant theory – advanced by Darwin in *The Origin of Species* and accepted by Herbert Spencer – explains instinct as hereditary habit.

This theory is as follows:

When breeders want to produce animals with certain qualities, they begin by selecting those possessing this quality and then have them mate.

The quality then appears – with great intensity – in their descendants, while those lacking the required variation are eliminated. Only those possessing the desired quality are allowed to survive.

What breeders do artificially, nature does mechanically and fatalistically. In the "struggle for life," only those animals possessing some quality that renders them superior to others will survive. Long ago, the economist Malthus observed that agricultural production is rapidly overtaken by the growth of population, so that the earth provides less for people to eat and becomes a place besieged. The quantity of food is finite, while the number of mouths increases. Only the strongest survive, and in the struggle natural selection is born.

Darwin and Spencer argue that the origin of instinct can be explained in the same way. At first, what's now an instinct was merely a fortunate habit, one that gave certain animals an advantage over others. Those possessing this advantage then eliminated the others, and the habit – now fixed by heredity – became instinctual. This also explains how instincts became common to all individuals of the same species.

But this theory runs aground on the following objections:

First, it can't be verified experimentally. At present, all we can see is an abyss between the various species; we can't actually witness their transformation. The crossbreeding of different species fails, for the offspring either return to one of the original types or are themselves sterile.

Second, even where the line of descent is discontinuous, some instincts continue to be perpetuated in the species. Among bees, for example, neuters are born not of neuters but from the queen, yet all have the instincts of neuters.

Finally, the problem with Condillac's theory resurfaces here. There are some instincts that experience just can't explain. If the instinct of self-preservation hadn't protected animals from the very beginning, for example, they would have died. The same is true of the instinct of nourishment.

So instinct is a simple, irreducible fact that resists explanation. Recognizing this characteristic, we define instinct as a natural predetermination of activity, a unique phenomenon in its own right.

THIRTY FOUR

Habit

Habit is often defined as a tendency to repeat an action that's already been performed many times. But this definition, which goes back to Aristotle, is subject to several objections. First, if an action is simply continued over an extended period, it can become habitual without being repeated. Even with this correction, however, Aristotle's definition still might be criticized. It's true that a habit grows stronger with repetition, but the self has a tendency to reproduce an action after performing it just once. Continuity or repetition develops but doesn't constitute this initial seed. So to study habit in itself, and to really understand it, we'll have to take a fresh approach and examine habit in its normal state, as it develops after the single performance of an action.

Looked at this way, habit has two characteristics. First, it's a faculty of preservation – it ensures the survival of our past actions. The second characteristic is that the action preserved tends to reproduce itself, so that later it seems to appear out of nowhere.

So habit is the faculty that preserves our past actions as well as the force that tends to reproduce them.

We might also say that habit has almost all the characteristics of instinct, but to a lesser degree. First, instinct is unconscious, while habits become more unconscious the stronger they are, so that an extremely strong habit can make us act almost as unconsciously as does instinct. Second, just as instincts are perfect, habits are more perfect than voluntary actions, for they force us to act precisely, eliminating hesitation and deliberation. The only difference is that, in habit, this perfection is a consequence of education. Third, instincts are immutable, and though habits can certainly be modified, they always resist such modification – a resistance that's greater according to the strength of the habit. Fourth, like instincts, habits are specialized, with precise ends and objects. We acquire the habit of taking a certain action, for example, or of displaying a certain kind of style. This specialization is less perceptible than that of instinct but becomes just as noticeable in the case of strong habits.

But here's an important difference. While instincts are common to all members of a species, habits are individual. But for this, habit basically converges with instinct, although the convergence is never complete. The two faculties might be compared to mathematical series that converge more and more, becoming equal only at infinity. However unconscious, perfect, immutable, and specialized a habit may be, it can always be altered by an act of the will, which is enslaved by habit only so long as it wishes to be and can always recapture, so to speak, the empire that it has temporarily lost.

Instincts are nature speaking and acting within us. Since habits are acquired instincts, we can say that habits are an acquired nature that emerges from the will but that – once constituted – continues to exist outside the world of voluntary activity. Spinoza said that God is the unique substance and that the world is God realized, an idea epitomized in his phrase: "God is nature naturing; the world is nature natured." Similar terms might be used to characterize instinct and habit – the former is nature "naturing," natural nature, while the second is nature acquired, nature "natured."

Having defined habit, let's examine its laws.

A number of important studies have been published on this topic. The most noteworthy are the *Mémoire sur l'habitude* – the first work by Maine de Biran – and the *Thèse* of Ravaisson on the same subject. What emerges from these studies is that there are two laws of habit:

1. Habits tend to excite active phenomena.
2. Habits tend to diminish the intensity of passive phenomena.

When a psychological phenomenon is active, habit excites it, making it still more active and allowing the phenomenon to be more easily reproduced. But if the phenomenon in question is passive, habit weakens it, even to the point that it becomes imperceptible.

What is habit's effect on the different faculties of the mind?

First consider the passive component of sensibility – the faculty that experiences pleasure or pain. Assume we have an agreeable sensation. Repeated frequently, this sensation may become a matter of indifference. Habit might dull our sensibility. What's agreeable to a man of simple tastes, little accustomed to the pleasures of the world, may leave another man – who knows this sensation too well to have a taste for more – blasé and indifferent.

But there's also another component to sensibility – one that's active and composed of inclinations and passions – and it's this component that habit excites. The more our passions are satisfied, the more they demand from us. Always looking to go further, our passions demand all that we can give them, and as a consequence our sensory activity may become intensified.

For the most part, intelligence is an active faculty. But some of the lower kinds of knowledge are almost entirely passive. Habitual perceptions aren't even noticed. The atmosphere weighs on us, for example, but we don't feel its weight; or if we stay for a long enough time in a warm room, we stop noticing the unusual temperature.

But intelligence is mostly active, and where it is, habit excites the phenomena encountered. The more we explain things to ourselves, for example, the easier it becomes and the more pleasure it affords. A student beginning to study mathematics experiences a thousand difficulties; but over time, he becomes more accustomed to it, finds it easier, and, understanding it better, discovers its pleasures. Similarly, a student studying abstract ideas for the first time may find himself uncomfortable and exhausted; but little by little, he acquires the habit of study, understands more, and then finds his study more agreeable.

Of all the faculties of intelligence, none depends more heavily on habit than memory. Habit – the faculty of preservation – is responsible for a large part of memory, and the habitual exercise of memory can help us remember things we might otherwise forget – although it can't, of course, provide memories the mind has never held.

Since there's nothing passive about the will, here habit acts on phenomena that are essentially active, making our voluntary movements easier and increasing their tendency to repeat themselves.

Having examined the laws of habit, let's try to explain it.

Here again we encounter a theory that came up in our discussion of instinct, that habit can be reduced to a purely physiological phenomenon. According to Descartes,[79] the minds of animals follow routes already opened by preceding passages. Because movement of this kind is the very condition of thought and will, the phenomenon tends to reproduce itself.

---

79. See Lecture 25. Lalande.

But this theory runs aground on the following objections. First, it doesn't explain very well the tendency of an action to be reproduced. Second, habits depend on the will, which always remains their master and could, if it wished, shake off their influence. Unable to draw a clear distinction between habit and will, we conclude that the first must be a psychological phenomenon.

Other philosophers have tried to reduce habit to the association of ideas. Dugald Stewart, for example, described habit as no more than an association of movements. Just as ideas that the mind has experienced together or in succession tend to attract one another, Stewart says, so it is with movements. If this were so, habit would be only one form of a more general faculty – the tendency of different psychological phenomena, under certain circumstances, to attract one another.

But our analysis suggests that this theory doesn't account for all aspects of habit, for it explains only reproduction, and habit is also a faculty of preservation. On Stewart's account, where would the reproduced actions be preserved? Nor is there any reason to believe that the tendency for repetition derives only from the affinity that movements might have for one another. An action – even a simple action – tends to repeat itself. The fact that movements come to be associated with one another facilitates their reproduction, of course, making them easier to perform and explaining why we like habit so much. But it's not a necessary condition of the tendency to repetition.

Since these explanations of habit won't do, let's look for one that's more consistent with our analysis and explains both components of habit – preservation and reproduction.

1. Preservation can be explained by the general principle that "every being tends to persevere in its being." When a phenomenon affects us, we tend to preserve our being as modified by the phenomenon. This explains how habit can be a faculty of preservation.

2. The action's tendency to be reproduced can be explained by a kind of unreflective spontaneity that develops in the wake of the action and outside of the will. The will congeals, so to speak, on some specific point, determining what our action will be once and for all, so that we needn't act anew.

This explains how habit can excite activity. But how does it explain the weakening of passivity? Every sensation involves a relationship between some need and an object that might satisfy it. The object remains constant, while the need – which is active – becomes excited by the habit. As a consequence, the pleasure of the satisfaction becomes less intense, and sensibility is dulled.

What's the role of habit in life?

Habit allows us to preserve the past, which is an essential condition of progress. Thanks to habit, we move forward without always needing to return to where we've been. But this isn't the only condition of progress. In addition to clinging to what we possess, we have to continue to learn new things. Insofar as it maintains the past within us, habit is an enemy of change and an obstacle to progress that, though not insurmountable, must be acknowledged. There's much to fear in living an overly habitual life, in allowing ourselves to be its prisoner and letting it render us immobile. Habit is a necessary – but insufficient – condition of progress.

THIRTY FIVE

On the Will and on Freedom

The will is the faculty by which we become the primary cause of some of our actions, which might thus be said to come about through our own impetus, emanating from us and us alone.

To better understand the will, let's examine a voluntary action and its different phases.

1. Every voluntary action begins with a conception of one or more ends to be achieved.
2. This end conceived, we consider our reasons for acting – the conception of motives.
3. Because not all motives have equal value, we compare them to decide which are strongest – deliberation.
4. We then choose the motive we prefer and in so doing decide to act in a specific way – the decision.
5. Finally, we carry out this decision – the phase of execution or action.

An action has to pass through all five phases to be considered truly voluntary. Otherwise it is not a willful action and must have some other cause.

Is there such a thing as free will? This question dominates every discussion of this topic. But to answer it, we first have to ask another: What is freedom?

Kant defined freedom as our capacity to set in motion a series of actions. For him, the distinctive character of the will is precisely this capacity. For while the first in the chain of events leading to some physical phenomenon is difficult to establish, the will is always first in the chain of events it initiates and is not itself caused by any prior event.

But is it true that the will itself has no cause? Is it really capable of setting a chain of events into motion?

Freedom can be proven either directly or indirectly.

The direct proof focuses on the fact that we have the idea of being free. This idea couldn't be a function of experience, for everything in the external world is subject to an absolute determinism. So if we have the idea of our freedom – which we do – it's because we see and feel ourselves to be free, and thus we are.

Some philosophers, however, suggest that the origin of the idea of freedom lies not in introspection but is rather a construction of the mind – an illusion.

But then we'd have to explain the origins of this illusion. Bayle compared the human will to a weather vane that's conscious of its movements. Suppose that every time the weather vane wants to turn in one direction, the wind comes along and blows it that way. The weather vane would believe itself the cause of its movements. So it is, Bayle says, with the human mind. Its causal pretensions are illusory, for our will does no more than obey outside forces to which we're oblivious.

This argument assumes that will and desire are very much the same and that – at least in most cases – our desires are finally realized. Both assumptions are questionable.

First, will is different from desire. They've often been confused but shouldn't be. For we desire things we know we can never have. We might wish that the impossible were possible, for example, or that the ideal were real. In fact, it might even be said that, in most cases, the object of our desire is ideal. We desire what's real only insofar as it resembles some cherished ideal. But the will, the practical faculty par excellence, dwells within the realm of what's possible and real. We can will only what we can accomplish.

Second, we often will something without desiring it, deciding to do our duty even as our sensibility secretly wishes to avoid it. This struggle between duty and passion is, in fact, one of the great wellsprings of dramatic interest, especially in the work of Corneille – Curiace and Chimène are striking examples. And such a struggle takes place only because desire and will are very different forms of activity. Will is the strength by which we maintain our individuality, while desire opens us to the external world. Desire makes the self leave itself, while the will tries to rein it in.

So these phenomena are really very different. But even if they weren't, we still couldn't accept Bayle's theory, for it presumes an almost perfect correspondence between our desires and the causal circumstances in which we find ourselves. Yet almost always the opposite is true – how few of our desires are realized and how rare it is that things are as we wish them to be!

Spinoza proposed another, more rigorous explanation for the idea of freedom.

We're conscious of our actions, he suggests, but not of their causes. I sense that I'm moving my arm, for example, but I don't sense all the bodily phenomena of which this arm waving is a mere consequence. Spinoza explained the idea of freedom as a function of this consciousness of our actions combined with an ignorance of their causes, an ignorance that leads us to imagine that we ourselves are the cause.

But we don't accept Spinoza's theory either. If every time we're ignorant of the causes of a phenomenon we attributed causality to ourselves, then freedom would increase in proportion to our ignorance. But the very notion of acting freely implies complete consciousness and rational intelligence.

Second, when we're ignorant of the cause of a phenomenon, we don't attribute causality to ourselves. We actually endure our ignorance quite well, and our minds don't force us to fill in the lacunae of science haphazardly.

Since these various explanations for the idea of freedom won't work, we accept the direct proof discussed above.

An indirect proof of freedom consists in showing that, without it, we couldn't explain certain facts of daily life like contracts, promises, and so on. How could we be held responsible for our obligations if we didn't freely incur them?

The same question can be asked with respect to civil punishment. If man isn't free, such punishment makes no sense, and neither does the idea of a reward.

There's one additional indirect proof of freedom.

Kant proved that the will is free by first postulating the moral law and then showing that it's possible only because of man's freedom. But we won't say more about this proof here, for in this course we intend to take just the opposite approach – to use the proof of freedom to establish the moral law.

THIRTY SIX

On Freedom (Continued). Psychological Determinism

Serious objections have been raised to the idea that we have free will.

Several systems of thought have claimed that man isn't free, that everything he does follows well-determined laws. Hence the name "determinism." Fatalism and determinism have often (and mistakenly) been confused. Fatalism assumes that all beings depend on a higher will that's omnipotent but also arbitrary and capricious. This assumption lay behind the ancient notion of *fatum*, or fate, as well as the Mohammedan notion of destiny. But fatalism has since fallen away, and we needn't refute it here.

The key argument of determinism is the irreconcilability of free choice and the principle of causality. Some determinists, wanting to demonstrate this alleged irreconcilability without leaving the world of inner experience, have tried to identify fixed psychological laws that govern our actions. Others have pointed to the contradiction between the principle of causality, as used in science, and the principle of freedom.

Today we'll discuss psychological determinism.

Here's an action: I go outside. Why? Because my health requires me to exercise, or because there's some task I must perform. These are the causes of my action, the motives that lead me to it. And because my action has a cause, it's not free. Freedom is only an illusion.

Determinists go on to pose the following dilemma:

- either the act we thought free was actually caused by a motive and thus wasn't free; or
- it didn't have any cause at all – which violates the principle of causality.

Since the second hypothesis is unacceptable, our actions must be guided by motives – which derive from intelligence, the accidents of life, our character, and our habits. Where actions are brought about by motives, they contain no element of contingency.

In most situations, however, we have several different – even conflicting – motives. How could a single action result from multiple motives?

Determinists reply that a kind of struggle and appraisal takes place among the different motives, in which the strongest gains the upper hand and causes the action. They compare what happens to a scale where the weights represent motives and the beam symbolizes the will. Just as the scale tips toward the side on which the weight is heavier, so the stronger motive will cause our action.

So whether there's one motive or several, determinists assert, in the will everything happens mechanically. The motives that derive from our constitution bring about our actions automatically.

This was the position taken by Mill and Leibniz.

To refute this doctrine, other philosophers have claimed there are actions without motives.

Reid made such an argument. "I have twenty guineas in my pocket," he observed. "If I pull one of them out, why the one rather than another? When I begin walking, why do I start out with my right foot rather than my left? These actions have no motive."

Similarly, assume that I have a sharp stiletto, placed at the middle point of a line. Then assume I have to move it to one end of the line or the other. I do so. Why did I choose one rather than the other?

Reid calls this the freedom of indifference.

While we won't discuss his examples in detail, it's clear that Reid's hypothesis makes no sense. There are no actions without motives.

If I pull one guinea rather than another from my pocket, it's because of the way the muscles in my hand conform to the arrangement of guineas. In Reid's hypothetical case of the stiletto, there's also a reason for the choice – the need to cover one of the points. After hesitating, the mind, wishing to complete the task, simply chooses the end on which its attention is fixed at that particular moment.

But even if there were actions without motives, this would still be a poor objection to determinism. For if Reid's theory were correct, the trivial actions of life would be free while the more important would be determined, thus granting his adversaries the major part of their thesis – that our most important actions are determined.

Jouffroy reformulated this doctrine, distinguishing two kinds of causes of our actions – dispositions, which come from sensibility, and motives, which come from intelligence. The love of our neighbors, for example, is a disposition that encourages us to be charitable; but if we're charitable out of duty, we're acting on the basis of a motive.

Dispositions are forces, so it's easy to understand how they might affect the will. But motives are ideas or states of mind – inert things that have no power to act upon the will. If it's true that actions performed under the influence of dispositions are determined, then actions produced by motives are free. So there are free actions.

But this argument rests on the shaky assumption that we can act under the influence of an idea alone. Ideas can't bring about actions, for between actions and ideas there's an abyss. Like desire, ideas aren't restricted to the domain of the real, and this means that intelligence can have no effect on the will without stirring up sensations that give it the strength it lacks.

This is why Kant argued man can and should act according to his duty alone, because he loves his duty. The mere idea of the good has no influence on the will.

In short, motives must always be accompanied by dispositions. If actions caused by dispositions aren't free – as Jouffroy believes – then no action is free. Determinism wins again!

Determinists insist that when one motive strikes us as better than the others, we necessarily decide in its favor. This we grant. Once we've decided which is the strongest motive, the action has been determined. But this doesn't mean that our actions aren't free. Once we've finished with our deliberations, of course, there's no room for freedom; but freedom resides, not between decision and execution, but between the conception of an end and the choice of the strongest motive. Once we've conceived of some end, we have the capacity to deliberate and to make this deliberation last as long as we want. This is where we find freedom.

So the only thing determinists are mistaken about is the place of freedom in voluntary action. We are distinguished from lower beings by our faculty of suspending action. Things don't deliberate or choose among alternatives. An animal conceives of an end and moves toward it ineluctably, without the capacity to stop and reflect. Man alone can restrain himself, stop, reflect, and choose.

THIRTY SEVEN

On Freedom (Conclusion). Scientific Determinism. Theological Fatalism

As we've seen, those who believe in psychological determinism try to show that there's a contradiction between the principle of causality – when applied to the inner world of the mind – and human freedom. Scientific determinism tries to show that a similar contradiction obtains when the principle of causality is applied to the external world, the world outside the mind. Applied to this world, the principle of causality would have us understand all things as composing an immense chain of causes and effects, in which every element is connected. Each term is an effect in relation to its cause and a cause in relation to its subsequent effect. Now, assume that man has the power to act freely. A defining characteristic of a free action is that it can change the world in some way. But this requires that the world is changeable, that it must be possible for us to disrupt these causal chains at will. And the principle of causality makes this impossible, for it denies that there's any contingency in the external world. So our actions can't be free.

This isn't to say that there's no such thing as freedom – only that, according to the scientific determinists, it remains bottled up in consciousness and can't express itself in the world outside the mind. So freedom has only a virtual value. We possess it, but we can't do anything with it.

But the scientific determinists actually go further. Not only can freedom not express itself – it can't exist at all. For physiological phenomena are determined like all others, and, as we've already established, the soul is closely linked to the body. Every psychological phenomenon is accompanied by a physiological phenomenon. If physiological life is completely determined, then psychological life, which is parallel to it, must be as well.

Every act of the will, for example, is accompanied by certain cerebral modifications. But these belong to some causal chain and are thus determined — as is the act of will to which they're bound. So free will can't exist at all.

Such is the theory of scientific determinism.

Perhaps the strongest response to this theory was provided by Kant, who recognized that in man there are really two distinct beings, and in the self, two different selves — one that is phenomenal and has only a virtual existence, the other noumenal or substantial. The origin of this duality is as follows.

The one real self can be known only by conceiving itself under the form of the principles of reason — which is, after all, the condition of all knowledge. In other words, to become conscious of itself, the real self has to reflexively apply the a priori forms of sensibility and the categories of the understanding. But these laws of the mind are no more the actual laws of the inner than of the outer world. Phenomena inside the mind are no more in time than phenomena outside the mind are in space. And the same is true with respect to causality. So when it becomes conscious of itself, the self denatures and transforms itself. The real, primitive, noumenal self isn't subject to the principles of reason; but the conscious self must conceive itself in terms of temporality and causality. The consequence is that there come to be two selves — one that exists but isn't known and another that is known but doesn't exist.

This distinction allows Kant to resolve the tension between freedom and scientific determinism. Science assumes determinism, while ethics presumes freedom — the two theses that Kant placed in opposition. He even conceives the entire problem of philosophy in this way, as an attempt to show how we can resolve the tension, reconciling freedom and determinism. To this end, he assigns science and ethics to different worlds — the principle of causality, he says, reigns supreme in the phenomenal world, while freedom reigns in the noumenal world. So the laws of science are true with regard to phenomena, and the laws of ethics are no less true for noumena. It's the phenomenal self that's subject to determinism, while the noumenal self remains the seat of freedom.

But an extremely serious objection can be made to Kant's theory: It preserves a possible but not a real freedom. Because our life activities take place in the phenomenal world, they're determined. The will — imprisoned within the noumenal world — can't escape to exert its influence on phenomena. So the freedom that Kant offers us is metaphysical, virtual, sterile. His theory is also subject to a number of other, more important criticisms, but this alone is enough to refute it.

Since Kant's theory is an insufficient refutation of scientific determinism, let's look for another way to reconcile human freedom with the principle of causality.

That science assumes determinism is undeniable. The elements that make up a series of phenomena are clearly linked in causal chains. From the vantage point of causality, there's neither contingency nor freedom.

But while the relationship between phenomena in a series is determined, this isn't so for the direction in which the series is heading. All that the principle of causality requires is that phenomena be closely interconnected. But the end of each series is determined by the principle of finality, and the necessity called for by this principle is far less than that demanded by causality. The same goal can be achieved by different means, the same destination reached by different roads. And if the end of things happens to be freedom, then means must exist to realize this end. There would have to be a substantial amount of contingency in things.

In other words, the order called for by the principle of finality isn't an absolute determinism. The ends assigned to the billions of series of phenomena that traverse time and space might be achieved in very different ways. Here freedom might be introduced into the external world, and change might occur.

This is how freedom and scientific determinism can be reconciled.

Although now of mere historical interest, we must say more about fatalism, if only to complete our discussion of the theory of freedom. Since the rise of theism, the main form taken by fatalism has been a theological one – the view that there's a contradiction between human freedom and the nature of God.

In particular, two attributes of God – prescience and providence – have been seen as irreconcilable with freedom.

1. If God foresees everything that happens, then he's already foreseen anything and everything I'm going to do. If this is so, I'm bound to do those things, and as a consequence I'm not really free. In this equation, either the perfection of God or human freedom has to be sacrificed, and fatalists sacrifice the latter.

    This contradiction arises from the fact that fatalists imagine God existing in time. But for God, there's no past, present, or

future – only an eternal present. He doesn't see "at present" what's going to happen "in the future." He sees eternally whatever human beings do, so there's no contradiction.
2. If God can intervene in the course of human affairs, then He can change our conduct at will. While this doesn't mean we have no freedom, it does imply that we have much less of it than might otherwise be the case.

We'll return to this matter in our discussion of metaphysics and show how the contradiction might be resolved.

PART THREE

Logic

THIRTY EIGHT

Introduction. On Logic

The science of logic studies the rules the mind should follow to arrive at truth. Logic is distinguished from psychology by the extent of its domain, for logic is concerned with but one specific category of states of consciousness – intelligence – while psychology studies all aspects of the self. The perspectives of the two sciences are also different. The only goal of psychology is to understand the nature of the mind, while logic studies the mind with the more practical aim of helping us reach the truth. Psychology describes the mind as it is, logic how the mind should be used to achieve the goals of science.

While logic is thus distinct from psychology, they nevertheless remain closely related. First, both are concerned with the nature of man. While logic applies the findings of psychology to a particular end, psychology, as a theoretical science, necessarily precedes its practical counterpart. We must understand intelligence before deciding how it's to be used.

Second, intelligence isn't an isolated faculty capable of acting on its own but rather always acts in concert with the other faculties – will and sensibility, for example, also play a role in religion. Here again, psychology must precede logic.

To some extent, however, psychology presupposes logic, for the latter deals with the theory of certitude, which is the foundation of every science. This makes logic so important that – had it not been for the need to provide a complete inventory of the states of consciousness – we'd have discussed logic at the very start of this course.

Some philosophers have questioned the importance of the study of logic. Doesn't our very nature teach us how to reason properly? Must we know the mechanics of a syllogism to make a sound deduction? Innate in every mind, these philosophers say, natural logic makes the formal study of logic – which neither improves faulty minds nor advances the progress of science – irrelevant.

Our first response to this objection is that sciences needn't have a practical use. If geometry could never be applied in practice, for example, it would still have a right to exist as a pure science. The mind has an innate need to understand, and every science that satisfies this need – whether practical or not – performs an important function. So it is with logic. Even if it had no application whatsoever, it might still exist as a pure science, as long as it helps us to know its object – the laws the mind follows when reasoning correctly. So there's a perfectly legitimate speculative interest in being able to solve the problems of logic.

Moreover, logic does have a practical use. Human beings might naturally reason well, but they still make mistakes. Our instincts lead us to false as well as true judgments. So we must somehow guard against error, and the best way is to determine the nature of truth, the nature of error, and the conditions of each. Armed with this information, we're in a better position to figure out what's true and what's not.

Some might respond that we'd often be better off if we relied less on logic, which can lead us astray. But is the fact that we sometimes misapply the principles of logic a reason to do away with it? For every case where we've made a mistake by relying too heavily on logic, how many cases are there where we've erred from not relying on it enough! Let's not be intimidated by a few troubling examples proving only that even the best of things can be abused.

So logic is simultaneously a science, since it tries to explain a specific object (reasoning), and an art, since – unlike logic – science has no practical goal in mind and lacks any concern for how such a goal might be achieved.

The practical side of logic is most obvious in methodology, where it's clearly an applied science or art.

This double character of logic represents yet another difference from psychology, which is a science – of states of consciousness – and nothing but a science. Ethics and logic, by contrast, are both art and science – that is, on the one hand, they try to explain their objects, and, on the other, they put their findings to practical use.

Logic can be divided into two major parts.

First, logic studies the rules that the reasoning mind follows, not concerning itself with how these rules should be applied. The only interest of this "general or formal" logic lies in what the mind actually does to reach truth.

The second part of logic – applied or special logic, or methodology – concerns how the various procedures analyzed by general logic might be combined to arrive at truths about different kinds of objects.

THIRTY NINE

On Truth. On Certainty

Truth is the conformity of the mind and things. When the mind is adequate to things (as the expression goes), it possesses truth. Certainty is the state of a mind that knows it possesses truth, the effect of truth on the self. The opposite of certainty is not ignorance (whose opposite is science) but doubt, the state of a mind that feels itself not in possession of truth.

The main question about certainty is: "What brings it about?" The immediate answer is: "Truth." And since truth brings about certainty, there must be a sign that allows us to determine what's true. This sign – the real cause of certainty – is called "the criterion of truth."

What is this criterion?

Many philosophers answer that it's evidence, something objective that clearly distinguishes truth from falsity. Descartes argued that there's a kind of light intrinsic to truth and that this light illuminates the mind. This is why the theory of objective evidence has often been attributed to Descartes; but he understood evidence differently than we do. For him, evidence is produced only if the will directs our understanding in an appropriate way, which isn't the same as relying entirely on a sign outside the mind. The theory of objective evidence should actually be traced back to Spinoza (*Verum index sui* [truth the index of itself]).

But this theory can't explain differences of opinion. If evidence were objective, the judgments of all men would always concur, while in fact there are many controversial propositions. The loftiest questions, those that have the greatest significance for our lives, haven't yet been answered so as to command universal assent. Yet most people are certain that their own beliefs about these questions are true. So there's clearly no unmistakable, objective sign that a judgment is true.

It might be said that differences of opinion stem from the differences among various minds, that there is some objective criterion but not everyone recognizes it. But the differences among minds aren't sufficient to explain how people can have such completely contradictory opinions.

Since evidence isn't the criterion of truth, let's take another approach. We've just identified two kinds of judgments – those universally accepted and those that are controversial, appearing true to some people and false to others. So there must be at least two kinds of certainty.

In fact, there are three. We'll examine each and see what kind of evidence brings them about.

1. Mathematical certainty, which results from mathematical demonstration. When we're mathematically certain, we can prove why it is that we are, and everyone will accept the truths so established.
2. Physical certainty. When we see some object, we're sure that we see it. Our certainty here is purely intuitive, but it's every bit as strong as mathematical certainty. As with mathematical certainty, the truths of which we're physically certain are universally recognized. Not all philosophers agree that man is free, for example, but all agree that we possess the idea of freedom.
3. Moral certainty. We're often sure of things that are neither proved by mathematics nor based on observation. An architect, for example, may build a bridge and believe it solid even though he can't supply mathematical or empirical proof. Similarly, a religious believer's faith may transcend mathematical demonstration. Faith is the epitome of certainty. We're never more convinced than when we believe by faith, and yet truths of this kind are proven neither by fact nor by demonstration. This represents a third kind of certainty – the kind most common in everyday life – in which we're convinced of something despite our inability to provide rigorous proof.

Now let's consider the different causes of certainty.

1. Mathematical certainty is always the result of deductive reasoning. All deductive reasoning can be reduced to the form $A \to B; B \to C; A \to C$. Here reasoning consists of a series of identities. How can we be certain that the three angles of a triangle are equivalent to two right angles? Because we establish an identity between the properties of the alternate internal and corresponding angles, on the one hand,

and the sum of the angles formed around a right angle, on the other. This demonstrates that the proposition is true.

So the cause of mathematical certainty is the identity of the proposition being considered with another proposition already recognized as true. The criterion of mathematical certainty is identity.

2. When we see some object, we're certain that we see it. It's endowed with an authority that imposes itself on the mind, and this authority constitutes physical or factual evidence.

The objection might be raised that we sometimes see things that don't really exist. But when this happens, it's not because the evidence is misleading but because we go beyond the evidence and affirm more than it warrants. If a person who's hallucinating sees a ghost, for example, his mistake is not in affirming that he "sees" a ghost but in affirming that there is a ghost.

Physical certainty is thus produced by fact alone.

FORTY

On Certainty (Conclusion)

The judgments about which we're morally certain aren't universally regarded as true. So judgments of this kind lack any objective criterion that would allow us to decide at once whether they're true or false. Such a criterion exists for the other two kinds of certainty; but with moral certainty, there's simply no objective sign, and this accounts for the diversity of opinion.

What explains the certainty we feel in these cases? It can't be purely logical, for when we're morally certain, we feel no need to prove logically – to ourselves or others – the judgments we affirm. Were we to draw up a list – as complete as possible – of the purely logical considerations that go into an architect's plans, we'd see that these bear no relation to the strength of the architect's conviction. The same would be true of the purely logical motives we might list for some of our political or religious opinions. We would see a huge gap between their value and our certainty. With moral certainty, therefore, we must acknowledge the intervention of nonlogical psychological elements. In fact, intelligence often acts together with will and sensibility, so it's not surprising that these faculties influence our certainty. Our sensibility has a more or less vague affinity with one side or the other in a dispute, which is explained by our temperament, education, habits, and heredity. This sensibility provokes the will, which acts on the understanding, directing our mind's eye in a particular direction and deflecting it from considerations that might lead us in another. Seeing only this one side of the argument, the understanding then affirms or denies with certainty.

This means that moral certainty is a result not of the judgment acting on the mind but rather of the mind acting on the judgment. This is why it's essentially personal in nature, because sensibility and will are personal faculties par excellence. If the understanding, which is common to everyone, acted alone, we'd all have the same opinions; but sensibility varies from one individual to another and from moment to moment. We don't all have the same passions, habits, temperament, or even the same amount of intellectual autonomy. This is why opinions vary.

Moreover, sensibility and will constitute our most personal faculties – this is why we hold so strongly to our judgments of moral certainty. We die for our faith but not for a theorem. Our differences of sensibility and will are thus responsible for the infinite diversity in opinions.

We've already seen that moral certainty is more common than it might seem, and now we can see why we believe with moral certainty every judgment for which there's no mathematical or physical evidence. Mathematical certainty is possible only in mathematics, for there alone can we establish absolute identities between terms. Only in mathematics are terms sufficiently simple and without qualities.

Physical certainty, for its part, comes about only with statements – not interpretations – of fact. The vast majority of judgments, however, involve interpretations. We see things only in the light supplied by the mind. And even if judgments without interpretation were more common, they're not terribly instructive. The consequence of all this is that only a very small number of judgments can be the object of universal certainty – those pertaining to mathematics and, among physical judgments, those pertaining to mere statements of fact. Most judgments involve neither mathematical nor physical certainty, and these are judgments of moral certainty.

From this, it doesn't follow that we should always be skeptical. All we've established is that – having no objective criterion – the truth is difficult to find. But this isn't to say it's impossible. Pursuing truth with our temperament, instincts, and passions, we conceal it from ourselves. But this personal element gradually disappears under the influence of discussion, which, by comparing different opinions, reveals what they have in common and what's objective in them. The share of [im]personal truth[80] grows as the discussion becomes freer and more inclusive.

The intervention of sensibility and will isn't an insurmountable obstacle to the attainment of truth, and these faculties allow us to acquire new ideas. So there's no reason to lament the absence of a condition

---

80. The original manuscript reads "vérité personnelle," but the context makes clear that Durkheim's intended meaning was the opposite. Eds.

in which the mind might easily distinguish truth from error without investigation – as if judgments had already been clearly labeled true or false.

What follows is that we must be, if not skeptical, then at least tolerant with regard to opinions of moral certainty. Since truth isn't self-evident, we shouldn't expect to find it in those who think differently from ourselves.

FORTY ONE

On False Certainty or Error

When we know the truth, we're sure of it. But sometimes we have the same degree of certainty even when in error. So error is simply false certainty – certainty with no foundation in reality. A theory of error, therefore, should be included in our discussion of certainty.

What's the cause of error?

Spinoza as well as others believed that error is simply partial truth. Errors arise when, seeing but one part of the truth, we mistake it for the whole. Spinoza liked to give the following example: If we think of man in isolation, abstracted from everything else, he seems to be an independent and complete being, free and self-reliant. Yet this is wrong, for we've seen but one part of the truth. We've forgotten that man is part of a larger world from which he can't be extracted. If we'd seen the whole picture, we'd understand the depth of man's dependence. Rather than appearing to be an empire within an empire, man would appear one part of a whole.

But is Spinoza's view correct? Is error simply partial truth? Not at all. For if seeing "less than the truth" leads us to err, why doesn't seeing "more than the truth" have the same effect? The mind is no more "adequate for things" in the one case than in the other. For example, in a vacuum, water rises to ten meters. To explain this, we say that nature abhors a vacuum. But the reality is that in a vacuum water won't rise higher than ten meters. When we grant nature a sentiment it doesn't have, we go beyond what the facts allow. In this case error isn't a matter of partial truth.

Moreover, even if we accept Spinoza's theory, we must still explain how we end up deforming the truth, how we come to believe that we're seeing the whole when in fact we're seeing only a part. Spinoza doesn't explain this, but this is the important problem, for if we want to avoid errors, we must know their cause.

So what leads to false certainty?

Human beings have both intuitive and discursive faculties. The first lead us directly to truth, while the second do so by means of reasoning. In which kind of faculty might error occur?

Not in the intuitive faculties, for these are infallible. We can't see anything but what we see! Hallucination is not false intuition, but – as we've already said – a false judgment superimposed on this intuition. From the intuition of a representation, I might falsely conclude that the object represented exists.

This leaves the two discursive faculties – analysis and synthesis. Should we be suspicious of these?

To analyze is to deduce one idea from another, where the first is contained in the second. Synthesis, by contrast, involves adding to one idea another not contained in the first. When I say that $2 + 2 = 4$, I'm using the analytic faculty. By contrast, I'm using the synthetic faculty when I say that metals are good conductors of heat, for here I'm adding the idea of conduction, which isn't contained in the idea of metal.

By definition, analytic errors are impossible. Consider the false analytic judgment $2 + 2 = 5$ or, better yet, $A = B$. To say that the latter is false is to say that we're wrong to believe that A contains B. If, nevertheless, we conclude that $A = B$, it's because we've mistakenly subsumed B within A. We've erred by illogically adding B to the number of properties constituting A. The error is one of false synthesis, not false analysis.

So we can say that every error is an error of false synthesis and as such can take two forms: A diminutive error is a synthesis that falls short of reality, whereas an augmentative error is one that goes beyond it. This theory again refutes Spinoza's, showing that an error isn't simply a partial truth.

But what's the cause of error? How do we arrive at false syntheses?

We explained this in our discussion of moral certainty. Error is a form of certainty. But it can't be a form of either mathematical or physical certainty, for both are infallible. Only moral certainty can deceive us. So if we arrive at false syntheses, it's due to the intervention of sensibility and will, which cause the understanding to augment or diminish the truth. If reason were our only faculty, there'd be no such thing as error, but intelligence can be diverted from its normal course by the will, which is an instrument of sensibility. Of course, moral certainty isn't always false, but it's the only kind of certainty that can be false. From an internal, subjective point of view, we might even say that error and moral certainty are the same. The only thing that distinguishes them is that the former is discordant – while the latter is in harmony – with things as they are.

FORTY TWO

Skepticism

As we've seen, the opposite of certainty is doubt. Any doctrine that regards certainty as the normal condition of the human mind can be called dogmatism. Skepticism, by contrast, considers doubt the normal condition and even a logical necessity. Skepticism is suspicious of our faculties, where dogmatism considers them reliable. The former would have us remain in a state of equilibrium, adhering to no opinion whatever, where the latter would have us choose and commit ourselves.

Between these two extremes lies the doctrine of probabilism, which holds that probable truths – those that we can neither affirm nor negate completely but that can't be altogether doubted – exist. Practically speaking, we must have opinions about things. Those we adhere to are neither absolutely true nor absolutely false but simply have a greater likelihood than others of being true. Probabilism was the doctrine of the philosophers of the New Academy, including Arcesilaus and Carneades.

Let's begin by arguing against probabilism. The state of mind it deems appropriate – one of neither affirmation nor doubt – is unintelligible outside the context of certainty. For to say that one thing is more probable than another is to say that we are more certain of it. Remove certainty and all probability disappears. To say that one thing is more true than another, we must already have a criterion of truth. But if it's impossible for us to know what the truth is – if we can't be certain of it – then probabilism loses its reason for being. By the same token, if certainty is possible, there's also no reason for probabilism.

Now let's move on to examine skepticism.

Those who argue in favor of skepticism rest their case on three alleged facts: man's ignorance, his errors and contradictions, and the incapacity of his reason to prove itself.

1. Man's ignorance. With Pascal, we might say that we don't know anything at all in its entirety, that there's no object, not even a property, of which we have a complete science. Isn't this enough to prove that we're incapable of attaining truth?
2. Errors and contradictions. How can we hope to arrive at the truth when on every question our opinions are divided? How can we believe that the truth is available to us when all around us we see the errors and contradictions in human thought? None of the attempts to discover universal truth has amounted to anything at all. When the efforts of all past generations have run aground, why should we hope to be successful? So prolonged a failure is clear proof of some radical incapacity. Moreover, the astonishing diversity of human judgment provides a striking argument for the skeptics. It seems that the more human beings progress, the more they disagree. So the lesson of the present is the same as that of the past. Reason is incapable of conquering truth.
3. Reason's incapacity to prove itself. Beyond the arguments just considered, the skeptics see a radical problem in our understanding. Reason may be able to prove all of science, but what can prove the validity of reason itself? Who's to say that reason isn't wrong? The only way to be sure that reason won't lead us astray is to prove it, but the only way to do so is by means of reason – a vicious circle.

These are the three essential arguments of skepticism. But what's their value?

1. The first argument isn't terribly important. We are, in fact, ignorant of a great many things, but that we know even the little bit we do gives us the right not to be discouraged and not to renounce the possibility of greater knowledge.
2. The second argument is stronger. We readily admit, of course, that human opinion is diverse and contradictory. But does this admission require a radical condemnation of human reason? If the only source of certainty were the understanding – which clearly doesn't lead everyone to the same opinions – the answer would be yes, for reason would be a flawed instrument to which no credit should be granted. But if we accept the explanation of certainty discussed earlier, then the understanding can no longer be held responsible for these contradictions. The understanding is naturally sound and is led astray only by the intervention of sensibility and will. It's true that the judgments

of men aren't all the same, but the fault lies with sensibility and will rather than with the understanding. Once we know the cause of these contradictions, we also know that they can be remedied by limiting the role played by faculties other than the understanding. We need sensibility for the acquisition of new ideas, but once they've been acquired, only the understanding can be responsible for judging, appreciating, and controlling them. Its only defect is that too often it remains under the yoke of the other faculties. The way to free the understanding is through discussion, in which judgments become more and more universal and objective and escape the harmful influence of sensibility and will.

3. Finally, let's consider the so-called radical problem in our understanding – the *diallele* the skeptics claim to show us.[81] It consists, as we've seen, of the claim that reason, which proves everything, can't prove itself, for every demonstration of it would merely beg the question by relying on the very faculty it seeks to prove.

    A common response to this charge is that, while reason can't prove itself true, neither can it prove itself false, so that the skeptic might doubt his own doubt. If he doesn't, he holds at least one truth, the necessity of doubting, to be certain, and by so doing restores the legitimacy of reason.

But this argument isn't decisive. Committed skeptics don't hesitate to doubt their doubt and recognize that even the existence of uncertainty is uncertain. The real problem with the position is that it isn't philosophical. It represents nothing less than a complete decay and exhaustion of the mind – something we can't accept.

Also, consider the skeptic's argument that, since reason can't prove itself, we've no right to believe it. By what right do we believe only that which is proven? Skepticism would have to begin by demonstrating this.

Moreover, before we dismiss reason, we have to do more than simply show that it can't prove itself. Beyond this, we need positive reasons for treating it with suspicion, and those given by the skeptics – examined earlier – aren't justified.

Given this, the distrust of the skeptics is appropriate only with regard to certain uses of our faculties. Absolute skepticism is as illogical as absolute dogmatism. The latter begins with an act of faith, the belief

---

81. From the Greek word for "crossing," *diallele* refers to the opposite of parallel. Eds.

that our faculties are reliable, laying down the principle that reason can't fail us, that the laws of reason govern all things as they do the mind. But dogmatism can't demonstrate this principle. Skepticism, by contrast, asks us to doubt all of reason without considering whether it has the right to do so and whether its arguments impinge upon all – or only some – aspects of our understanding.

But between dogmatism and skepticism there's a middle ground, space for a doctrine that, predicated on no a priori affirmation, examines our reasons for believing and for doubting and decides on the basis of this examination. This doctrine studies our numerous faculties, identifies the domain over which each can be trusted, and specifies the conditions under which they can be believed. In short, it critically examines the mind and bases its decisions on this examination.

This doctrine is called criticism.

FORTY THREE

Ideas. Terms. Judgments. Propositions

All truths can be formulated as judgments, and all judgments can be formulated as propositions. While judgments are made up of ideas, however, propositions are made up of terms.

An idea is an act of representation by the mind in which a specific object is represented. Every idea is a representation, and ideas are signified by terms. So everything that's true for a term is true for the idea it signifies. But as a term can express only one part of an idea, it isn't always the case that what's true for an idea is true for the term that signifies it.

Terms are general when they express a general idea and particular in the opposite case.

General terms have two characteristics — comprehension, which refers to the collection of characteristics that distinguishes the signified idea from all others, and extension or scope, the collection of things covered by the term.

Extension and comprehension follow this law: "Extension varies inversely with comprehension."

This means that if many characteristics distinguish the term from all others, the number of things it will cover will be small. Conversely, if the term covers many things, it must be because it has fewer distinctive characteristics.

The upper limit of comprehension is infinity, and the lower limit of extension is unity. When an idea is infinitely comprehensive, it has an infinite number of characteristics and could apply to only one single thing. There couldn't be two distinct objects that share an infinite number of characteristics.

A judgment expresses a relationship between two ideas, and a proposition states this relationship verbally. Every judgment is composed of three ideas, and, consequently, every proposition contains three terms:

1. A subject;
2. An attribute or predicate that applies to the subject;
3. A copula that ties together the other two terms, expressing how the predicate applies to the subject. Every copula makes use of the verb "to be."

What's the exact meaning of a copula? It's often been asked whether, with respect to a copula, the verb "to be" has an objective or subjective meaning. Our view is that every judgment is subjective. When I say, "God is good," all I'm doing is affirming that the predicate "good" applies to the subject "God." I'm not making any reference to the idea of existence. So a copula never indicates more than a relationship of covering or applicability between two ideas and says nothing whatever about the objective existence of this relationship.

Judgments can be considered from either a qualitative or a quantitative point of view. The quantity of a judgment refers to its universality or particularity. A universal proposition is one that takes the subject in its full extension: "All men are mortal." "No man is immortal." In both cases, the word "man" is taken in its fullest extension. A particular proposition is one in which the subject is taken in only one part of its extension: "Some men are intelligent." The term "singular proposition" is often used to refer to one variety of particular propositions, those in which the subject is a proper name.

From a qualitative point of view, propositions can be distinguished as either affirmative or negative. "All men are mortal." "No man is immortal."

Every proposition has, at the same time, both a qualitative and a quantitative aspect. Combining these two facts about propositions yields a fourfold classification of them, which the Scholastics designated by the letters A, E, I, and O.

1. A universal affirmative proposition, or A;
2. A universal negative proposition, or E;
3. A particular affirmative proposition, or I;
4. A particular negative proposition, or O.

This classification proves convenient for developing a theory of syllogisms. The classification can be expressed in two Latin verses:

Asserit A, negat E, verum generaliter ambo;
Asserit I, negat O, sed particulariter ambo.

[A asserts and E denies some universal proposition;
I asserts and O denies, but with particular precision.]

The conversion of a proposition refers to a transposition of subject and attribute in which the proposition remains true, as in the example: "Every man is an animal; certain animals are men."

Here are the rules that determine the new quantity of a proposition when a conversion is undertaken.

A universal affirmative proposition becomes a particular affirmative proposition. As the attribute, in the first case, is larger than the subject, it must be less in the second.

Particular propositions don't change in quantity. "Some men are mortal = some mortals are men." Since the extension of both attribute and subject is restricted, no change is necessary.

A universal negative proposition doesn't change either: "No animal is a rock; no rock is an animal."

Finally, a particular negative proposition can't be transposed. "Not all people given to vice are rich" can't become "Not all rich people are given to vice."

FORTY FOUR

Definition

A definition is a proposition that tries to make a thing's nature clear to us. The terms of this proposition must be transposable without requiring a change in either quality or quantity. In definitions, in other words, extension and comprehension must be equivalent in the subject and attribute, as in: "Every man is a two-handed mammal = every two-handed mammal is a man."

It's often said that there are two kinds of definitions – of things and of words.

Definitions of things reveal their nature, while those of words reveal their meanings. The Port-Royal logicians insisted that the difference between these two kinds of definitions is so great that each follows its own laws. Where definitions of words are arbitrary and nominal in the sense that a word might be given any definition whatever, definitions of things try to explicate the nature of real objects and thus can't be arbitrary. Definitions of words are incontestable, whereas definitions of things can be false and subject to debate.

But is this distinction valid? It doesn't seem so to us. Whenever we define something, whether it be a thing or a word, we're expressing its idea in terms of a proposition. Here's a definition: "Geometry is the science of sizes." Now, how could we accept that this definition, as a definition of things, is so different from what it would become if we substituted some other word for "geometry"? The Port-Royal logicians assume that a definition is of things wherever a word already has a well-established meaning. But this is too vague a point on which to have the distinction rest. The Port-Royal logicians also assert that definitions of words can be taken as the point of departure for deductions, which isn't the case for definitions of things. But if there are some definitions that can serve as foundations and others still must be proven, it's only because the former are obvious where the latter are not.

So in fact there's only one kind of definition – of things. Let's examine the many ways things can be defined.

One frequently used technique for defining things is to explain how they come about. This is called definition by generation. A cylinder, for example, is the volume obtained by a rectangle that is wrapped around one of its sides.

Without a doubt, this is the best way to define something. When we know how a thing is made, we can reproduce it at will, and we know it perfectly.

But definition by generation is appropriate only for things that are so simple that the mind can possess them in their entirety – things mathematical that are simplified, constructed, and given their qualities by the mind itself. To define things by generation, the mind has only to observe the way in which it proceeds when it constructs them.

But concrete things are of a completely different nature. They're not constructions of the mind, so it's quite difficult, even impossible, to define them by generation. Instead we must define them by comprehension, by enumerating all their characteristics. If I want to define man, I say that he's a being, a vertebrate, a mammal, and has two hands. Some of these characteristics are more general than others, and the least general characteristics presuppose the most general. So there's no need to enumerate them all. We must only indicate the least general characteristic of the things being defined. Then, in addition, we must specify another characteristic that distinguishes such a thing from all others. To this end, we'd say that man is a two-handed mammal. This is called definition by *genus proximum* and *differentiam specificam*.

Finally, a thing can be defined from the perspective of extension by enumerating all of its forms. To define the mathematical sciences, for example, we'd simply list them all. But this is the most problematic way of defining things. As we can never be sure we're giving a complete enumeration, the length of this kind of definition tends to make it less clear.

Every definition should be short and clear – two conditions required by the nature of definition itself, whose aim is to render things perfectly intelligible to the mind. The third condition is that the definition must be adequate to its object, including everything defined and nothing more.

FORTY FIVE

On the Syllogism

In our discussion of psychology, we identified two forms of reasoning – deduction and induction. In this lecture, we'll study the former.

The most perfect form of deductive reasoning is the syllogism, which allows us to establish the truth of a new proposition on the basis of a proposition already recognized as true. For example, if the proposition to be proven is that "Paul is mortal," we proceed by deducing it from another proposition recognized as true – "All men are mortal" – by means of the intermediary proposition "Paul is a man."

All men (M) are mortal (T);
Paul (t) is a man (M);
Therefore, Paul (t) is mortal (T).

The last proposition contains two terms and an attribute with an extension greater than that of the subject. For this reason, the attribute is called the major term (T). The subject, by contrast, is called the minor term (t). Finally, the first two propositions contain a common term by means of which the major and minor terms are compared. This is called the middle term.

The third proposition of a syllogism is called either the question or the conclusion, depending on whether the demonstration has already taken place or not. The first two propositions are called the premises – the one in which the major term is compared to the middle term is called the major premise, while that containing the minor term is called the minor premise.

ON THE SYLLOGISM

Now let's turn to the mechanism of the syllogism, whose function is to demonstrate the truth of the question or conclusion. Every proposition contains two terms – a subject and an attribute. To say that a proposition is in need of demonstration is to say that we don't know if these two terms belong together. To establish that they do, we search for a third term that would allow us to decide. What we have to do is demonstrate that T contains t – from the point of view of extension, of course – which we can write as "T > t." To do this, we compare T with M and find that M is contained in T. This gives us T > M (men are included in the class of mortal beings). Now we compare M with t. We find that M > t (Paul is included in the class of men). Knowing that T > M and M > t, we derive T > M > t. Therefore, T > t (Paul is included in the class of mortal beings).

Such is the theory of the syllogism from the point of view of extension. If we want to develop a theory about it from the point of view of comprehension, we need do nothing more than reverse the order of the preceding inequalities. We can show this by relating it to the following law: In principle, extension is the inverse of comprehension. So, if from the point of view of extension T > t, then from the point of view of comprehension t > T. It's obvious that the number of characteristics that define Paul is greater than the number of characteristics that define mortal.

In his *Lettres à une princesse d'Allemagne*, Euler offered an ingenious theory of the syllogism, using a circle to represent the extension of each of its three terms and representing relationships of containment by placing some circles inside others.

In the following figure, for example, circle H represents the idea of man, circle M the idea of mortal, and circle P the idea of Paul. H is contained in M (all men are mortal), and P is contained in H (Paul is a man). Even a quick glance at the figure is enough to show that P is contained in M (Paul is mortal).

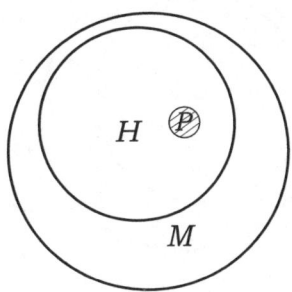

If, on the other hand, the syllogism is presented in this form –

No man is immortal;
Yet Paul is a man;
Therefore, Paul is not immortal;

– then we could, using Euler's method, designate man, immortal, and Paul by circles H, I, and P, respectively, as in this figure:

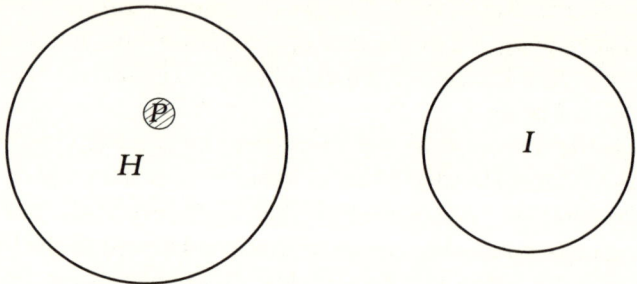

Since P is outside of I, the idea of immortality doesn't contain the idea of Paul.

Now, consider the following syllogism:

Some A are B;
Every B is C;
Therefore, some A are C.

This could be drawn thus:

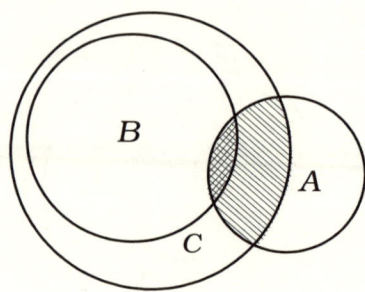

Or consider the opposite syllogism:

Some A are not B;
Every A is C;
Therefore, some C are not B.

We could depict this as in the following figure:

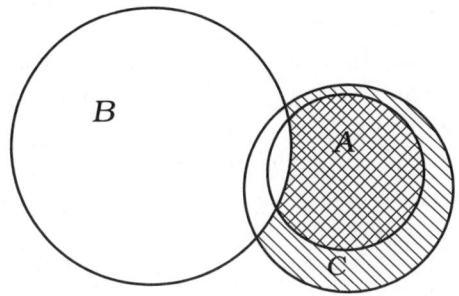

This notation has the advantage of clarifying the essence of the syllogism. This essence doesn't involve comparing unequal quantities, as the notation given earlier might suggest, but rather involves the expression of relationships of containment. Moreover, Euler's method clearly shows that syllogisms are purely formal. We could substitute any proposition whatsoever for the letters in the preceding examples and the syllogism wouldn't be any less rigorous, regardless of whether the premises are false or even meaningless. To show this, let's consider several examples of syllogisms that are in themselves perfectly valid and that, illustrated using the method of Euler, take the form of three concentric circles representing the major term, the middle term, and the minor term, respectively. As syllogisms, they're irreproachable, but they're nevertheless false either in their premises or in their conclusions.

The first example contains three false propositions:

Every courageous sentiment is commendable;
Imprudence is a courageous sentiment;
Therefore, imprudence is commendable.

In the next example, two false premises lead to a true conclusion:

My snuffbox is on the moon;
The moon is in my pocket;
Therefore, my snuffbox is in my pocket.

The third example contains two true premises that lead to a false conclusion:

Every rat eats lard;
Rat is one syllable;
Therefore, a syllable eats lard.

Later we'll consider how two true premises can lead to a false conclusion. But however this may be, these examples clearly show that syllogisms are purely formal.

The principle of identity governs the operation of syllogisms. The conclusion can be considered included in the premises only because it's identical to one part of the premises.

The modes of the syllogism depend on the quantity and quality of the propositions of which it's composed. From this double point of view, there are four types of propositions, which we've designated using the letters A, E, I, and O. These propositions can be combined in 64 different ways, yielding 64 modes of the syllogism. But when we apply a certain number of general rules to which syllogisms must conform to be valid, it turns out that 54 of these modes are invalid. This leaves a possible 10.

But according to the school that formulated them, there are really 7 such rules. Hamilton reduced this number to 3:

1. Every syllogism must have no fewer and no more than three terms. The corollary of this law is that no word in the syllogism is allowed to shift its meaning, for such a shift would be the equivalent of introducing a fourth term.

2. The major term must be universal and the minor term affirmative. The major term must be universal because, if it weren't, the middle term wouldn't have the same extension with respect to the minor term as with respect to the major term, which would corrupt the reasoning. This is why the following syllogism is inexact:

Certain works of art have a cubical form;
A table is a work of art;
Therefore, a table has a cubical form.

In addition, the minor term must be affirmative. This is because it announces the application of the general rule furnished by the major term to the subject at hand and so must affirm that this rule applies to the subject. This is why the following syllogism contains an error:

Every man is an animal;
No horse is a man;
Therefore, no horse is an animal.

3. The conclusion must agree with the minor term in quantity and with the major term in quality. The subject of the conclusion is the smaller term, the larger term its attribute. But because the relationship between these is determined by their relationship to the middle term, because the latter is compared with the larger term in the major premise, and because the minor term must always be positive, it necessarily follows that the conclusion must always be positive if the major term is positive, negative if it's negative.

Moreover, in the minor premise, the smaller term is affirmed as being contained in the middle term. Yet in the conclusion, the larger term can't be attributed to a greater number of individuals than are contained in the middle term. So if one of these propositions is particular in scope, the other must also be; if, by contrast, one is universal, so too will be the other.

A syllogism can take different forms, and which it takes depends on the place the middle term occupies in the premises. This term can be an attribute in the major and minor premises, an attribute in the former and a subject in the latter, or vice versa. In this way we can distinguish four forms that syllogisms can take.

Syllogisms are susceptible to changes that render them more or less complete. The different forms a syllogism can take are called the different species of syllogisms.

Hypothetical syllogisms are those in which a conditional major premise contains the conclusion:

If there is a God, we must love him;
There is a God;
Therefore, we must love him.

In this syllogism, the major premise can be divided into two parts. The first is the antecedent, the second the consequent.

Disjunctive syllogisms are those in which the proposition of the major premise poses an alternative:

Those who killed Caesar were either parricides or defenders of freedom;
They were not parricides;
Therefore, they were defenders of freedom.

In disjunctive syllogisms, the division must be exact and complete, and the first proposition must enumerate all possible cases. A disjunction that omits a term is false.

Reasoning can also be clothed in a number of other forms, but these can all be reduced to syllogisms:

1. The enthymeme, a syllogism in which one proposition remains implied: The more there is of love, the more joy there will be everywhere.
2. The epichereme, a syllogism in which one or two premises are accompanied by their proofs. Such, for example, is the case with the *Pro Milone* of Cicero: It is justifiable to kill those who lay in ambush for us; proof, Clodius wanted Milon to die in a trap; therefore Milon had the right to kill Clodius.
3. The prosyllogism, an argument composed of two syllogisms such that the conclusion of the former becomes the major premise of the latter. We could also have a prosyllogism composed of multiple syllogisms such that the conclusion of each one of them becomes the major premise of the one following.
4. The sorite is a polysyllogism, an argument composed of an indeterminate number of propositions tied together in such a way that the attribute of the first is the subject of the second, the subject of the second the attribute of the third, and so on, the conclusion uniting the subject of the first proposition with the attribute of the last.

As an example of a sorite, consider the following, found in Montaigne's discussion of a fox who, before crossing the ice, listened and heard the sound of the water:

That which makes noise moves;
That which moves is not frozen;
That which is not frozen is liquid;
That which is liquid gives way under weight;
Therefore, this river which makes noise will give way under weight.

5. The dilemma has for its major premise a disjunctive that distinguishes two parts, and it concludes about the whole that which has already been concluded about one part of the disjunctive. Such, for example, is the reasoning of an English minister who demanded money for the clergy:

If you spend a lot, you are rich, and you should pay;
If you spend nothing, it's because you economize, and you should still pay.

What's the value of the syllogism? In the scholastic period, philosophers relied almost exclusively on syllogisms. The Renaissance began a reaction against them. Bacon and Descartes attacked the syllogism vigorously. More recently, Mill did the same, insisting that – since there's no more in the conclusion than in the premises – the syllogism teaches us nothing. When all is said and done, every syllogism can be reduced to a tautology. The only thing that has logical value is induction, because it alone can furnish us with the principles for deduction. When we assert that all men are mortal, we implicitly assert that Paul is mortal. The syllogism, which does nothing more than extricate the second proposition from the first, yields nothing new.

Yet however much the syllogism itself might be entirely formal and insufficient, it's something other than mere question begging or a tautology. To be sure, the conclusion is contained in the premises, but it's present there only in a weak way. It must be extracted and brought out, and this is the work of the syllogism, which brings together two ideas that were not previously attached. In this sense, at least, it makes known something new. Moreover, its importance is well established by the mathematical sciences. Each of these sciences is an immense prosyllogism, and, unless the utility of these sciences is denied and it's asserted that there's nothing more in the most complex formulas they arrive at than there is in the definitions that serve as their base, the utility of syllogistic reasoning must be recognized.

FORTY SIX

On Induction

Induction is the form of reasoning that allows us to move from the particular to the general, or from facts to laws. Laws state causal relationships between two or more observed facts. So there are two steps to every induction:

1. We seek out a causal relationship between two facts.
2. This relationship identified, we extend it to all empirical cases where it might apply.

Here's an example of an induction where these two steps can easily be distinguished: Pascal wanted to determine the cause of fluctuations in the column of mercury in a barometric tube.

First Step. Pascal noted that, in a certain number of cases, the cause of the fluctuations is the weight of the air. In other words, he discovered a law that governs the phenomenon in the cases he's observed. A causal relationship has been established.

Second Step. This relationship – which has been observed in a certain number of cases – is then extended to all possible cases, and Pascal asserts the general claim that the cause of variation in the height of the barometric column is variation in the weight of the atmosphere.

In the first step, Pascal sought to identify a causal relationship. How can such relationships be determined?

Mill, in his *Logic*, gave four methods for doing so – concordance, difference, concomitant variation, and residues.

1. The method of concordance. If, in every observed case, the phenomenon for whose cause we're searching is regularly preceded by the same antecedent, we say that this antecedent is its cause. Suppose we're trying to determine the cause of A. We see BCD preceding A one time, BC*D* preceding it another time, and BC**D** preceding it a third time. In other words, A is always preceded by the same phenomenon B. This creates a strong presumption that B is the cause of A.
2. The method of difference. This involves suppressing the presumed cause of the phenomenon and examining whether the phenomenon itself also disappears. Suppose BCD are the phenomena that always precede A. If B disappears and C and D by themselves don't produce A, we can conclude that B is the cause of A.

    For example, in order to establish that air is the condition of sound, we note that sound is always produced in air and can't be transmitted in a vacuum.

    The method of difference is the best way to determine the cause of a phenomenon, for the most the method of concordance can give us is a strong presumption. Were we to rely exclusively on this method, we'd very often mistake a relationship of sequence for one of causality. This fallacy is called *post hoc, ergo propter hoc*.
3. The method of concomitant variation. This consists of varying the presumed cause of the phenomenon and seeing if the phenomenon varies in the same proportion. If the expansion of a body increases as it gets hotter, for example, we can assume that heat somehow expands bodies.
4. The method of residues. To the first three methods, which had already been identified by Bacon, Mill added a fourth, of residues. If we take away from a given phenomenon all that which, by virtue of previous inductions, is the product of already known causes, that which remains would be the effect of heretofore neglected antecedents.

    For example, research on the cause of sound and how it's transmitted shows us how to calculate precisely its speed in the air. Yet when we conduct experiments, the results don't confirm our predictions (the predicted speed is less than it should have been). When the known causes are accounted for, there remains a residue to be explained, the difference from the predicted speed. Laplace had the idea that this difference might be due to the expenditure of movement the sound represents, which increased the heat of the air and explained the difference.

In the second step of the induction, we extend to the universe of possible cases the relationship we observed in several particular cases. What justifies this extension from the particular to the universal? What's the principle of induction?

From one of his texts, it appears that Aristotle founded induction on the principle of identity. In fact, he seems to have reduced it to a syllogism, of which the following is an example:

The donkey, the mule, and the horse all live long lives;
These are all animals without malice;
Therefore, all animals without malice live long lives.

In this example, Aristotle moves from a fact to a law, so it would seem that inductive reasoning can be reduced to a syllogism and that there's actually only one kind of reasoning – deduction.

If we examine Aristotle's syllogism more closely, however, we see that its nature is quite specific. The middle and minor terms have an equal extension. The minor term asserts that all the individuals who have the characteristics suggested in the conclusion have already been observed. But almost always we use induction to generalize when we haven't observed all possible cases. Through induction, for example, we determine the laws of gravity without having verified them in relation to all bodies. So Aristotle's inductive syllogism works only if all the possible cases have been observed and are enumerated in the minor premise – which is virtually impossible.

So induction can't be reduced to deduction. It involves moving from the particular to the general, and this movement can't be explained by the principle of identity alone. Between the particular and the general there's an abyss – an abyss that induction leaps across – but by means of what principle?

According to Reid and the Scots, this principle is simply an instinctive belief of the human mind in the stability of the laws of nature. It's this belief that permits us to generalize from the particular. If we believe that everywhere and for all time bodies with mass obey the same laws, it's only because we believe in an immutable nature.

Such a belief is undeniable. But for it to serve as a solid foundation for induction, it must rest on one of the principles of reason – causality. Every phenomenon has a cause. From this it follows that, if everything else remains the same, the same cause will always produce the same effects. If nothing prevents A from producing B, then A will always produce B. As every law states a causal relationship, a law that is true in one case will be true in all identical cases.

Here we find a new fact that contradicts the empiricist theory of knowledge. According to this theory, reason is formed through induction. But we've shown that induction assumes the principle of causality. So the vicious circle is flagrant. For laws to have universal value – without which science would be impossible – they must rest not on a contingent principle derived from experience but on a necessary truth derived from the very nature of the mind. If not, the principle of causality would be nothing more than a perpetual hypothesis to which new facts might one day give the lie.

Fallacies

We've just examined the conditions under which induction and deduction yield valid results. Now let's consider the errors that result from illegitimate reasoning or fallacies.

One well-known classification of fallacies is that of Bacon, who called them εἴδωλά or *idola* and compared them to phantoms that cloud and muddy our understanding. Bacon distinguished four different forms of fallacy:

1. *Idola tribus* are errors common to the entire species, which stem from the nature of the human mind itself – from the limits and narrowness of the mind, for example, from the need for harmony inherent in human nature, from the natural errors of our senses, and so on.
2. *Idola specus* are idols of the cave, which stem from individual defects. Having a predilection for science, we denature nature to transform it into material for our understanding.
3. *Idola fori* are errors born of language. The "forum" here refers to the place where conversations occur.
4. *Idola theatri* are errors born of philosophical sects, stemming from the spirit of various philosophical systems. Bacon always depicted philosophers as actors on a stage.

But these terms used by Bacon (like the ideas they express) are quite vague, so this classification is important only from a historical point of view. It shows that Bacon clearly saw that the cause of error is often subjective. His list of fallacies is neither exact nor complete.

Let's see if we can improve upon this classification. We'll begin by noting that just as there are two kinds of reasoning, so too are there two kinds of errors – fallacies of deduction and fallacies of induction. Here are the fallacies of deduction:

1. Ignorance of the subject, or *ignoratio elenchi*, consists in proving too much, proving too little, or making an argument that's beside the point. In an assembly debating whether to wage war, for example, an orator who proves that war in general is unjust may be committing an ignoratio elenchi. For he has proven too much. It makes little sense to speak of war in general. If he proves that war is advantageous, he proves too little. This is insufficient for the particular case at hand. If he speaks of the grandeur and glory of country, he's making an argument that's beside the point, for it's not clear that war has this result.
2. Begging the question, or *petitio principii*, consists in assuming what's in question. The positivists beg the question, for example, when they construct the self out of states of consciousness, thereby already assuming the existence of the self.
3. Vicious circle fallacies consist in proving two propositions with one another. There's a vicious circle in the reasoning often (but wrongly) attributed to Descartes, for example, in which he's said to prove divine truth by the authority of evidence, and the authority of evidence by divine truth.
4. Ambiguity of terms. A syllogism must contain three terms – no more and no less. The syllogism becomes false if a term shifts meaning, for, in effect, this introduces a fourth term. This explains the falsity of the following syllogism:

   Schemers do not merit confidence;
   This man has a scheme;
   Therefore, he does not merit confidence.

Here are the fallacies of induction:

1. *Post hoc, ergo propter hoc.* This consists in mistaking for a cause that which is only an antecedent – for example, taking the cause of a great person's death to be an astronomical phenomenon that happened to coincide with it.
2. A second form of inductive fallacy consists in passing from the contingent to the necessary, from the relative to the absolute, and vice versa. We might say that so-and-so has cured an illness and therefore

that he's a good doctor, or that so-and-so is a good doctor and therefore that he will cure some particular illness.
3. Imperfect enumeration, which consists in drawing a general conclusion without having examined all the relevant cases. From the fact that water always rises in a vacuum, for example, it's been concluded that nature abhors a vacuum; but this conclusion fails to account for the case where the water is higher than ten meters (thirty-two feet) and rises no more.

FORTY EIGHT

On Method

A method is a set of procedures the human mind follows in order to arrive at truth. These procedures differ depending on the object of study, so each type of science has its own method.

Let's begin by examining the different procedures the mind follows in order to arrive at truth.

There are two general procedures – analysis and synthesis. We'll have to define these words clearly, for they're often given different meanings.

For Condillac, analysis is the method followed by the mind when it breaks down a whole into its parts. Synthesis, by contrast, is the procedure of recomposition. When I dismantle something, I can be said to be analyzing it, and when I restore it to what it was previously, I'm synthesizing.

The Port-Royal logicians, however, gave these words a completely different meaning. For them, analysis is a regressive procedure that examines the conditions of a proposition until it arrives at something true. Synthesis is the inverse, as it begins with the proposition at which analysis arrived and ends at the proposition from which analysis began.

This definition was taken from geometry, which defines the two words in this way. For the Port-Royal school, analysis finds new truths, while synthesis proves to others what we already know to be true.

In the search for truth, the inventor follows the analytic method, while the synthetic method is – according to an expression of Port-Royal – one "of doctrine."

Kant gave these words yet another meaning.

For him, analysis is the method that starts with one or several principles accepted as true and develops everything contained within these principles, adding nothing to them. So the analytic method reveals only what we already know from prior knowledge. From the definition of a triangle, for example, we can use the analytic method to deduce that the sum of the angles will equal two right angles. The conclusion contains no more than the premises. The synthetic method, by contrast, adds something new to prior knowledge and lays down principles that analysis then develops.

We used these two expressions in this Kantian way when we distinguished synthetic from analytic judgments. In the Port-Royal definition, analysis and synthesis are distinguished only by the order in which they supply truth. They both establish the same things, but in a different way. There's no more difference between them than between "the path one takes in climbing from a valley up a mountain and that which one takes in descending from a mountain into a valley."

But in the Kantian sense, synthesis doesn't repeat what analysis has already done. Instead, the two follow from and complement one another. Analysis and synthesis can't be separated and reciprocally presuppose one another. We can make deductions only from principles accepted as true, yet these principles will be of little use if they've not been developed by synthesis.[82]

Now let's consider how useful methodology is.

There's very little agreement on this question. Some regard method as useless, for example, while others consider it the whole of science.

It's clearly an exaggeration to say that methodology is responsible for discoveries. Inventions are a product of genius, which no method can supply. Method can regulate the force of genius, keep it from going astray, but can't create it. So while method is necessary for science, it's not the source of all invention, for it would have to have discovered itself – and without being regulated by some method, it would be hard pressed to do so.

But this doesn't make methodology any less indispensable to science. Method is to the mind what an instrument is to the hand. To proceed methodically is to act rationally, and this, for man, is the best way to act.

---

82. The original says "analysis," but "synthesis" makes more sense given the context. Eds.

FORTY NINE

Method in the Mathematical Sciences

There are two distinct parts to mathematics, as there are to all the sciences. The truths that together compose mathematics must first be invented and then demonstrated. Consistent with this, there are two parts to the method of mathematics: one pertaining to invention, the other to demonstration.

It might seem at first glance that invention has no place in mathematics, for in mathematics truths are all deduced from one another. But there's a difference between geometry as taught and geometry as practiced. Once a theorem has been found, of course, the way to demonstrate it is to tie it to another that's previously been demonstrated. But first the theorem has to be found, and thus demonstration presupposes invention. What's the basis for the faculty of invention? The answer is – imagination. Those who invent are endowed with the gift of imagination, while others try to understand and develop their inventions. There is no fixed rule for the use of the imagination. Only one is imposed on the inventor – to submit his discovered proposition to a rigorous verification.

Invention represents the synthetic part of the mathematical sciences. But to demonstrate propositions once they've been found, they must be tied to previously demonstrated truths by means of the laws of deductive reasoning. Mathematical demonstration is carried out with the aid of definitions, axioms, and deduction.

Definitions are the material of the demonstration, which merely develops whatever is contained in the definition.

Axioms are the regulative principles of mathematical reasoning.

Deduction, by conforming to these axioms, does the work of developing whatever's included in the definition. Axioms don't provide us with any new information but merely guide the march of the reasoning mind. Upon closer examination, it becomes clear that there's only one axiom in mathematics – the principle of identity and contradiction. All the others can be reduced to this, and it's this principle that guarantees their value. Of deduction properly so-called, there's nothing more to say, as we already studied it in detail when we discussed the syllogism – its most important form.

FIFTY

The Methodology of the Physical Sciences

The methodology of the physical sciences comprises two components:

1. the invention of laws;
2. the demonstration of laws.

To find the laws that govern phenomena, we must begin with observation, the simple ascertaining of facts as they are. Before explaining a phenomenon, we must understand it precisely, and this is the goal of observation.

In the physical sciences, observation involves the use of the senses, whose reach is extended by various instruments. The observant individual should have four characteristics: attentiveness, intelligence, exactitude, and impartiality.

To say that an observer should be attentive is to say a bit more than that he should merely observe. He should neglect no detail whatsoever and, without being distracted, pay attention to everything that occurs before him. For observation to be a fruitful activity, the observer must also be sufficiently intelligent to distinguish important from less important facts. Finally, the observer shouldn't add to or subtract from the phenomena observed and – as completely as possible – should embrace the role of faithful witness. He must remain impartial, for if he doesn't, he risks seeing what he wants to see rather than what's really there.

Observation reveals facts as they are, but this still leaves us far from the discovery of laws. For laws aren't inscribed in things from which their secrets must be wrested. It's up to us to extract laws from the material provided by observation, and here invention plays an important role. Confronted with facts, the man of genius gets the idea for a law and develops what's called a hypothesis. It's impossible to say just how hypotheses are developed, but the most common procedure – and the one that yields the best results – is analogy.

Analogy is a kind of reasoning in which we draw a conclusion about one fact from another that it resembles. If the two facts are identical, we reason not by analogy but by induction. Analogy requires that facts have both resemblances and differences.

Analogy often suggests new ideas, and to it we owe many discoveries. We have made a discovery when we apply to one fact the law of another that it resembles, finding that the law remains true in the new case. What we can't explain is why a particular hypothesis is developed by one thinker instead of another. Creativity – which is entirely a function of imagination – intervenes even in cases where a hypothesis is drawn from analogy. So not everything in analogy has a logical base – contingency plays an important role in the invention of every hypothesis.

Whether the mind proceeds by analogy or in some other way, the term "hypothesis" can be used to describe the anticipated idea of a law. Indeed, we could define a hypothesis as a law that hasn't yet been verified. As we previously noted, for example, Pascal observed variation in the height of mercury in a barometric column and believed that the cause was the variable weight of the air. At this point, the law was merely a hypothesis, and it became a true law only later, when it was verified by the method of concomitant variation.

As this shows, hypotheses are indispensable in all the physical sciences. Without hypotheses, no discoveries would be possible. Hypotheses aren't, nor should they be, the last word of science, but they're nonetheless crucial. Yet this isn't always recognized. Philosophers have often distrusted hypotheses. Many logicians have believed that the true method of science consists simply in observing facts without adding anything to them. This, they claimed, was the only sure path to knowledge, for every other method runs the risk that simple mental conceptions will be mistaken for truth. Bain was among the philosophers who took this position.

While relying on hypotheses might be risky, however, there's simply no way around it. We might very well be fooled by hypotheses, but we can't reach truth without them. As we've already shown, the laws of things don't leap to our eyes. Moreover, all hypotheses must be rigorously verified.

So hypotheses have great scientific value, and we have rules that keep them from being a source of error. Good hypotheses must have the following characteristics:

1. Simplicity. This requirement has its basis in a kind of a priori conception as well as in the facts themselves. Our view is that, in general, nature doesn't follow complicated paths, and this is supported by the simplicity of the laws discovered thus far.
2. Explanation of all the known facts. Obviously, just one fact that contradicts a hypothesis is a sufficient cause to reject it.
3. Predictive power with respect to new facts. This requirement is the best guarantee of the truth of a hypothesis. On the basis of known facts, we may construct a hypothesis and deduce from it certain consequences. These observations represent new facts predicted by the hypothesis. When these have been verified, the hypothesis acquires an air of certainty it wouldn't otherwise possess.

A comparison will summarize the role of hypotheses in the physical sciences. To form a curve, we specify as many points as possible and then connect them with a curved line. The points represent the facts, while the line is the hypothesis.

Once a law has been found, how can it be demonstrated?

The answer is – through experimentation. We begin with a hypothesis and then test it through an experiment. Many philosophers have commented on the difference between observation and experimentation, some suggesting that the former is passive while the latter is active. But this way of characterizing observation and experimentation is not only inadequate but in some cases false (an astronomer, for example, letting his telescope wander randomly across the sky and happening upon a previously unknown star, is quite active – despite the fact that he has engaged only in observation, not experimentation).

Some say experimentation is characterized by the fact that the experimenter acts on the observed phenomena. But this, too, would exclude astronomy from the experimental sciences.

So what's experimentation? It's simply the use of a hypothesis. Experimentation is observation intended to prove a hypothesis. A hypothesis, Claude Bernard said, is the guiding idea behind experimentation, regardless of whether we artificially create the phenomena studied by the experiment. From the moment the observer's goal becomes that of verifying a preconceived idea, the situation is an experiment. The hypothesis needn't be precise, and it doesn't matter if the aim of the experiment is to clarify it. From the moment a guiding idea exists, an experiment is taking place.

Once a law has been found, it has to be extended to cover all possible cases. As we've seen, here induction comes into play. In all the physical sciences, experimentation and induction compose the method of demonstration.

Some have asked if there are physical sciences based on pure observation. Isn't meteorology such a science? Yet meteorology is devoid of experimentation, so it does nothing but ascertain facts. The same is true of natural history.

But this theory is highly problematic. No science void of experimentation can have laws because their existence implies hypotheses, experimentation, and induction. And because every explanation is based on a law, such a science couldn't explain facts. So investigations based on pure observation are not true sciences but histories that recount and classify certain facts. The word "science," in its proper meaning, can't be separated from explanation.

FIFTY ONE

Method in the Natural Sciences

The term "natural sciences" is quite vague and is often used to refer to things as different as natural history and physiology. So it's important to begin by determining its exact meaning. We'll use it to describe those "sciences" that don't rely on experimentation – especially natural history.

As we just argued, sciences of this kind don't establish laws but merely ascertain facts. Since it's impossible to study facts without putting them in some kind of order or imposing some kind of limit on them (the mind can't do so, and – if it could – wouldn't find any satisfaction in it), the essential procedure of these sciences is to place facts in some sort of classification.

Classification serves two ends:

1. It aids memory. The number of natural phenomena is infinite, and even the best of memories can't retain them all. Classification facilitates the study of such phenomena by placing them in order, enabling us to recall facts more easily and to recognize them more readily than when they simply appear in nature.
2. Classification allows us to see nature's design. Nature has a certain plan, a certain way of classifying things, and because it's gratifying to recover this plan, the natural sciences satisfy us.

What exactly is classification? It's the operation by which we arrange observed beings or facts into distinct, hierarchically organized groups. Classifications can be artificial or natural.

Artificial classifications arrange facts or beings according to certain external characteristics. They achieve the first goal of classification –

aiding memory – but nothing more. Yet we shouldn't think that artificial classification is purely arbitrary. It has a foundation in nature and always rests on real characteristics – albeit those chosen to achieve its goal (those more apparent than they are significant).

Natural classifications, by contrast, divide beings according to their true relationships with one another. Such classifications rest, not on external characteristics, but on the intrinsic nature of the objects themselves. Above all, they achieve the second goal of classification – that of satisfying the mind through the recovery (in whole or in part) of nature's plan.

How are natural classifications produced?

1. through the comparison of beings or facts;
2. through the study of the hierarchy of facts or characteristics.

Comparison brings together all the characteristics of the beings in question in order to determine their differences and similarities. But comparison alone isn't enough. What's also required is study of the hierarchical organization of the characteristics. Certain characteristics seem superior to others, in the sense that the latter couldn't exist without the former. One can't be a mammal, for example, without being a vertebrate. It's by studying such hierarchical relationships that classifications are established.

What's the principle of classification? Because it's charged with the task of recovering nature's plan, classification assumes that there's a certain order in things. And what's the basis for this order? The principle of finality. Classification seeks to recover the order of things by recovering the ends to which they've been assigned.

FIFTY TWO

Method in the Moral Sciences

The moral sciences are those specifically concerned with the human spirit. In this lecture we'll examine the methodology of these sciences, of which there are four kinds: philosophy, social science, philology, and history. At the beginning of this course, we discussed the method appropriate for philosophy. Now we'll examine the methodology of the social sciences.

There are three kinds of social sciences: politics, law, and political economy.

Politics is the science of society, and its aim is to determine the best form for human society to take. What's the method of politics? It's often been approached in a kind of geometrical manner, as in, for example, Plato's *Republic*. But today this method has been abandoned and replaced by observation and experimentation, with history providing the facts.

Law, by contrast, concerns itself with legal rules and tries to determine – by deduction alone – how these rules apply in concrete cases.

Political economy used to be approached in the same way as politics, by studying in an abstract way the relationships between various human interests.

But this method too has been abandoned today. Political economists now study how these relationships play out in the present as well as in historical experience. Reasoning still plays an important part in what they do, but political economy is now richer because it attends to new facts made available through observation and experience.

The philological sciences study the laws of language – whether those of one particular language, a group of languages, or all known languages. Like all sciences that study laws, the philological sciences try to make sense of facts and so are inductive. Like the natural sciences, they rely heavily on reasoning by analogy to make sense of differences. This is the characteristic method of comparative philology.

The object studied by the historical sciences, of course, is the past, which can't be known except by relying on the testimony of those who lived in earlier times. So establishing the validity of testimonial evidence is an important part of the historical sciences.

Though testimony has no bearing on dogmatic philosophy or doctrinal questions, and though we must always be careful to preserve our absolute independence of mind, testimony is nevertheless indispensable to the determination of facts. Before the tribunal of history, we can't do without it. What's the basis for the authority of testimony? According to Reid and the Scots, it lies in the dual instincts of credulity and honesty. On the one hand, they say, we have a natural tendency to speak the truth, and, on the other, to believe what's said where we have no grounds for doubt. So the authority of testimony rests on a foundation that comprises the instinct of honesty in the person who testifies and the credulity of the person who listens.

There can be no doubt that we have these instincts. But in human beings, instincts are quite weak compared with voluntary activity. To a great extent, honesty and credulity depend on education and heredity; and while children naturally believe everything they're told, grown men are often more skeptical.

When do we take another person at his word? The answer is — when it's proven that he's neither mistaken nor deceiving us. So the authority of the testimony of others rests not on some general principle but on the particularities of each case. What steps can be taken to guard against error when it comes to the use of testimonial evidence? To answer this question, we must know something about the person testifying as well as about the facts being reported.

The two kinds of testimony are

1. that given by only one person;
2. that given by multiple witnesses.

With respect to the first, we must be assured that

a. the person giving it isn't mistaken;
b. he's not deceiving us.

For the person not to be mistaken, he must have a sufficient amount of general intelligence. We can't have faith in the testimony of a fool who's easily misled. In addition, he should have a specific competence in the type of facts about which he's testifying. A doctor has no more authority to testify about history, for example, than a philosopher does with regard to hygiene.

When the testimony is given by only one person, however, there's always a suspicion that what's said might be tainted by personal bias. The chances are good that this isn't so, but in all such cases there's at least the possibility.

If there's more than one witness, we can have more confidence in the testimony. And when there are many, many witnesses, we can be sure that personal bias hasn't intervened.

But it might be that these witnesses are engaged in a conspiracy. So we have to determine if they have an interest in collectively deceiving us as well as the means to carry it out. If so, we're thrown back into the situation faced in the case of the testimony of only one person. If not, the testimony can be believed.

But the facts testified to must also be considered. However great our confidence may be in those who testify, we can't believe what's absurd. So the facts reported must be possible facts and can't violate the laws of reason or science. Finally, the facts reported can't contradict another fact that's been previously established. Facts must be credible at both a general and particular level.

These are the rules that must be followed when we rely on testimony. When they are, we can believe the facts conveyed to us. But testimony alone is never sufficient to establish an idea, which must rest not on authority but on demonstration.

FIFTY THREE

Method in the Historical Sciences

The goal of history is to recount the past and return it to life. Where philosophy and the positive sciences study laws in the abstract, the aim of history is to show how laws play out in particular times and places. The other sciences try to draw out the resemblances between things, but history is more concerned with highlighting their differences. History shows how little two periods of time might resemble one another. Why does history focus on the particular? History's goal, as we've said, is to bring the past back to life, and what is general and abstract is dead. Life lies in the particular. Having analyzed the difference between two periods, however, history must then explain how one developed out of the other.

The material of history is furnished by three sources – each of them a form of testimony. These are legends, monuments, and documents.

1. Legends. Legends are stories that are passed down orally – typically within a single family. Yet stories might still be considered legends if they're written down, for while written stories aren't recounted by eyewitnesses, they remain legends. Their only proof lies in the oral tales on which they're based.

To be sure, the historian can't accept all legends on face value and must reject those that are patently absurd as well as those that, while consistent with reason, run contrary to the laws of science or to other known facts.

But even if a legend is false, it must always be respected as a fact. The events it recounts may not have actually taken place, but the legend still exists and must somehow be explained. A legend, in other words, should never be completely discounted – we should either accept it as true or regard it as an indicator of the beliefs and spirit of a prior age.

If a legend is false, it must be interpreted and its origin explained. We might even say that – if we can explain how it emerged and came into men's minds – no legend is false.

2. Monuments. Monuments are relics from the past that have reached us more or less intact. These include monuments properly so-called (temples, tombs, medallions) and especially inscriptions, which are the object of study of the recently founded science of epigraphy. The most important materials of epigraphy have been provided by the ancients, who inscribed on monuments records of their most significant public and private activities. Some of these inscriptions have survived, and they help us to imagine what life must have been like at the time.

Monuments constitute credible historical evidence only if they have two characteristics:

a. Authority. The monument must have been built during the period about which it informs us.
b. Sincerity. We should be particularly skeptical of funereal inscriptions. Regret or vanity have often made their way into memorials for the unworthy.

3. Documents. There are several kinds of historically significant documents – memoirs, records, histories, and journals kept by those living through a historical period. Literary works are an especially good source of information – they help the historian grasp the spirit of the period he's studying. There are entire centuries that can't be understood without a firm knowledge of their literatures.

These three sources provide the material of history. But what do historians do with this information?

They can't be content simply to recount the facts pieced together from different sources. Historians must go beyond this, reconstructing the past on the basis of these facts. Historical reconstructions are acts of imagination. The historian might have to reconstruct an entire constitution from a limited number of facts or describe some belief or practice from what one author alone has said. So in history there's more than enough room for a kind of inductive interpretation – indeed, this is a defining characteristic of history. Interpretation of this sort corresponds to the invention of hypotheses, just as the facts conveyed by documents correspond to those gathered through observation.

Once a historical hypothesis has been formulated, however, it must be demonstrated by showing that it conforms to known laws and explains the facts. This demonstration will be especially convincing if the hypothesis leads to the discovery of new facts – historical experimentation.

What we've said about history shows that, in principle, there's no reason to doubt its findings and that we might be able to be as certain about them as we are about those of the other sciences. But this has been contested. Some argue that the claims of history should be dismissed, because the facts on which they're based are inevitably altered, consciously or unconsciously, by those who pass them down to us. If this is so, what faith can we have in these facts or in the historical reconstructions built upon them? Indeed, critics argue, the more ancient a fact, the less faith we can have in it. Someday in the future it will no longer be possible to know precisely what happened today. So the limits of history constantly change. They extend from a point just before humanity made its appearance and advance as humanity marches forward through time. On this view, history isn't at all scientific, and we can't be certain about its findings.

But this skepticism is ill founded. The facts on which history relies are provided by sources that we can believe or not as the circumstances warrant. When we can't be certain about facts, we can reject them. But when we've proven that there's no reason to doubt them, it's perfectly legitimate to believe them. History should always be careful about which facts it trusts, but when its trust is well placed, its findings are certainly credible. For this reason, history should be counted among the sciences.

FIFTY FOUR

Language

Each man is enclosed within himself. None of us, as Leibniz said of the monad, has windows onto the rest of the world. So how do we communicate with one another? By means of external phenomena called signs.

A system of signs is called a language, which can be made up not just of words but of any signs whatever. Although the term "language" is customarily used to refer to spoken words, in our definition the signs of deaf mutes would also qualify.

Scholars often distinguish between natural and artificial signs. The first arise spontaneously, without reflection, while the second develop slowly and are the result of reflection, meditation, and progress. This distinction doesn't lack foundation. Some signs are established deliberately by human will, while others have an instinctual origin. But it's important to pay close attention to the meaning of the word "natural." Some signs are natural in the sense that they involve spontaneous behavior that, much later in our development, serves to communicate our thoughts. A child laughs if he's happy, for example, and does so spontaneously. Yet if he sees others laugh or cry, he doesn't consider this a sign of joy or happiness, for experience teaches him this only later.

But some have argued that there are natural signs in the proper sense of the word – that for children laughter and crying function as signs and are taken as such even before experience intervenes. Seeing a smiling person approach, doesn't a child himself smile? Seeing an angry face, doesn't he experience a real feeling of fear? The child thus grasps instinctively the relationship between certain signs and the states of mind they represent.

This theory, which assumes that children have well-developed instincts, is associated with the various Scottish philosophers who have exploited the notion of instinct. In France, Garnier has been its major proponent. But there's no proof children have such instincts. The faculty of interpreting signs might as easily come from heredity, a notion the Scots don't even consider. But even if this weren't so, the instinct of imitation is sufficient to explain why a child hearing laughter laughs or seeing crying cries. Approach a child with a sufficiently large object, perhaps with movable parts, and the child will cry. Hector's son cried on seeing his father's casket, of course, but we've no reason to consider these tears a sign of reflection or the result of an instinct of sadness. The conclusion that there are "natural signs" just isn't supported by the facts.

Neither do we believe that – prior to experience – the child has any ideas whatever. Nor do we believe that he's capable of understanding the relationship between a material and a psychological phenomenon experienced but imperfectly before. Signs are "natural" only if we mean that they involve spontaneous behavior – not that they can be understood from birth. This invites us to consider the origin of language.

How did language come about? The philosopher Bonald thought it impossible for man to create a system of signs without another system of signs at his disposal. For how could we understand that a certain word expressed a certain idea if we didn't already have a system of signs that allowed us to communicate? It seems to be a vicious circle.

If language wasn't created by man, Bonald reasons, its source must lie in divine revelation – a view he supports with passages from the scriptures. We won't follow him into this part of his argument, focusing instead on what the theory might be worth.

A Talmudic legend says: "One must have pliers in order to make pliers; therefore, pliers are the product of divine intervention." Bonald's reasoning is the same – most human inventions are due to divine revelation.

Yet the so-called vicious circle on which his reasoning depends is hardly indissoluble. We wouldn't be able to create language without nature's help, of course, but nature provides this by granting us those external physiological phenomena that accompany our psychological phenomena. Possessing intelligence, we soon understand that certain natural phenomena might be used as signs. We make others understand our experience by means of these signs, and the communication proves so easy that these others soon begin to express the same phenomena by means of the same signs. Eventually, these signs become more complex and more refined.

Bonald challenges us to discover the genesis of the very first sign. But we have a challenge for him. To create language, God would have had to make man understand the relationship between certain phenomena and certain feelings. But if man had been able to understand these relationships, he would also have been able to construct a system of signs and wouldn't have needed God to do it for him. So if we grant this capability to man, we must also grant him the capacity to create language. Thus we reject Bonald's theory.

Language wasn't taught to man by God but was rather acquired through our very nature. But this still leaves two possibilities:

1. We acquired language spontaneously at the moment the human species emerged. As soon as our intelligence began to show itself, we spoke – as simply and with as much comprehension as we thought – and what we said was understood by others.
2. Language was created slowly over time. At the beginning of human thought man possessed no system of language and had to make it himself. According to this hypothesis, human beings not only had to develop a language but had to conceive the idea of language itself.

Which of these theories should we adopt?

Given our conclusions about natural signs, we can reject the first, for it assumes that a system of such signs existed right from the start. Yet Renan cites a fact in support of this theory. If language had been created by man, he would have perfected it over the years. Many of the languages that exist today, however, are imperfect. This being so – as it requires less intelligence to perfect a language than to create it – language must have been received by man already made (*Thesis on the Origin of Language*).

Our answer to Renan is the same as Garnier's. While no actual person has ever sought out a syllable to represent an idea, the association of a syllable with an idea is a function not of instinct but of experience and reflection. While language wasn't created by one man and then taught to others, it might still be a product of human reflection.

So language was given to us neither by a supernatural being nor at the origin of our experience. Neither was it created by a genius and then spread by authority or violence. Here's how it came to be. Some men noticed that certain external phenomena were always accompanied by certain feelings or ideas – states of consciousness. So they tried to communicate to others their thoughts or feelings by means of these phenomena. It required a great deal of effort for them to understand one another, of course, but time is nothing in this context. In this way, little by little, a system of signs emerged. In the beginning, the signs were very simple and expressed ideas only in vague terms. But over time they became more analytic and were employed to express not just haphazard collections of ideas but nuanced ideas as well. They became particularized and better adapted to thought. This is what we mean when we say that signs are a product of reflection, and it's in this sense that language is artificial.

Now let's see how useful language is to thought. Is it essential or can we think without signs?

To answer this question, let's distinguish between three kinds of ideas:

1. concrete or particular ideas – for example, the idea of this paper;
2. abstract ideas;
3. general ideas.

1. Can we conceive of particular ideas without signs? At first glance, the answer seems to be yes. I see an object before me. For me to think of it, the object need only avoid contradicting the laws of my intelligence. I don't have to name the object or designate it with a sign. But this assumes that the object is present. What if it's not? Here the same thing seems to hold true. All I have to do to recall an object is remember its forms. I don't have to give it a name, which means that, with particular ideas, we can indeed think and recollect without signs.

But this kind of recollection is very difficult and demands intense effort. If we had to think about an object's forms and qualities every time we wanted to bring it to mind, we'd never reach conclusions or be able to communicate. If, when I think, "I saw the *Noces de Cana* at the Louvre," I have to represent to myself in its entirety the Louvre and the painting, the thought would take a long time to be expressed, and others would find it hard to understand me.

So how do signs aid memory? While they don't allow us to dispense with thinking about the things that they express, they do exempt us from one part of the operation necessary for thought. With signs at our disposal, we need no longer represent to ourselves all the forms of the object but can make do with the fragments of memory attached to the sign. All of our more or less confused recollections about the object group themselves together around this sign, so that the sign brings the object to mind immediately, without our having to work so hard to remember it.

2. Now let's consider abstract ideas. Can we conceive of these without signs? Condillac denied this categorically. Since what is abstract doesn't exist, how could we represent it without a sign? The intervention of signs is necessary to bring the abstract into existence.

But we can't agree with Condillac. We believe it's possible to think about an abstract thing in the absence of signs. Here's a table, for example. Without using signs I can certainly formulate an abstract idea of its length. I can separate its length from its other qualities, and I can repeat this operation whenever I want.

At least in theory, therefore, we can think of abstract things without using signs. But if we had to go through the same procedure every time we wanted to think of an abstract thing, thought would be too laborious. Considering the central role played by abstract ideas in the sciences, it's not hard to see why, in this realm, language is absolutely essential. Words serve to fix abstract ideas, preventing their flight from the mind. When we encounter them, they awaken our memory, relieving us of the need to formulate each abstract idea anew.

3. General ideas – like those of genus and species – are those that apply to a large number of individuals.

Can we think of these without signs? Without signs, for example, could we think of the idea of humanity, of all the characteristics possessed by human beings? Could we think of these without signs? Suppose we define humanity as the collection of free and intelligent beings. How could this be represented without signs? The most we can do is think of a single being who is intelligent and free, but then we're thinking not of humanity but of an individual with humanity's characteristics. It's true that, when we think about the intelligence of this hypothetical individual, we can't help but think about the many different forms intelligence might take. But without signs, even this would be quite difficult. Words relieve us of – or, so to speak, abridge – this effort, and do so once and for all.

All this brings us to the following conclusion. In theory, thought could exist in the absence of a system of signs, but it would be distorted and impoverished and would require tremendous mental labor. Progress would be impossible, for we'd have to repeat the same mental operations over and over again. To relieve us of this burden is the very great service that language renders to thought.

But we might go further. Thought is mobile and fleeting and easily escapes the mind. To this mobile, hazy something, words grant a real solidity. An idea becomes attached to a word that, because it can be clearly defined, keeps the idea from being confused with other ideas. This is the second service that language renders to thought.

Is this to say that – thanks to habit – we can think using signs alone? This is the theory developed by Taine in the first chapter of *Intelligence*.

We don't believe this is possible, because we must always think something, and we can't think except in ideas. Our nature forces us to see some idea lying behind every sign. This idea might be extremely vague, but it exists nonetheless. The condition for thinking in signs is that we see at least the shadow of an underlying idea.

By itself, though, this shadow is insufficient. Ideas must be expressed in words, which give them a kind of body. So language aids thought but isn't a complete substitute for ideas.

PART FOUR

Ethics

FIFTY FIVE

Definition and Divisions of Ethics

Ethics is the science that studies what humans should do in the various circumstances in which they find themselves.

When ethics poses this question in a general way – not concerning itself with particular cases – it's called general or theoretical ethics. When it seeks to understand how a general ethical law, once established, should be applied in particular situations, it's called particular, applied, or practical ethics.

The former is a pure science, whereas the latter is both a science and an art – thus paralleling the distinction between general and applied logic. Insofar as either ethics or logic is concerned with abstract and general laws, the term "science" applies to it. These forms of inquiry become art when they consider how these laws apply in practice.

FIFTY SIX

On Moral Responsibility

Each of the arguments we're going to advance in the field of ethics rests on the single fact of moral responsibility. The entirety of ethics can thus be revealed by explaining moral responsibility and examining its conditions. The main condition we'll consider is the moral law and its consequences.

Undeniably, man is a responsible creature. He judges his actions, declaring them good or bad, and recognizes that others also have the right to judge them. This is the essence of responsibility, which has also been called imputability.

Let's consider this idea further. Someone who's responsible is accountable to a law. For when we feel we have to account for our actions, we do so by considering whether they've violated some law. In such a circumstance, we feel dependent on the authority of this law.

Yet responsibility also has another characteristic. In twenty or thirty years, I'll still feel responsible for an action I commit today. It's true that civil law recognizes that we're no longer culpable after a certain amount of time. But when it comes to the moral law, there's no such recognition. Moral responsibility survives the act in perpetuity. The act may take only a moment to complete, but we'll be held accountable for the rest of our lives. So there are two components to moral responsibility:

1. We're responsible, accountable for our actions before a law;
2. This responsibility is perpetual.

What are the conditions of moral responsibility? To be held accountable, I must be the cause – and the only cause – of my actions, for otherwise it would be some other cause, and not me, that incurred the responsibility. This is why those who act under the influence of passion or illness are never held responsible for their actions – they're not their own masters. So the first condition of moral responsibility is freedom.

Despite this, some determinists have tried to reconcile their position with the notion of responsibility. According to Plato, for example, man isn't free, but this doesn't mean that he's irresponsible. (For Plato, responsibility consists in being rewarded or punished according to one's actions.) Plato argues that, if a man has acted badly – whether or not he's done so of his own free will – it's good that he be punished so that he might be corrected. In the opposite case, it's good that he be rewarded. An evil person, according to Plato, is a dangerous malady. If we're not rid of him, he may entrench himself in society. This is how Plato tries to reconcile determinism with the existence of punishments and rewards.

We don't contest Plato's logic, but the kind of responsibility he's concerned with is civil rather than moral. The latter involves more than just the meting out of punishments and rewards. Moral responsibility hinges on our dependence on a higher authority, on a law to which we declare ourselves subject. And responsibility of this sort is irreconcilable with determinism. If we're not free, we can't reproach ourselves for violating the moral law or be satisfied because we've acted consistently with it. Yet, properly speaking, it's precisely this remorse and contentment that constitutes moral responsibility.

We noted earlier that we're responsible for our actions in perpetuity. What's required for the present-day self to be held accountable for an act committed ten years ago? What's required is that the two selves form one – that is, that the self be identical to itself. Freedom and identity of the self – these are the two necessary psychological conditions for moral responsibility.

FIFTY SEVEN

On Moral Law. The History of Utilitarianism

We've just examined the conditions that must be met for us to be held responsible – in perpetuity – for our actions. But to give a complete account of moral responsibility, we must also consider the nature of the authority to which we're accountable. To be responsible, we must have a rule to which we try to conform, in terms of which our responsibility is measured. In other words, we must be subject to some law, which is a moral rather than a psychological condition.

Let's examine the characteristics of this law. Philosophers generally agree that the moral law has three characteristics – it must be absolute, universal, and obligatory:

1. Absolute. There can be no exceptions to the moral law. Its commands must be relative, not to this or that individual, but to humanity as a whole. Moreover, the moral law can't be relative to this or that end. Its commands apply in every circumstance.

2. Universal. Here we face a difficulty, for some say that the moral law isn't the same everywhere. For example, there's a significant difference between the law of the savage and that of civilized man, suggesting that the moral law isn't universal. But all this objection really shows is that the material of the moral law varies – not the law itself. It's true that, when different peoples try to define the moral law, their mutual understanding breaks down. But they're still searching for a universal law. The savage considers his morality to be that of all peoples, so the facts particular to his circumstances don't contradict the universality of the moral law. In our discussion of logic, we noted that, while there's only one truth, it can be obtained in various ways. The same holds in

ethics. While there's only one moral law, it can be reached in various ways.

3. Obligatory. The moral law takes the form of commands, and those commanded to do something are bound to obey. But where things that are subject to physical laws can never escape them, we can disobey the moral law. The sense of necessity associated with the moral law derives from its obligatory nature. To use Kant's expression, the moral law is imperative.

What kind of law satisfies all three of these conditions?

Many philosophers point to self-interest, which commands us to do what's most advantageous to us. This is the principle of utilitarian ethics, which has changed considerably over time, growing from an apology for hedonism almost to the point of appreciating the most noble and most disinterested sentiments.

In our view, the Cyrenaic school offered the first version of utilitarian ethics. Aristippus argued that nothing is good but pleasure – and immediate pleasure at that – unless it would lead later to pain. As Aristippus saw it, the sole condition of taste is the abandonment to pleasure.

Epicurus went a step further. Noting that pleasure is always followed by a pain of greater intensity, he believed that interest properly understood required a renunciation of pleasure. For him there are two kinds of pleasure – short but intense "pleasures in movement" and long but weaker "pleasures at rest." Experience shows that the former are always followed by great pain, which upsets the soul, throws it into disequilibrium, and causes moral maladies. "Pleasures at rest," by contrast, are less intense but more continuous – and they don't expose us to the risk of violent pleasures. So the instinct of reason advises us to choose these pleasures over the former. Where can they be found? In work, meditation, sobriety, and the study of philosophy. In the name of interest, therefore, utilitarianism came to recommend a virtuous life.

So Epicurus, on the basis of interest, recommends something noble; but his method is quite arbitrary. It's not easy to determine the intensity of any particular pleasure. While Epicurus offers some excellent maxims, therefore, these don't constitute a well-built system. Bentham, who sought a more certain, scientific criterion in his arithmetic of pleasures, had much the same response. Epicurus had also suggested that his followers only associate with one another, pursuing a way of life that was strict and of a higher order but as egoistic in its consequences as in its principles. The Epicurean was required to disengage himself from society, flee from public affairs, avoid the responsibilities of family or friendship, and live for himself alone. By contrast – even as he sought a more scientific utilitarianism – Bentham tried to reintegrate altruistic sentiments into utilitarian ethics. Let's examine how Bentham's utilitarianism improved upon that of Epicurus.

Although there are many different kinds of pleasures and pains, there are only a few dimensions on which they vary – intensity, duration, certainty, and proximity. But these dimensions concern only the intrinsic value of pleasure and pain. Another important way in which pleasures and pains vary lies in the consequences of some act for us and those around us. So how should we determine whether an act is good? We should consider the pleasure or pain that might result and then ascertain the extent to which these pleasures or pains have the characteristics we've mentioned. This done, we then make a list of probable losses and gains and decide in favor of the act that yields the biggest gain. The path is long but sure.

Simply by applying this method, Bentham made a significant improvement over Epicurus by showing that the most advantageous pleasures are those that don't concern the individual alone, that aren't purely egoistic. Believing that pleasure is in direct proportion to the number of people affected, Bentham recommended duty in the name of interest. His ethics was inspired by a great optimism, that our greatest pleasure can be found in the pleasure of others, for there's a natural harmony of all human interests.

In this way, Bentham integrated social duties into utilitarian ethics. John Stuart Mill tried to do the same thing for the love of goodness and truth. "Up until now," he said, "utilitarians have erred by considering only the quantity of pleasure, not the quality. Yet the two are quite different. Quality makes some pleasures superior to others. The pleasures of taste, for example, are significantly more vivid than those of sight, yet we find the pleasure of contemplating a work of art superior to that of eating a delicacy. So let's seek out pleasures which are qualitatively superior."

But how can this criterion be applied? How can the quality of pleasures be compared? To know which of two pleasures is preferable, Mill says, we have to ask those who have experienced both and rely on their judgment. But what if they don't agree? What if competent judges differ? Then what we do is vote and regard as superior the pleasure that's been declared so by the majority.

Recently, Herbert Spencer has revived Mill's approach, with a few modifications. What distinguishes the two philosophies, as Spencer himself says, is less a difference of doctrine than of method. Spencer criticizes Mill for proceeding too empirically, for suggesting that the qualitative comparison of pleasures should be more scientific. As Spencer sees it, our knowledge of human nature alone should be enough to allow us to figure out what makes us happy: "It falls to the moral law to deduce from the laws of life and the conditions of existence those acts which tend to produce happiness, and those which produce unhappiness. This done, these deductions must be recognized as laws of conduct to which we must conform." Instead of proceeding empirically, Spencer pursues a method analogous to that taken in the physical sciences, attempting to discover the causes that produce happiness.

Such is the history of utilitarianism.

FIFTY EIGHT

Critique of Utilitarianism. The Morality of Sentiment

In every utilitarian approach to ethics, the moral law is based on self-interest. So to evaluate utilitarianism, we'll ask whether self-interest satisfies the conditions of the moral law.

We noted earlier that the moral law must be universal. Would a moral law based on self-interest have this characteristic? No. Interest, by its very nature, is personal. It's nothing more than immediate pleasure, and pleasure varies from one individual to the next. What pleases me may make you unhappy, and, conversely, what distresses me might be a source of great pleasure to you. Some people can't stand mental labor, for example, while others live for it. What's considered pleasurable also varies from one land – and one epoch – to the next. How could we found a universal law to cover something so variable? This objection applies whether we're dealing with forms of utilitarianism that stress quantitative or qualitative pleasures. Epicurus found more charm in tranquil retreat than in the active life of the public forum. But a more active person would find such tranquility intolerable, preferring the excitement of the crowd and the emotions associated with public contests. How can Epicurus claim that his tastes are shared by everyone? He has the tastes he does only because he happens to have a serious disposition, a calm temperament, and a love of peace. But if I'm of a different mind, following his advice will lead me – as I seek my greatest interest – to act differently.

Mill's doctrine is subject to the same objection. He finds one pleasure qualitatively superior to another, according to his particular taste. But why should it be mine? Pleasures are subjective, and there's no way to make them otherwise. But Mill insists that he doesn't adjudicate among pleasures on his own but rather bases his judgments on the testimony of others, those who have experienced the pleasures and said which is superior. But by what right do these judges decide for anyone else? When intellectuals say to the common man that there's more pleasure in intellectual labor than in the senses, they won't be believed. And with good reason, for there's simply no justification for imposing on others our own views as to what's pleasurable.

Furthermore, why should I believe that this judge is infallible, that what he's observed is true even for himself? Mill recognizes that this is a possibility – it might explain what happens when multiple judges disagree – and his solution is that in such cases we should yield to the decision of the majority. But today's majority can easily become tomorrow's minority, so that the moral law would fluctuate as much as its civil counterpart. In short, there's no reason to believe that this utilitarian tribunal is infallible, and no reason to think it can pronounce universally applicable sentences.

Since Spencer did nothing more than revive Mill's theory and give it a more scientific formulation, the same objection applies to him.

There can be no universal formula for happiness because there exist within us two beings – a general and an individual man. What's pleasurable is a function not just of our general but also of our individual natures. So pleasure necessarily varies across individuals and can't form the basis for a universal law.

But the moral law must also satisfy a second condition. In order for it to be obligatory, it must be universally observable and thus universally recognizable – regardless of experience or education. This means that the moral law can't be a privilege reserved for a chosen few, a favor bestowed on a small aristocracy, as some of the ancients believed. Neither is it a luxury, something superfluous to life that we can simply pass over. Everyone must be able to comprehend the moral law at a glance.

Could a moral law based on self-interest satisfy this condition? Obviously not. It takes a great deal of experience to know what our true interests are; and even after such experience we may not really know – indeed, nothing is so difficult. So a moral law based on self-interest can't be obligatory and can't satisfy the essential conditions of the moral law.

Other philosophers, without falling into the trap of regarding the good as simple or undifferentiated, have sought to rest the moral law on an alternative foundation. These philosophers include Hutcheson, Rousseau, Jacobi, and Adam Smith; and among these, it was Smith who offered the best formulation of what's called "the morality of sentiment."

These philosophers recognize that most moral judgments don't stem from self-interest. Nevertheless, they claim that we needn't abandon the search for a general principle that guides our actions. For each of us has within us an instinct that allows us to judge some actions bad and others good. If we follow this instinct or natural sentiment, they argue, we'll never be led astray.

In the specific version of this argument advanced by Smith, the sentiment that serves as the foundation of the moral law is benevolence or sympathy, a natural sentiment which draws us toward certain people and leads us away from others. The good is simply another term for whatever characterizes those we like, while the bad characterizes those we dislike. Since sympathy demands reciprocity, we follow the example set by our friends. This is how the good should be practiced.

Does Smith's theory satisfy all the conditions of the moral law? It rests on an accurate observation, for there's no doubt that for many people sentiment is the only guide to action. But does this mean that sentiment is the true and only foundation of morality? That's the important question.

Our view is that sentiment is rather fallible. When we act on instinct, we end up doing the wrong thing almost as often as we end up doing right. So instinct is an extremely uncertain guide, all the more so because it doesn't always mislead us – as Pascal noted of the imagination – and because we can't know when it misleads us and when not.

Moreover, sentiment doesn't command us to obey. There's something predetermined about sympathy, for we're hardly free to like or not like someone as we choose. But if choice is lacking, how can it command us to like one type of person rather than another? A moral law founded on sentiment can't be obligatory.

Finally, sympathy assumes the presence of at least two people. But if morality were to rest on such a sentiment, it would disappear in the absence of society. In Smith's theory, it's as though morality becomes incarnated in the other and ceases to exist without him – which makes virtue depend on quite contingent conditions. But the moral law must exist for itself, independent of all conditions. For these reasons, Smith's theory of the morality of sentiment can't satisfy the conditions of the moral law.

Beyond this, the theory mistakes an effect for a cause. What's the origin of our sentiment of sympathy or aversion? It's hardly an ultimate fact that must be left unexplained. If I instinctively like one person and not another, the reason is that the former has respected the moral law, whereas the latter has violated it. If I have sympathy for the first, it's because he's good. He's not good because I have sympathy for him. This critique of Smith thus leads us to assume that there must be some moral rule that guides our judgments about other people. Smith simply stopped too soon – had he gone further, he'd have found the cause upon whose effects he heaped so much attention.

FIFTY NINE

The Morality of Kant

The lesson of the preceding discussion is as follows: There is such a thing as the moral law, but it doesn't rest on experience. Yet experience is the stuff of which knowledge is made. Prior to experience, there's nothing in us but forms, of which we're barely conscious. So Kant reasons that the moral law must be purely formal. The material of knowledge – derived as it is from experience alone – lacks moral value. So experience is not immoral, but amoral, foreign to morality.

What do we know of the moral law? One thing we know is that it's a form of the mind and that as such – forms being universal – it exists in all people. How can we know whether or not we should perform a certain action? Every time the maxim that guides our action can be elevated to a universal rule of conduct, Kant says, the action is good. In the opposite case, the action is bad. Kant formulated the moral law as follows: "Always act according to a maxim that you could will to be a universal law" (*Groundwork of the Metaphysics of Morals*). He went on to apply this formula to many specific cases. Should we steal? No, because we couldn't will theft to be a universal law, for to do so would spell the end of private property. The moral proposition being considered can't be elevated to a universal rule of conduct, so the action in question is bad.

But how would the moral law thus formulated act upon the will? Why should we engage in actions whose rule can be elevated to a universal law? According to Kant, there's only one answer. The moral law simply commands us, and we must obey its authority without question. For this reason, Kant called the moral law a categorical imperative.

An imperative is a formula that commands, a maxim of action. Kant distinguishes between a hypothetical imperative, which commands something as a means to an end (for example, "We must stay sober in order to be healthy") and a categorical imperative, which commands something unconditionally, as an end in itself. "A categorical imperative," he says, "unconditionally demands of us a certain conduct, without any consideration of the end to which it may be a means."

But for an action to be moral, it's not enough that it merely conform to the letter of the moral law. According to Kant, it must do so solely out of respect for this law. If you help someone because you like them, the action conforms to the law, but it isn't moral, as it's not done solely with the law in view. On the other hand, a man who, though no longer happy with his life, rejects suicide out of respect for the moral law is engaged in a moral action. The moral law demands to be obeyed for itself, and an action ceases to be moral from the moment it becomes intertwined with calculations of interest.

What should our position be with respect to this theory? Before going further, we should pause to note that – giving the word "interest" an expansive definition – it's clearly impossible for man to act without having some interest in his actions. A maxim of action that doesn't work on us through some motive will necessarily be ineffective. It's useless for Kant to say that we must respect the moral law because it's the law. This reason alone is never enough. Man must have an interest at stake if he's to avoid violating the moral law. To act as Kant would have us is to act without reason. So an absolutely categorical imperative is impossible.

Nevertheless, there does exist a reason – implied in Kant's categorical imperative – for us to respect the moral law. But this reason transforms the categorical imperative into a hypothetical one. We must act in such a way that the maxim of our actions can be elevated to a universal law if we want to be truly human. This is the reason for us to act one way rather than another, and it is also the end that human beings seek.

What do we mean when we say this reason is implied in Kant's categorical imperative? Our view is that Kant himself doesn't remain faithful to the purely formal theory of morality he lays out. For having declared that the moral law must be purely formal, he then gives it content. For his first formulation of the moral law, he substitutes the following: "Act in such a way that you always treat human beings – yourself and others – as an end and not as a means." In other words, respect for the human personality is an aim of morality. This need to respect the personality contains and becomes the reason for the moral action. With this formulation, Kant is no longer content to determine the external or formal characteristics of morality but actually tells us what moral action should be in itself. He seems to have been led ineluctably to sense that a purely formal moral law can't really shape human conduct. He's forced to recognize, in short, that in order to establish the authority of this law he must give reasons.

Also, having declared that sensibility should never play a role in morality, Kant even comes close to integrating motives of sensibility into his ethics. By what intermediary, he asks, does the moral law have an effect upon activity? He answers that it's by means of a half-sensible and half-rational motive that he calls respect for the law. But try as he might to depict such a feeling as intellectual in nature, it clearly remains a phenomenon of sensibility, which proves that man can't act without having some interest as a motive, whether it's an interest of a higher order or not.

Kant's ethics is one of the greatest efforts ever made to push humanity toward the ideal. Kant's wish was to draw mankind away from the world of the senses and make him live a purely rational life – thus creating a distinctive place for us in the universe, even if doing so runs contrary to our nature. But however beautiful it may be, Kant's effort was doomed to fail. A purely formal morality is close to being an empty morality, and the only way Kant can escape this consequence, as we've seen, is by contradicting himself.

Our discussion of morality up to this point has taught us that there does exist a moral law that guides our activity, that it precedes experience, and that it's this law that explains moral judgment. From our discussion of Kantian ethics, we've also learned that this law has to agree with our nature and speak to our interests if it's to command our obedience.

SIXTY

The Moral Law

What is our duty? It's to do that for which we're made. Here I don't mean an end determined by some higher power, only that we're fashioned in a certain way, disposed toward some actions and unfit for others. The same is true of us as of other things, that we should do what we're good at. So the question we have to ask is: What is man's proper employment? The answer to this question will be the moral law itself.

Because that for which we're made is nothing other than our end, the moral law commands us to achieve our end. This end is the ideal terminus of the development of the human being, and it's toward this terminus that we must march. As human beings are constantly changing, we can and must work at becoming more and more what it's in our power to be, at fully realizing all the powers of our nature. To accomplish this, all we must do is attend to the direction toward which these powers naturally orient us. So the first formulation of the moral law is: "Move in the direction of your end."

But what does this end consist of? If we arrived there, our being would be actualized, would be an absolute and perfect version of what it is now in a limited, imperfect way. At present our being is essentially – but incompletely – a person. So to move in the direction of our end is to develop our personality, and from this can be derived the second formulation of the moral law: "Always act with the goal of developing your personality."

But what's a person? It's a being who's identical and free. The most important of these two characteristics is freedom. The opposite of a person is a thing, and what characterizes a thing is that it lacks initiative. It's put into motion by external forces rather than by itself. As Malebranche said, things don't act but are acted upon. A person, by contrast, being free, can remove himself from the influence of external forces and engage in action all by himself. No matter how powerful these forces may be, a person has the capacity to cast off their influence, at least in the internal realm of consciousness. So the essential characteristic of a person is freedom. But what does it mean to be free? To be free is to not be used as a means, either by external forces or by other men. The slave is an instrument in the hands of his master, where a free man is the instrument of no one. Because the essence of personality is freedom, and because being free means not being used as a means, we can substitute for our earlier formulation of the moral law the following: "Always act in such a way as to treat yourself as an end and never as a means."

Despite how it might seem, this formulation isn't a recipe for egoism. The moral law commands us to respect our personality, but it certainly doesn't rule out maintaining relationships with other people. Indeed, it's impossible to avoid the company of others, and one of the tasks of the moral law is to tell us what our relationships with others should be like. When we are reminded that the moral law is universal, we immediately see that not only ourselves but all other men as well must develop their personalities. They too must treat themselves as ends and not means. But to respect the personalities of others is to recognize that what's important to us may not be important to them and that – given the universality of the moral law, as we've just pointed out – we can't substitute what we think is important for what others do. This leads us to the definitive formulation of the moral law: "Always act so as to treat the human personality, everywhere you encounter it, as an end and never as a means."

This formulation makes clear that the moral law, although universal, can vary from one individual to another. All men advance toward their end, but they don't all have the same idea of what this means. This is why the moral law – universal though it is – has taken various and sometimes even contradictory forms.

SIXTY ONE

On Duty and the Good. On Virtue. Rights

The approach to ethics we've been developing rests on a single principle – moral responsibility. Up to this point, on the assumption that moral responsibility is a function of moral consciousness (consciousness in the realm of moral affairs), we've merely postulated this principle, not fully discussed it. Moral consciousness is a kind of judge that pronounces sentences on our actions and those of others. Because we judge ourselves as well as others, we felt justified in arguing that moral responsibility is the foundation of theoretical ethics. Moral consciousness can be clear or muddled, conscious or unconscious, mistaken or sound, enlightened or ignorant – but no one is completely without it. And because moral consciousness is universal, so is moral responsibility.

From this we deduced that human activity is governed by a moral law. Inquiring into the nature of this law, we examined, in order, morality and interest, the ethics of sentiment, and the morality of Kant. We concluded that the foundation of the moral law lies in the idea of finality – a conclusion that has two advantages:

1. The idea of finality has immediate implications for action, so that passion and calculations of interest need not play any role in ethics;
2. Men need not attempt actions that would be absurd or impossible.

The very conception of our end implies the will to realize it. Far less dour than Kant's morality, our formulation of the moral law doesn't mean giving up the quest for happiness, which can be found in the realization of our end. If we make happiness our life's goal, we find that the greatest happiness lies in obedience to the moral law. Happiness is a necessary consequence and natural complement of the moral life. Where Kant saw a radical antinomy between the two, we see a harmony that in no way compromises the dignity of the moral law.

We can now move on to discuss a number of related ideas, beginning with duty and the good.

Duty is the obligation we have to respect the moral law. We have to advance our end.

The good is simply the end for which we've been made. The idea of the good is logically prior to that of duty, for if we're obligated to respect the moral law – and this is the meaning of duty – it's because the law is good. But this wasn't the case for Kant, for whom duty is logically prior and who claimed that duty is an absolute without providing any justification for doing so. As Kant saw it, the moral law is above criticism because of its higher authority, and the good consists in obeying this law.

Virtue is the constant practice of duty. I say that virtue is a practice because it involves a deployment of activity. And this practice must be constant; it must be a habit (Aristotle). To be virtuous, we must do more than be good once – we have to do so continuously, always respecting the moral law. Virtue is to be found, not in one or even several isolated actions, but rather in a kind of disposition, a special temperament of the will.

But do we have to respect the moral law to the letter? Clearly not, for this offends common sense, and with good reason. Some say the opposite. But this would mean that those who are mistaken about the nature of their ends are incapable of virtue, sinning because of their ignorance. We've already discussed this criticism in our treatment of the morality of interest, and it isn't one to which we can remain open. So our view will be that virtue requires obedience, not to the letter of the moral law, but to its spirit. Men are virtuous when they advance what they sincerely believe to be their end. To be sure, they must be absolutely sincere as they set out to determine what this end is and in the course of so doing should ignore every consideration foreign to reason. They should be impartial as they take up the question and seek a solution to it. But once they've decided, on the basis of reason alone, what their end is, virtue is simply a matter of their consistently advancing this end. This is why we can say that virtue consists in good will. Good will is actually required in two areas: A person must show good will by banishing from consideration any motives that stem from sensation (leaving the question to reason alone) and also by applying the verdict thus rendered. These two conditions are both necessary and sufficient for virtue.

But must we dismiss each and every motive stemming from sensation? To be virtuous, must we – as Kant says – love virtue? Or does the idea of moral sentiment corrupt morality by making it too easy to demonstrate good will? Our view is that it's irrational to condemn men for their good sentiments. Moral sentiment, no matter what its form – contentment, remorse, sympathy, or antipathy – is an aid to virtue, and there's no reason to lament this fact. Of course we can't command sentiment or expect it to be the whole of morality, but where sentiment exists, there's no need to uproot it for the sake of morality. Its absence may make virtue more beautiful, but its presence is certainly no obstacle to virtue.

A right is a moral authority with which, in certain situations, human beings may be invested. This authority is "moral" in the sense that its existence doesn't depend upon the availability of the material means necessary to enforce it. A child lost in the middle of the woods, left to his own devices and without physical strength, still has the right to others' respect for his life.

What is the foundation of rights? According to Hobbes, it's might. In the state of nature, the right of each man has no limit other than his strength, so he has the right to do whatever he can. But such a hypothetical situation couldn't last indefinitely, as each man would kill anyone weaker than himself, and life would be perpetually endangered. Because the strongest instinct is that of preservation, however, all men – acting out of self-interest, with the goal of providing the security so lacking in the state of nature – agree to give up some of their natural rights in order to respect the lives of one another.

According to Hobbes, this is how rights are established. But if rights rested only on this simple agreement, they'd vanish in a second. For them to be secure, they must be removed from the caprice of individual wills. But how? Hobbes's answer is that a man invested with absolute power will emerge out of the crowd and guarantee the permanence of the social contract.

This absolute monarch will be the guardian of rights, protecting them against the whims and weaknesses of the masses. So according to Hobbes, rights rest on a contract that has self-interest as its foundation, and this contract is guaranteed by a man armed with absolute power.

Let's evaluate this theory. No matter how great the strength of a monarch may be, all men are at bottom quite fragile, and therefore inadequate guardians of rights. What good is it to remove rights from the dangers they face from the errors or faults of the crowd, only to place them in the hands of a single man, with his own errors and faults? For this reason, our view is that Hobbes's theory doesn't achieve its aim of establishing rights on a stable foundation. Neither the will of a man nor the traditions of a family are sufficient guarantees. In fact, there would probably be more security if we were to leave the contract in the hands of those who came together to make it.

Moreover, the nature of the moral law makes us doubt that in the state of nature the right of each man was equal to his strength. The moral law limits these rights by commanding that we perform certain actions and not perform others. We have more power than rights in the state of nature.

But if might isn't the foundation of rights, what is? Clearly there's a connection between the idea of duty and that of rights. Cousin has said that a right is simply a demand for the performance of duty. If another person has the obligation to respect my life, I have the right to demand of that person that he do his duty – and thus the right to not have my life cut short.

According to this theory, my rights are based on the duty that you have in relation to me. But why do we have the right to demand of another that he do his duty? Is it because it's our job to make virtue reign in the world? Not at all. If others fail to do their duty, they'll suffer the consequences. Why should we intervene? Moreover, if rights consist in a demand for the performance of duty, the consequences would be very serious indeed and would make even Cousin himself hesitate. Demanding the performance of the duty of charity, for example, amounts to socialism. So this theory strikes a blow against individual freedom.

But what, then, is the foundation of rights? We've already established that human beings have duties. The corollary of this is that we have the right to do everything necessary in order to fulfill our duties. I have the duty to preserve my life. If you threaten it, I have the duty to defend it by every means possible. So the foundation of my rights is my duties, not those of others. We should even say that "man has only one right: that of doing everything which is necessary in order to accomplish his duty, which is to say, in order to realize his end."

Division of Practical Ethics

Practical ethics, which is concerned with what human beings should do in specific situations, has four branches:

1. Individual morality – at least in the abstract, we can imagine a man living alone, trying to figure out his duties.
2. Domestic morality – man's duties to his family.
3. Civic morality – man's duties to those who inhabit the same country and to those with whom he shares certain tastes and interests.
4. Social morality – again abstracting from the particular, the general duties man has to his fellow man.

Individual Morality

Of the four branches of practical ethics, individual morality – in which man is treated as though living an isolated life, having no relationships with others – is the most elementary. So natural is individual morality that we needn't go to great lengths to establish its importance. Insofar as man is isolated, either in fact or in principle, what duties does he owe to himself?

To answer this question, we need only apply to this particular case the general formula of the moral law. Man must treat his personality as an end and never as a means. In other words, he must always respect and develop his personality, never allowing it to become a means to some other end; assure himself that everything within him might be perfected; and then try to achieve this perfection. Now, man has both a body and a soul, and the two are closely connected. So let's begin by asking: What are our duties to our body?

The first is to preserve it. We have no right to take our own lives. Suicide is immoral for three reasons:

1. We have duties that must be fulfilled. Even in the hypothetical situation in which man is isolated, we're duty-bound to develop our intelligence, sensibility, and activity. Killing ourselves makes it impossible to perform these duties.
2. In general, people commit suicide in order to avoid pain or escape the fatigue of life. But in doing so, they treat their bodies as instruments of pleasure, which they feel free to destroy when they no longer play this role. But the human body isn't a means for pleasure, and to treat it as such is contrary to the moral law.

3. Finally, while suicide runs contrary to individual morality, it violates even more the strictures of social morality, for killing ourselves makes it impossible for us to fulfill our duties to others.

For these three reasons, suicide is a crime. But some go further than this, insisting that suicide is not only criminal but cowardly – that men kill themselves because they lack the courage to deal with adversity. Without entering this debate (which seems to us insoluble), we'll simply note that there are instances of suicide that seem to require real courage – the man who kills himself to avoid dishonor, or Cato preferring death to the yoke of Caesar. Surely these men aren't cowards.

Just as it's immoral to kill oneself in a single stroke, so too is it wrong to commit suicide slowly over time, through willful suffering, self-deprivation, or self-mutilation. The body is no more an instrument for pain and suffering than for pleasure. The one end for which we're made is morality, the development of our personality. In itself pain has no greater moral value than pleasure. It might sometimes be a moral remedy – a means of perfecting ourselves – but it isn't an end in itself. This refutes the widely held belief that we were put on earth in order to suffer. On the contrary, we were put here to do no more and no less than play our designated role, to be a moral person.

For the same reasons, we're duty-bound not only to avoid harming our bodies but also to maintain and improve our physical well-being. Hygiene is a moral matter. The moral law prohibits us from abusing pleasures that might harm our bodies – which explains why temperance is a duty.

Now let's move on to examine man's duties to his soul – to his intelligence, sensibility, and activity.

1. Intelligence. Because its goal is to achieve truth, our first duty to intelligence is honesty. Lying in any form – whether deception of self or others – is prohibited.

But it's not just that intelligence mustn't be diverted from its natural aim; it should be positively led in the direction of truth. For this reason, we have a duty to develop our intelligence as much as possible. Our view – in opposition to Rousseau – is that there is no tension between morality and the progress of civilization. For there can be no antinomy between nature and the moral law. We can perfect ourselves without any fear of being immoral. If we're endowed with intelligence, our duty is not to do nothing with it but rather to use it to bring us closer to its end, which is truth. We can devote ourselves entirely to the pursuit of the arts and sciences without being unfaithful to the moral law. Man's aim or ideal lies not in the past but in the future.

2. Sensibility. Here our duties are analogous to those to intelligence, for in this realm too we're obligated to develop our being. But our sensibility is made up of strong passions, emotions, and inclinations, which are disparate and sometimes contradictory. How can these be developed simultaneously? Clearly it's not possible, for to do so would be to introduce anarchy into the life of the soul. So not all of our inclinations can be developed at once, and those that are must be developed harmoniously. But which sentiment should be first? We respond: human dignity, our pride in being human beings, which is to say moral persons. We must never allow the veritable majesty with which we're invested to be damaged or offended. All that debases or diminishes our personality must be repugnant to us. Pride of this sort is perfectly legitimate.

Pride doesn't exclude modesty, of course, for our sense of the grandeur of our nature contains an understanding of our weakness, from which modesty is born. The sentiment of dignity is neither arrogant nor vain. Arrogance is the sentiment of dignity taken to such an extreme that it insults others, whereas vanity is pride in petty superiorities, a cheapening of oneself with petty preoccupations. True dignity is as far from one as the other.

3. Activity. The duty we have to activity is to exercise it – to work. So work in all its forms is a duty. Some have drawn a distinction between noble forms of work – letters and the arts, for example – and manual labor, which was considered degrading. But with regard to morality, there's no distinction to be drawn. All forms of work are noble, and all are moral. What matters is that we exercise our activity and not allow ourselves to wither away. Activity is best exercised according to our aptitudes, of course, but this is really a secondary concern. Our primary obligation is to keep the human personality from rusting away through inactivity. Laziness is the great solvent of our individuality and is repugnant to anyone who has even a slightly refined sensibility. Laziness is a weakening of the personality. A lazy person, his will numbed, easily falls prey to the influence of other people and things. This makes laziness the worst of all dangers.

But in developing our activity, we must also avoid the twin dangers of laxity and obstinacy. On the one hand, we should achieve clarity of will and have enough self-discipline to keep our will from being diverted from its end. We can't allow variations in our sentiments or the influence of other people to distract us from our primary aim. From laxity comes laziness. And when we no longer know what to will, we must devote all our energies to figuring it out. On the other hand, this isn't to say that we should never deviate from our previous lines of conduct, never diverge from our primary aim even when novel circumstances arise. In fact, we're duty-bound to change when necessary, for unwavering obstinacy is irrational. We must be firm, which means being neither weak nor stubborn.

SIXTY THREE

Domestic Ethics

The aim of domestic ethics is to determine what duties are owed to one another by the members of a family. By "family," we mean a group of people who share a common origin. Some moralists have denied that the family is a good and useful institution, viewing it rather as a kind of unnatural association, a small society formed within the larger mass – one in which people love one another intimately, with greater strength and intensity than can be found elsewhere. To such thinkers, it seems unnatural that people should feel any sentiment other than the love of humanity in general. But we believe that these philosophers – whom we call communists – fail to understand the very foundation on which society rests. A position similar to that of the communists was taken by Plato, who also tried to do away with the family, not for the benefit of humanity but for that of the city.

In light of the fact that such a position has been advanced, the question we'll have to consider first – before asking what duties family members owe to one another – is whether the family has any right to exist. We think it does, for two reasons. First, the family is the sole institution in which children can be properly raised, the only environment in which a child can receive his earliest education and instruction. For it's by nature alone that parents love their children at an age when there is, so to speak, very little about them that's human, when they inspire no affection from strangers. Children benefit from an instinctive parental love that is irreplaceable. This instinctive feeling changes over time, becoming a more reasoned form of affection; but in whatever form, it's the strongest of social bonds. A child deprived of access to this natural bond is isolated and lacking the protection that nature itself affords.

This alone is enough to show that the family is a good and healthy institution.

Second, the family is the principal school where children learn disinterest. Left to themselves, individuals would probably fall prey to egoism. Yet within the small circle of the family, they're forced to take into consideration interests other than their own, to make sacrifices and dedicate themselves to the good of the family. This is an excellent form of instruction, and as society demands an enormous amount of disinterestedness and reciprocal sacrifice, the family renders a great service to man by so habituating him.

History confirms this. How did cities come into being? By the coming together of individuals? On the contrary, social unity is familial. Cities are populated by different families, just as nations are made up of different cities. Society is like a large organism in which there's a central brain issuing commands and other small, secondary centers – families, for example – which are its subordinates. Dissolve these centers and – the societal bases destroyed – the brain's activity could no longer be transmitted to the body as a whole. The family is the primary and most natural grouping of individuals.

There are two reasons, therefore, why the family has a right to exist – because it serves the interests of children and because it has social utility. The basis for the family is marriage – an association between a man and a woman who commit themselves to sharing all of life's pains and joys. Marriage is defined by mutual commitment, and this alone makes it moral. In marriage, one spouse gives a gift of himself or herself to the other, in so doing diminishing his or her personality. This would run contrary to the moral law were it not for the reciprocity of the gift (Kant: "Doctrine of Right"). Every association between a man and a woman that lacks this mutuality is necessarily an immoral enslavement of one to the other.

Let's move on now to consider the duties of family members to one another. We'll examine:

1. Duties of parents toward one another. Marriage is a commitment entered into freely and in utter sincerity. So the first duty is fidelity, or the duty to respect this commitment. Beyond this, each spouse has different duties resulting from the differences of their positions. By virtue of his physical strength and intellectual aptitudes, the man finds himself better able to protect the family. This is incumbent upon him, and to

the woman fall more humble duties. But different though their functions may be, the two spouses are equal.

2. Duties of parents toward their children. Parents must first provide for their children materially – an obligation implied in the very idea of marriage. Parents also have a duty to educate and instruct their children. On this matter there are two schools of thought. One holds that parents have both the right and the duty to exercise as absolute an authority over their children as possible and are responsible for instilling in them all of their ideas and habits. According to this view, the child is the property of his parents, and there can be no limits on parental power.

Opposing this is the liberal doctrine of Rousseau (*Émile*), for whom "the best way to educate is to educate as little as possible." Rousseau holds that children are naturally good and should be left to their natural instincts, free to do whatever they want. The father, already corrupted by civilization, should exercise as little influence over his child as possible. This is why Rousseau raised Emile far from the life of the city, where his nature could be free to develop as it might.

The first of these schools of thought seems to us immoral and the second fanciful. The first violates the rights of the human being – rights which children have, despite the fact that their being is not yet fully developed. But should we substitute for utter enslavement complete freedom? Of course not. Rousseau assumes that children are naturally good. But why? They're neither completely good nor completely bad, for a child's character depends on heredity and circumstances. Rousseau's method of abstention also gives the child neither education nor instruction, leaving him defenseless in the struggle for life, where he'll be torn apart by competition. We're duty-bound to prepare our children, to educate them, to teach them habits, and a certain amount of authority is required to do this effectively. This authority should never be excessive, and it should be used not to shape the child in the image of his parents but rather to prepare him for the development of his personality. The habits we teach our children should all help to make persons of them. As we've said, authority is useful in this regard, but its ultimate aim should be freedom. It has to prepare the child for being a free person one day. So what parents owe to their children is that they must provide for them materially and morally. Parents owe these duties to all their children equally: they've no right to favor one over others. This is why our laws prohibit the practice of birthright.

3. Duties of children toward their parents. The most important duty here is obedience. Children must obey their parents because they lack

the intelligence necessary to understand how they should act in accordance with the moral law, with the requirement that they develop their personality and respect that of others. Parents make up for this lack through the instruction they offer. In addition, obedience is in the material interests of children, for their propensity is to ignore what's good or bad for them. They can profit greatly from the experience of others.

But children have to be obedient to their parents only until they become adults, after which parents no longer have the right to demand their submission. The grown man, free, must alone direct his conduct, initiating and taking full responsibility for his actions. But love and respect should survive. Although he no longer owes obedience to his parents, the child should continue to love and respect them in recognition of their many services.

4. Duties of children toward one another. Children should be united in fraternal love, which is the most perfect form of friendship. Friendship is defined by absolute confidence in, and complete equality to, the other; and as an essentially leveling sentiment, it should be unreserved. Two men of unequal intelligence may be friends, but their friendship will be one of equals. These two characteristics of friendship are most obvious in fraternal love, where – owing to their common origin – siblings are equal and have total confidence in one another.

Such are the duties that bind together the members of this small society called the family, which is the seed from which society as a whole is born.

SIXTY FOUR

Civic Ethics

Civic ethics asks the question: "What are the duties that the individuals who form a nation owe to one another?" It assumes the existence of societies of people united by special bonds.

On what foundation does society rest? Some philosophers believe that society is unnatural, that the normal condition of human beings is one of solitude and isolation, and that it's only by artificial means that we emerge from this state. According to Hobbes, societies are formed because of the threat of violence. For Bossuet, divine revelation causes us to leave the state of savagery. And according to Rousseau, society is formed when we agree to place our common fate in the hands of the most intelligent among us. For all of these philosophers, therefore, society is a more or less artificial condition. Had we listened only to the voice of nature, we'd have remained isolated.

But the facts suggest otherwise. Altruistic sentiments are as natural as their egoistic counterparts, so that the voice of nature – so frequently mentioned by Rousseau – actually moves us toward association. We have an almost irresistible need to seek out the company of our fellow man. Solitude has few charms for us and is often quite disagreeable.

Isn't it natural for parents and children to become attached to one another? Far from tending toward isolation, we are, as Plato said, πολιτικὸν τὸ ζῷον – social animals. Indeed, society is so far from being artificial that isolation can be considered a mere abstraction. Rousseau, Hobbes, and Bossuet don't recognize that society exists even in the individual, that man himself is a society. As Claude Bernard has said, each individual is composed of millions of anatomical elements, each with its own individuality and vitality. This proves that isolation is an unnatural state, that everything that exists clamors to be associated with something else. The great society that unites individuals is no less natural than the smaller one constituted by each. Like a natural organism with its brain, nerves, vessels, etc., the former is simply more complex.

So society is natural. People join together naturally because no one can be self-sufficient and carry out by himself all the tasks that Europeans consider essential to life. The solution to this problem is the division of labor. Each individual, charged with a specific task, performs it better and more quickly and – by exchanging the fruits of his labor – acquires the goods essential to life. In this way, the division of labor – as Bastiat observed in *Harmonies économiques* – enhances the well-being of each to the benefit of all. Each individual receives much more than he could on his own. This is the advantage offered by the division of labor, and this division is the foundation of society.

Now let's consider how society should be organized. Clearly, care for the common good should be entrusted to a certain number of people specially charged with this function. These people constitute a government, which is armed with various powers. To keep these powers from being abused, they should be apportioned among various categories of government officials. This principle is called the division of powers.

There are three such powers: legislative, executive, and judicial. Legislative power establishes the laws which govern society, executive power applies these laws, and judicial power punishes violations of the law through the use of penalties.

What is the foundation of punishment? It's often been said that punishment is expiation, that someone who's violated the law should be punished so that his misdeed can be expiated. But how could a punishment erase a misdeed? And what right does a government have to enforce morality and impose virtue? If society ever tried to assume this role, it would quickly discover that it lacks the means to do so. In order to expiate a misdeed, we have to be able to judge precisely what's good and bad about it – "to fathom hearts and minds" – thus going beyond the limits of our vision. But in fact all we see is the act itself. The intention behind it – the only thing that's morally significant – escapes us. So punishment can't be expiatory.

Some say that the goal of punishment is to reform the guilty. But this isn't our responsibility, and in any case punishment doesn't always bring about such reform. Inflicting pain on a man's body or soul can make him worse rather than better. Some say that if someone is punished for a misdeed, the fear of further punishment will keep him from doing it again. But to terrorize someone does nothing to improve his heart.

The real foundation of punishment, therefore, is the right to self-defense. A society, no less than an individual, has the right to live and defend its existence. This right can be exercised in two ways – immediately (by imposing a punishment) or in a preventative manner (by threatening pain against whoever commits an illegal act).

What are the functions of government? Here we confront the same theories encountered earlier, when we discussed education. One theory, called socialism, denies the rights of individuals, insisting that all citizens are property of the state. Having abdicated their individuality by entering into society, individuals are reduced to nothing, while the state is everything. The role of government, according to this theory, is to lead society toward its proper end – whether the individuals composing it desire this end or not. As long as it performs this function, the government is permitted to do anything whatsoever. So socialism endorses an absolutist government, whether it's a king or an assembly that governs. Rousseau's *Contrat social* epitomizes this theory. When men come together to form society, according to Rousseau, they abdicate their personality, renouncing their freedom in order to profit from the association. This makes them slaves, but by virtue of the fact that the government they've agreed to obey is their own, they regain their autonomy. I may give up my freedom, but there's a kind of compensation if my neighbor does the same.

Opposing this is an entirely different theory – liberalism or individualism – which holds that society is an abstraction and the individual the sole reality. The only things of value, according to liberalism, are the ends of individuals. The function of government is to protect citizens from one another, to safeguard the individuality of each, to exercise authority and guard against encroachments upon individual freedom.

We believe that socialism undermines the personality of the individual and is therefore clearly immoral. Socialism regards an individual's personality as simply a means, an instrument employed by society to achieve its ends. Nor is the compensation offered by Rousseau enough. As soon as I give up my personality, it doesn't matter that others do so as well, for I've still committed an immoral act.

Should we accept the alternative theory? While it doesn't contradict the moral law, liberalism does conflict with the interests of society. Each society – like each individual – has its own proper end. If only because we're west of Germany and north of Spain and Italy, we – as a society – have certain specific interests that differ from those of other countries. Our end is different from that of England, Switzerland, or Italy. Given this, certain individuals must of course be granted the power to direct society toward this end; and to know what this end is, what the best means are to realize it depending on the circumstances, and to make ready these means – all this forms a science, or a set of pursuits that fall to certain people specifically charged with these tasks.

So government has every right to guide society toward its end; and because government – according to our theory – is born of the people, it can perform this role without diminishing the personality of the citizen. Because the government exercises the will of the nation, it's subject to perpetual control – one word from the nation is enough to change the course of its actions. So we can entrust government with this twofold role:

1. Government must protect its citizens from one another.
2. Government must guide society toward its proper end.

Because these are the functions of government, it must be given sufficient powers to carry them out. But there are limits – the government's activities must immediately cease, for example, where they threaten to undermine the personality of its citizens. The government can demand that its citizens perform certain tasks but can never descend into the realm of consciousness to impose an opinion. Thought must always remain free, shielded from the activities of government and provided with all the necessary means for self-expression. Every government must respect freedom of thought. Whatever the viewpoint or its consequences, all positions have the right to see the light of day; and what will lead some to triumph and others to fade away is discussion, in which no foreign power should intervene. But in any case, such intervention is destined to be ineffective. An idea might be suppressed for a certain period of time, but it wouldn't hesitate to reappear. Ideas die only when they're false. Persecution simply increases their strength. Of course, this applies only to freedom of thought and expression. Legislation can certainly restrict – by more or less moral means – our ability to propagate our ideas.

Citizens owe four duties to the state:

1. obedience to the law;
2. taxes;

3. military service;
4. voting.

    1. Obedience to the law. This is to be expected in a democratic society because the law is made by the same citizens who must obey it. But here a difficulty arises. Laws are never passed unanimously. Does the minority have the right to disobey? If so, society would always be threatened with dissolution. Secession might occur at any moment. But this is only a utilitarian consideration. From a moral point of view, does the minority have the right to disobey a law of which it disapproves? In every country that's not a democracy, the answer is clearly yes. The minority does have the right to oppose the law. But in free countries where everyone can express their ideas and become tomorrow's majority, the minority can't resort to brute strength or disobedience to advance its cause.

    2. Taxes. Public services can't be provided without money. And who should make this sacrifice other than those who benefit from such services, the citizens? So citizens should certainly be subject to taxation, but only to those taxes to which they've agreed.

    3. Military service. Of all taxes, the most noble and obligatory is that of blood. It's possible that someday all nationalities will merge into a universal republic; but for the moment not only are people divided into rival, frequently conflicting societies, but wars often occur within them. Every crime is a war, and to guard against this war an armed force must always be at the ready. For this reason, the tax of blood isn't owed just intermittently and must be paid by all without exception. But if society finds itself well protected and possessed of enough soldiers, certain classes of people – those better able to serve in other ways – can be relieved of military service (those who take care of the elderly, for example, or the oldest orphans, etc.). Society might also grant exemptions to those who devote their lives to the high culture of the mind. In fact, society should always try to exempt those who – thanks to certain duly ascertained capacities – can advance the progress of the sciences, letters, or arts.

    4. Voting. For every citizen, voting is not just a right but a duty. We're obliged to fulfill all the functions incumbent on members of society – one of which is to be concerned with the common good. Voting is the means by which the common good can be advanced. The more one abstains from voting because of a grudge or because it's inconvenient, the more the common good is sacrificed to particular interests.

SIXTY FIVE

General Duties of Social Life

A common way to classify duties has been to distinguish between positive (duties that prescribe certain actions) and negative (duties that proscribe actions). "Don't kill" is an example of a negative duty, while "Do right by others" is an example of a positive one. Negative duties, which must be observed absolutely, have often been called "strict," while their counterparts are called "broad." The prohibition against killing is absolute and therefore a strict duty, whereas one has a bit more latitude when it comes to positive duties. There are many ways of being charitable, for example, and one can be devoted to a greater or lesser extent.

There's some justification for this distinction, but its importance shouldn't be exaggerated. Clearly, some duties are positive and others negative; but no duty is less obligatory than any other, despite what popular sayings tell us. According to one such saying, "Justice is our most fundamental duty, and anyone who wishes to remain within the bounds of humanity must be faithful to it. Charity, by contrast, is a luxury we're not obliged to give." Another saying holds that "in rendering to each that which is his due, we do only what we must. If we go beyond this, we deserve special credit, because charity is less required of us than are other duties." On this view, negative duties are more obligatory, whereas positive duties are more meritorious.

Although many people think otherwise, positive duties are as obligatory as any. All duties can be traced back to the moral law, which doesn't recognize distinctions of degree of obligation. Since the moral law itself is absolute, so are all its applications. If the moral law orders us to be charitable, this is no less an absolute duty than that of being just. The widespread sentiment that there is a distinction to be made comes from the fact that positive duties – which are less important to society – have no civil sanction associated with them. But this doesn't mean that positive and negative duties have different moral characteristics, for the moral law supercedes society's law.

The consequence of this is that merit isn't to be found in doing what's right when it's not obligatory. Rather, merit can be measured in how difficult it is to carry out a moral action. Consider the following examples: A generous man shares his fortune with a needy person. Or the same man coolly and rationally pays a tax that the law would allow him to avoid paying. It's the latter action that's more obligatory and also more meritorious, because it's more difficult.

While sentiment very often comes to the aid of duty, making it easier to carry out, justice often must get by on reason alone. And despite appearances, it's justice that's more often meritorious. It's much harder to not speak ill of another person than to give a poor man money. Merit is a function of the difficulty overcome. This explains why we look back so favorably on antiquity, and why Rousseau could find society – which facilitates moral action – so immoral. Over time, society raises the average level of morality. But the fear that one's merit won't be acknowledged is among the greatest obstacles to moral action, and, as progress makes morality popular, such acknowledgment becomes harder to obtain. This is so because the smallest act seemed more meritorious when morality was less widespread. We can't say that antiquity was a time of greater morality, but the moral acts then undertaken did have greater merit.

All this having been said, we can still distinguish two categories of duties, which we'll now take up in order:

1. negative duties (justice);
2. positive duties (charity).

SIXTY SIX

General Duties of Social Life. (1) The Duty of Justice

Justice consists simply in respecting the personality of others. This is a straightforward application of the moral law. The only way to respect the personality of another person is to treat him never as a means but always as an end. Others, like ourselves, have both a body and a soul, and we should respect these in the same way we respect our own. To respect the body of another is to do nothing to undermine his life. "Thou shalt not kill" is the first formula of the duty of justice. While this formula seems to be among the most absolute of all morality, there are exceptions to it. If all men followed the moral law perfectly, of course, exceptions would be unnecessary. But this isn't the case, for there are men who constantly threaten others and remain outside the bounds of morality. The result is a state of war, which exists wherever there are criminals, more or less powerful men who consider themselves above the law. In other words, a state of war can exist regardless of whether or not nations attack each other. When dealing with criminals, the moral law no longer applies and must be altered. All the valid exceptions to this law have the following form: "All men whose lives are threatened have the right to defend themselves and, if necessary, to go so far as to kill their aggressor." This is the right of self-defense. Because I have the right to preserve my life, I have – as we discussed elsewhere – the right to do everything necessary to achieve this end, including, if necessary, the right to kill those who threaten me. Naturally, this right extends no further than the duty that lies at its foundation. As soon as the danger of death disappears, so does my right to kill. So if I show respect for my adversary and render him harmless without killing him, I lose the right to kill him.

What's true of the individual is also true of society. If a man threatens society, doesn't it have the right to defend itself by restraining him? It's been said that this is the basis for society's right to inflict the death penalty on one of its members. But when a criminal goes before a court, he's been disarmed, and society is no longer in danger. While society may take the precautions necessary to protect itself, it loses the right to kill him.

Some say the death penalty deters criminals. But which deters more – the severity of punishment or its certainty? Only a criminologist can say, but clearly the abolition of medieval torture didn't increase the number of crimes.

Moreover, the death penalty does the great disservice of habituating us to the sight of human blood. Human beings have an instinctive horror of murder that causes even the greatest of criminals to hesitate before killing someone. Executions diminish the strength of this instinct and thus compromise public security. Yet despite the advantages associated with the abolition of the death penalty, we shouldn't be dogmatic.

Society has the right to defend itself, not only against its own members but also against neighboring nations that threaten its existence. In defensive wars, this justifies the right of soldiers to kill. But what about offensive wars? Here too the soldier may unreservedly strike a blow against his adversary, for the latter still threatens to kill him. The immorality of war depends entirely on the leaders who willed it – the soldier and even those government officials who had no part in the decision remain innocent.

Moralists typically agree in condemning dueling, but our view is that it's justified in certain cases – for example, when a citizen is inadequately protected by the law. So dueling is justified by the right of self-defense. Still, it's quite absurd:

1. because the offense is considered to be as significant as the life of the offender;
2. because it's not up to the offended person to decide questions of right.

So our wish is that the law render duels unnecessary, condemning those crimes for which the duel is considered a form of redress. We must add that most duels have frivolous causes that render them indefensible. In sum, the duel is a remnant of conceptions of God and the spirit of chivalry passed down to us from the Middle Ages. The public will eventually come to a better understanding of duels, and then they will become less frequent, occurring only when absolutely necessary and provoking less public condemnation.

In addition to duties of justice toward the body of another person, we have duties toward his soul, toward his intelligence, sensibility, and activity. Honor – often considered a special faculty – involves additional duties concerning respect for one's word.

1. Sensibility. To respect the sensibility of the other is to be courteous. Typically viewed simply as a convention and not at all necessary for morality, courtesy too has its *raison d'être*. To be courteous is to avoid distressing another person unnecessarily. The candor of Alceste certainly has great aesthetic value, but this systematic discourtesy conflicts with the moral law.

Enemies of courtesy often cite its opposition to the duty of honesty. We should always tell the truth and nothing but the truth – yet we are supposed to do so without harming others. But being courteous often requires us to lie. And if we must choose between these two duties, why sacrifice courtesy? To avoid harming others is no less obligatory than to tell the truth. This conflict can be resolved if we attend to the facts of particular cases. As Rousseau said, virtue doesn't require complete candor. If the naked truth would cause another great pain and do him no good, then he should be spared our candor. Only the true egoist would make another suffer simply for the pleasure of speaking the truth. There's a haughty arrogance in the brutal truth of the misanthrope. Of course, there's no need to lie continually in order to bring pleasure to another, but we should seize every opportunity to spare him useless suffering. Between flattery and brutality, there's more than enough room for the happy medium of courtesy.

2. Intelligence. To respect a man's intelligence is to allow him to think, and to think freely, to be tolerant, to respect all ideas, no matter what they are, and to treat them with the greatest deference. Don't consider others mistaken just because they don't think as we do, or careless when they seem to reason poorly. Never judge the heart and sentiments of another by the nature of his opinions, for all opinions have the right to exist – not one warrants suppression by violence. Spiritualists, materialists, atheists, or deists, all opinions – so long as they are sincere – should be held in the highest regard. This duty of tolerance is a straightforward application of the moral law, which commands us to respect the personality of others and thus not thwart the growth of their intelligence.

Tolerance is recommended to us not just by morality but also by the interests of science. As we've seen and pointed out frequently, it's not easy to discover the truth. Human beings tend to see only one side of a question. Our passions, inclinations, and temperaments get in the way of our view, so to speak, and keep us from seeing the whole picture. So how can we enlarge the portion of truth we now possess? By allowing each person the freedom to see what he may of truth and speak about what he thinks he sees. Discussion allows a natural struggle among all opinions to take place; in this struggle, the most true opinion ultimately triumphs. But this progress is possible only if tolerance prevails and each person is allowed to pursue the truth as he understands it. To suppress a certain number of ideas is to hold back the light, so to speak, so that the truth can't appear.

So tolerance isn't founded, as certain narrow-minded people have claimed, on skepticism; and it assumes, not systematic doubt, but a profound sense of the difficulty involved in answering certain questions — as well as a great deal of scientific modesty.

3. Activity. Here we must distinguish between activity itself and the external conditions in which it takes place. To respect activity itself is to respect freedom. Hence the immorality of slavery. We have no right to enslave another and subordinate him and his activity. Moreover, because the moral law is formal and universal, we've no right to take another as our slave even if he consents. Finally, we must not even give indirect support to slavery, because it annihilates the personality and thus is completely immoral and abhorrent.

In the present state of things, human activity seems to assume the existence of an external condition that can be summed up in one word — property. If property is legitimate, we must respect the property of others. But is it legitimate? What's the moral basis for property? Clearly, it can't be made to rest on the right of first occupant or on the right of the strongest. Some say that property is a consequence of freedom. Having freely exercised my faculties, for example, I've acquired fungible or nonfungible property. By working, I've made the soil yield products that belong to me, for it's to me that they owe their existence. According to this view, property is only an extension of my personality and should be respected in the same way.

This theory explains how products of the earth become ours but grants little attention to the land itself. Some say that land is given value only by man's labor, that to have land alone is to have nothing. Our response is that, undoubtedly, in most cases land alone is without value. But if it doesn't constitute wealth in itself, it's certainly a condition of wealth. Land is unproductive unless it's cultivated, and until then it has no value. But to cultivate it – to draw from it products that give it value – we must first possess it.

Kant tried another way of demonstrating the legitimacy of property – one that was strikingly original but so closely tied to his larger system that it's now of merely historical interest. He distinguished between two types of property. Consider the first: I hold an object in my hand. To take it away from me would be to violate my freedom, which is immoral. Therefore, this object is my property. How can we move from this to property such as it exists today? Time and space have no objective existence but are purely subjective forms of sensibility. But freedom, as an attribute of sensibility, does have an objective existence. So freedom must exist independent of time and space. Applying this reasoning to the preceding experiment, we see that the object I hold outside of every idea of time and space must belong to me.

This demonstration assumes that time and space are purely subjective. Yet our discussion of psychology showed that time and space, like other rational principles, have an undeniable objective value.

So what is the foundation of property?

Let's recall the theory of right. Every right carries with it the right to exercise a duty. In the present case, that duty is to develop our activity and personality. But how could we develop our activity if we couldn't exercise it on external objects, if we had to keep it enclosed in the narrow walls of our person? We must add to our being, by extending it under the form of external objects. Such objects store up our actions, so to speak, and keep them from disappearing. So they're an indispensable condition for the development of the individual, and for this reason property is a right. At the same time, because property is necessary to the development of other personalities, justice requires that it be respected.

4. Respect for one's word. Sometimes we make commitments to other people, either implicitly or by giving our word verbally or in writing. We're obliged to carry through on these commitments for two reasons:

1. Not doing so would involve lying, which is proscribed by the duty of honesty.
2. Not doing so harms other people.

Our word concedes certain rights to the other person. These become his property, so to speak, and they must therefore be respected.

Nevertheless, it's well understood that a commitment is binding only if it's entered into freely – which is to say, if we weren't coerced into the agreement through violence or fraud.

SIXTY SEVEN

General Duties of Social Life. (2) Charity

The moral law requires more of us than that we not treat others as means; in addition, the personality of the other must be treated as an end. So beyond the negative duties of justice, there are the positive duties of charity. We can't remain content simply to avoid undermining the other's personality but should do everything possible to help him realize and develop it. To the formula of the moral law that sums up justice in the phrase "Don't do to others what you wouldn't want done to you" must be added the formula of charity: "Do unto others as you would have done to you." In other words, don't rest content with seeing to it that your own personality remains intact. Seek to enlarge your personality, and help others to do the same.

Like the duties of justice, those of charity can be deduced from the moral law. Because the person of the other consists of a body and a soul, we must work not just to avoid injuring both but to support them and, if the need arises, to care for them. The duty of charity toward the body of another requires that we look after his health.

As for the soul, we must again distinguish between three faculties: sensibility, intelligence, and activity. For sensibility, the courtesy demanded by justice becomes, in the context of the duties of charity, benevolence.

For intelligence, not only must we avoid stifling the ideas of the other through physical or moral intolerance, we must also work to develop this intelligence. We must spread and communicate our science to other men. The scholar shouldn't disdainfully retreat into what he knows. When someone has the privilege of knowledge, he must put it to good use by teaching what he knows to others.

Finally, for activity, we've already seen that we must respect property, which is its external condition. But people often lack property, so charity urges us to share our own with others as much as we can. Charity thus demands the giving of alms.

Such are our positive duties toward our fellow man. But no matter how obligatory it may be, charity must never conflict with justice. Whenever a conflict arises between these two kinds of duty, justice should take precedence. Our first obligation is to do no harm to the other, and only then to help him. Moreover, no matter what help we provide, we must never impose it. To do so would be contradictory. Why help the other in the first place? Only so that he can achieve his end, his personality. But by helping him despite himself, we violate this personality, this free activity. We can never save men despite themselves: *Invitum qui servant idem facit occidents* (To save a man against his will is the same as murdering him [Horace]).

Conflicts often arise between the duties of justice and charity. Should a father, with duties to his wife and children, risk his life in order to save someone else? Should a great man deprive his country of his services so that he may perform an act of charity? Theoretically, no. The duties of justice are more important. But practically speaking, no individual should proclaim himself indispensable, whether to his family or to his country. To do so would be arrogant and hurt others. This is why we hesitate to grant our approval to a man who refuses to risk his life under the pretext that he's essential to his family or fellow citizens. If such a man does sacrifice himself, however, we see in him such a substantial deployment of moral energy that we can't help but admire him.

SIXTY EIGHT

Summary of Ethics

The great philosophers have tended to rely on one of two mutually exclusive approaches to the study of ethics – the first entirely empirical, the second entirely a priori. Epicurus, Mill, and Spencer took an empirical approach, while Kant took an a priori approach. The first begins with observation and proceeds by way of generalization and induction, reaching the pinnacle of its development with Mill. It consists in observing man, either when he's alone or with others; noting the circumstances in which he's happy; and then deriving the moral law by generalizing from these findings. Kant, by contrast, begins with the abstract concept of pure morality, assumes that the will is capable of acting independently of sensibility, and then asks what the law of this will must be.

But empiricism, no matter what degree of generalization it's able to attain, can never achieve the universality that characterizes the moral law. All empiricism can formulate are local and provisional rules, good only for a certain time and a certain number of individuals. Conversely, despite the fact that Kant made many concessions and scaled back the rigor of his initial formulas, his ethics remained imaginary, providing us with rules that an ideal and hypothetical being should follow – not man as he is.

The method we've followed, in contrast to empiricism and apriorism, is both deductive and experimental. We began by postulating a fact of experience – moral responsibility. Deducing the conditions of this fact, we were then led to a law that is absolutely universal and obligatory. Finally, when it came time to specify the formula of this law, we were careful not to forget that its object is man, a being endowed with sensibility and having his own proper ends. Man's nature makes a great deal of difference to his activity, and there's an important connection between psychology and ethics. Mill wanted to reduce ethics to psychology, whereas Kant excluded psychology altogether. Instead, we've made ethics rest on psychology, for we believe that, to know what a man must do, we must know what he is. Psychology tells us that he's a person, so ethics concludes that his responsibility is to be a person. To be sure, our ethics has been governed by one a priori idea – that of finality. But a fact of experience – that of moral responsibility – is its point of departure. Experience has been consulted throughout, and the result is that our ethics is neither fanciful nor sterile.

PART FIVE

Metaphysics

SIXTY NINE

Metaphysics. Preliminary Considerations

Metaphysics is the science that studies the conditions of the states of consciousness, asking three basic questions:

1. Are the states of consciousness, taken as a whole, dependent on the existence of the soul?
2. Are the states of consciousness relative to the material world and therefore dependent on the existence of bodies?
3. Are the states of consciousness relative to the principles of reason and therefore dependent on the existence of God?

But metaphysics is concerned not just with what the conditions of the states of consciousness are but with their nature as well. After studying whether the soul, bodies, and God exist, metaphysics then examines the essence, nature, and attributes of each.

So metaphysics asks three sets of questions:

1. Does the soul exist? What's its nature?
2. Do bodies exist? What's their nature?
3. Does God exist? What's His nature?

In our treatment of psychology, we already discussed the existence and nature of the external world. So all that's left to consider are questions about the soul and God. To answer these, we'll rely on the following method – one suggested to us by the way we've posed the problems of metaphysics. We'll try to determine whether the states of consciousness can exist on their own or whether they depend on certain external conditions. So we must begin by considering the states of consciousness themselves, setting our sights only on what's absolutely necessary to explain them. Our method won't be purely a priori, since we'll start with the facts. Nor will it be purely inductive, since we'll do more than simply generalize from them. Rather, our method will be deductive. We'll deduce the conditions that make the facts possible.

SEVENTY

On the Soul and Its Existence

To say "the soul exists" is to say that, within us, there's a principle – distinct from matter and perceptible by the senses – whereby we understand our states of consciousness. Does such a principle really exist? In our lectures on psychology, we argued that extended matter is but an appearance, the real substratum of which can be conceived only by analogy with the forces that we ourselves are. So there's no need to ask if the principle to which the states of consciousness are connected is material in nature. Nothing can be extended, for the idea of extension is contradictory. In fact, it's quite possible that the principle perceived by our senses as material in nature is actually identical to the principle perceived by our consciousness as spirit. Still, to say that the soul is spiritual is to say that it's distinct from extended, perceptible matter.

Our theory of the world's universal spirituality is sufficient to demonstrate that this is indeed the nature of the soul. Yet the claim that this is so is also supported by four more specific arguments – the first three of which reveal a contradiction between the nature of spirit and that of matter:

1. Spirit has unity – this we've established in several ways in our discussion of psychology. Matter, by contrast, is multiple and infinitely divisible. In matter, no fundamental unity can be found beyond which division can't proceed. So matter can't be identical to spirit.

2. As we've shown elsewhere, spirit has identity. Yet matter has no trace of identity; it constantly changes. Over the course of several years, all the matter in our bodies will have been regenerated. It might still be said, of course, that our body retains its form, and this gives it identity. But this kind of physiological identity of form can be explained – as

Claude Bernard has said – only by the existence of a soul, a directing idea.

3. Matter is inert. It can make neither itself nor other bodies move. Spirit, by contrast, is active and spontaneous. I act only if I want to act. It's me – not an external object – that causes me to move. Inertia on the one side, spontaneity on the other – no principle can have both of these contradictory characteristics.

It's easy to see that these three arguments employ the same method of reasoning and that this method is analogous to that used by Descartes for the same purpose. Descartes, too, sought to understand the nature of the soul. Realizing that the mind could recognize the concept of the soul without making recourse to the concept of the body, he concluded that the two substances must be distinct. I can imagine perfectly well, he argued, that my body doesn't exist and that the external world is but an illusion. But it's impossible for me to imagine that I myself don't exist and that I don't think. Therefore I can recognize a soul defined over against the notion of materiality. So thought and extension must be attributes of different substances. This argument rests on the postulate that's the foundation of the entire Cartesian method: "Two concepts which can be conceived as separate must belong to different substances." Our argument, by contrast, rests not on this hypothesis, but on a principle that can be formulated as follows: "Two categories of phenomena having contradictory characteristics aren't connected to the same substance."

A fourth argument often made alongside the three preceding ones consists in proving the distinction between the soul and the body by noting the conflicts that frequently arise between them. These conflicts indicate that, in the soul and the body, two very different principles are at work.

Nevertheless, our theory escapes an objection often made against contemporary spiritualism – that it recognizes two kinds of reality in the world. This is indeed difficult to accept. We solve this problem by introducing the idea of continuity in nature. Our spiritualism doesn't assume that the soul arises all at once out of the chain of being. Spirit can be found in everything, in a more or less rudimentary form. Everything lives, everything is animated, everything thinks.

On the Spirituality of the Soul (Conclusion). On Materialism

The doctrine of spiritualism runs contrary to that of materialism. Having discussed arguments for the former, we'll now consider three opposing arguments for the latter:

1. The method of science demands parsimony. We shouldn't needlessly multiply causes and principles. Yet spiritualists postulate the existence of two principles – irreducible realities. This alone creates a presumption against them. They do this because they believe that perceptible matter can't have the property of thought. But why? The essence of things lies beyond our grasp, and every day new mysteries are solved. Perhaps one day it will be shown experimentally that matter is in fact endowed with spontaneity and thought.

Our first response to this argument is that, as we've seen, our own theory involves no such dualism. Viewed from the outside, reality is material, while from the inside, it's spirit. But it's always one and the same reality. Besides, the idea that one day perceptible matter may be shown to think is far-fetched. We've already shown that the qualities constitutive of spirit are different than those of matter, and the absence of these conditions means the absence of thought. A being that isn't unified can think no more than a being that isn't identical. No experiment can yield an impossible finding.

2. The second argument of the materialists turns on the fact that the physical can influence the moral. This influence is certain and considerable. It's clear, for example, that an illness weakens us psychologically as well as physiologically. It's also clear that thought is more active in the young than in the old. Women live more in the realm of sensibility and less in that of reason; the passions of southerners are more vivid

and their will less active than those of others. All this goes to show that psychological life is utterly dependent on physiology. The principle they have in common is the body.

But aside from the fact that these examples aren't as general as has been claimed, it's easy to cite many others where things are reversed, where the moral influences the physical. Joy or sadness can be the death of a man, pleasure is often the best remedy, and the imagination can have a remarkable influence on the body. But if the influence of the moral on the physical is reciprocal, and if this shows that they have the same principle, we've no more reason to believe that this principle is material than spiritual. Finally, the facts cited by the materialists can be explained perfectly well by the hypothesis that the body is but an instrument of the soul. And the best musician can't make a harmonious sound with a poor instrument.

3. Rather than concentrate on these examples, other materialists have tried to identify the physiological phenomena that produce thought. By studying the brain and thought together by means of the method of concomitant variation, they've shown that the former is the cause of the latter, that thought is a secretion of the brain. They've shown that thought varies with the brain's volume, weight, form, and quality – especially the quantity of phosphorous it contains. Finally, they've established experimentally that the circulation of blood in the brain is a necessary condition for thought. Flourens argued that certain lobes of the brain correspond to certain faculties. Removing the lobe that corresponds to sensation and thus depriving the animal of that faculty, for example, he observed that sensation returned when nutrition had restored the missing lobe. From this, some have tried to develop an entire system of cerebral localizations. Although their conclusions are exaggerated, it's well established that certain faculties – speech, memory, writing – are indeed lodged in specific parts of the brain.

But all these facts can be explained just as well if we consider the brain and the body in general to be the condition – and not the cause – of thought. To be sure, without the brain, without phosphorous, there wouldn't be any thought. But is this to say that the brain is thought? Certainly not. We mustn't confuse the ideas of cause and condition. A condition is that without which a cause couldn't produce its effect, but it's not itself a cause of that effect. A telegram can be sent only if the batteries, instruments, and wires are functioning properly; but sulfuric acid is only the condition of the message we transmit, not its cause. The same is true of the phosphorous in our brains.

So the arguments of the materialists don't amount to much, and the scientific basis for materialism can't be established. Moreover, the desire to reduce everything to extended, perceptible matter is fanciful. We've shown that it's contradictory. But beyond this, a world that rested on the principle of materiality alone would be unintelligible. What we call matter is no more than a collection of appearances, and the substance that serves as the substratum of these appearances can't be grasped by the senses.

SEVENTY TWO

The Relationship between the Soul and the Body

If the soul is distinct from the body, how can we explain the fact that there's an ongoing relationship between physiological and psychological life? How does the physical affect the moral, and vice versa? Numerous answers to these questions have been proposed — some metaphysical, others more physiological. Let's study these in turn.

Cudworth, for his part, imagined that there exists between the soul and the body a special substance called the plastic mediator — half body and half spirit. But clearly this theory does nothing but push back the difficulty.

Descartes sought to explain not the relationship between the soul and the body but rather that between the soul and those animal spirits that make the body move. He understood the relationship between thinking and extended substances to be an irreducible fact while at the same time believing that the abyss between them couldn't be bridged.

Malebranche, in his theory of occasional causes, did try to explain the relationship between these two utterly heterogeneous substances. Believing that individual beings are incapable of acting on their own impetus, Malebranche inferred that their movement must come from elsewhere — from God, who alone has real causal power. Indeed, Malebranche says, it would be impious to attribute this divine power to individuals. Human beings and things don't act but are always acted upon. Everything they do is willed by God. So it's in God, so to speak, that extension and thought are brought together. When God evokes certain sentiments and volitions within us, he also produces the corresponding movements in our bodies. It's not that one substance acts on another; rather, God presides over both, making them coincide. According to this "theory of occasional causes," individuals are not the causes of their actions but only the occasions – and thus only the "occasional causes" – upon which God exercises his causality.

Leibniz's theory of preestablished harmony was an effort to answer the same question. Like Malebranche and all the Cartesians, Leibniz – while diverging in several respects from the theory of his master – didn't believe that the soul and the body could act directly on one another, for the elementary forces he called monads have, as he said, "no windows on the rest of the universe." If the monads composing the soul and the body seem to interact, they do so only as the consequence of a preestablished harmony willed by God. For all eternity, Leibniz believed, God has governed the development of each monad. The soul and the body are governed in such a way that a perfect harmony always exists between them. "Suppose," he says, "that we want two clocks to keep perfect time with one another. One way to accomplish this would be to connect them with some mechanism to guarantee that they remain in time. Alternatively, we might place them in front of someone charged with constantly resetting each to the same time – Malebranche's hypothesis. Or we might build them so perfectly that, having been synchronized once and then left to themselves, they would remain forever synchronized. This is the hypothesis of preestablished harmony."

Such are the metaphysical hypotheses concerning the relationship between the soul and the body.

Now let's examine some other hypotheses that are more physiological in nature.

According to Descartes, life is basically a mechanical phenomenon. The bodies of animals and humans are nothing but machines, physiology is but a branch of mechanics, and there's nothing distinctive about life. But if we hold to this doctrine, it becomes very difficult to explain the relationship between things as different as extension (which is mechanical) and the soul (which is more dynamic). Other philosophers, however, do recognize that there's something special about life. Organicism, for example, describes the properties of life as disseminated in the various organs of the body. The life of the body is simply the aggregate of all the separate lives of its anatomical elements. But what's the cause of the organism itself? Organicism doesn't explain the harmony or unity of vital functions. The elements of the body are constantly changing. "They are constantly in movement," says Claude Bernard, "in a revitalizing whirlwind whose intensity measures that of life." In the midst of this continual change, however, there's something that doesn't change – the form of the body. Something – a principle, a law, an idea – must direct and organize all these changes, providing constancy even as there are ebbs and flows.

The Montpellier school calls this the vital principle. These "vitalists" explain the relationship between the soul and the body by saying that the entire life of the body can be reduced to a single principle – the vital principle; and, likewise, the entire life of the soul can be reduced to a single principle – the spiritual principle. Because these two principles are forces of the same nature, they're capable of acting on one another. It might be impossible to explain the relationship between thinking and extended substances, but we can certainly explain the action of two forces upon one another.

But this explanation is hardly satisfactory, for it's still hard to understand how two substances that are analogous but also as different as the vital principle and the thinking soul could act on one another. A later doctrine tried to solve this problem by simplifying things, explaining the relationship between the soul and the body by arguing that the two principles are actually identical. On this account, the vital principle is merely one of the faculties of the soul, such that the soul directs the body. This doctrine is called animism, from which Stahl, its founder, has drawn some very strange conclusions, such as that the soul consciously brings the body to life. This claim has undermined the doctrine's credibility.

More recently, however, animism has been revived with more moderation and good sense by Francisque Bouillier in a book titled *The Vital Principle and the Thinking Soul*, which cites the following facts. Man is one. In the abstract, of course, two beings can be distinguished in him; but man himself is one, for both popular sentiment and common sense affirm the absolute unity of the human being. Such a unity, Bouillier reasons, can't be explained by the association of two beings which are completely different. So these beings must come from the same source. Moreover, aren't we at least somewhat conscious of the action that the soul exerts on the body? Doesn't the vital sense indicate to us what's happening inside our bodies? "The subject," Peisse says, "avails himself of the vital effort which places the organs in play." We're able to locate sensations in different parts of our bodies only because the life of the body isn't entirely imperceptible to the soul. And when we're really sick, almost all of our organs become the site of more or less distinct perceptions. "It's a curious and painful spectacle," says a doctor, "to hear a hypochondriac list his sufferings. It might be said that, armed with a magnifying glass, he's examined every inch of himself and dissected each fiber of his being." Magnetism and hypnotism bring about the same results.

In addition, the soul can act directly on the body. The effects that emotions and passions can have on circulation are well known. We feel better, and we're better able to resist various distractions, when our lives are guided by a powerful motive. This explains the significance of moral hygiene for our health.

Is this to say that the action of the soul on the body is completely conscious, as Stahl would have it? Certainly not, says Bouillier. There's a difference between the soul and the self. And it's the unconscious part of the self that presides over physiological life.

We'll make no attempt here to choose from among these various hypotheses. In our view, the question of the relationship between the soul and the body seems insoluble. Before we can know if – and how – the life of the body might be reduced to that of the soul, we'd first have to reduce all physiological phenomena to a single phenomenon and then do the same for all psychological phenomena. Only then could we determine where these two facts might be reduced to one another.

SEVENTY THREE

On the Immortality of the Soul

We've now established that, within us, there's a spiritual principle called the soul. Experience suggests that the soul and the body are inextricably linked. But does this mean that the soul dies with the body? Few beliefs are more popular than faith in the immortality of the soul. What's the value of this belief? Three kinds of arguments – psychological, metaphysical, and moral – have been advanced in its support.

I. *Psychological Arguments*

Psychological arguments for the immortality of the soul point to a contradiction between the nature of our faculties and the view that the life of the soul is finite.

First, consider sensibility. Not all of our passions can be satisfied by the things offered to us by experience. In fact, we're always on the lookout for ideal objects, and we allow ourselves to rest for but a moment on objects that only resemble the ideal. Poets have conjured up beautiful verse to describe this sentiment, this longing for the infinite, and we've emphasized it ourselves. But why would humans have such a compelling need to reach beyond the finite if we were condemned to remain enclosed within it? Surely, therefore, death imposes no limit on our sensibility.

Next, consider intelligence. Human beings need truth, search it out, and slowly build up their stock of knowledge – yet we're far from possessing all of truth. Indeed, the more we progress toward it, the more it seems to elude us. In the present state of science, not only is there no one who can, during the course of his lifetime, know all of truth, but it even seems as if such an ideal man has never existed. So there's a conflict between our instinctual curiosity, which is infinite, and the limit imposed by death on the development of our intelligence.

Finally, there's activity. The lifetime of a man isn't long enough to allow him to achieve the good, yet we strive for it in its most perfect and complete forms. In short, our nature – as expressed in all our faculties – seems suited for infinite development. So isn't it true that we're duty-bound to attain this development, and thus we must be immortal?

In our view, this triple proof is far from decisive. Why shouldn't there be a conflict between our destiny and our aspirations? It's sad, but truth doesn't always side with happiness. As we see it, this line of argument hinges on the prior demonstration of the existence of a good and sovereign God. By this we mean a being infinite in benevolence, intelligence, and power, whose creations contain no contradictions, and who would not have given us tendencies destined to remain unsatisfied. But we must acknowledge that all hypotheses relating to the ends that God might have assigned to us are quite uncertain. Beyond this, what appears as a contradiction might not be so; we may simply be running up against the limits of our intelligence, which allows us to see only one side of things. Perhaps if we could contemplate the universe in its entirety, see the solidarity of all beings, if we knew the system of ends toward which the world is advancing – then what appears contradictory to us wouldn't turn out to be so.

II. *Metaphysical Arguments*

1. Death consists in a dispersion, a division of parts, a dissolution of being. Only divisible objects can die. Since the soul is unified and irreducible, it can't die.

2. The soul can't die because no object can. For to say that bodies die is to say that their elements dissociate, and these elements themselves don't die but are merely transformed. Similarly, by virtue of the principle of conservation of force and matter – which applies no less to the psychological than to the physical world – our force, our soul, can be transformed but not lost.

These two arguments are more convincing than their psychological counterparts. They establish that, after death, something of us survives. But they don't justify the kind of belief in the immortality of the soul held by most people. The immortality we hope for is personal, an immortality in which the self retains its memory and identity and continues to exist after the decomposition of the body. By contrast, the immortality established by these arguments is entirely metaphysical and impersonal. They show that the soul does continue to exist, but in a transformed state where it becomes something other than itself – animating another body, for example, or playing some other role. But if we cease to be ourselves, does it matter that we continue to exist? Given the transformation the soul undergoes, can we even say that what continues to exist is really us?

III. *Moral Proofs*

Moral proofs for the immortality of the soul rest on the idea that the moral law must have a sanction, a system of punishments and rewards attached to violation of or obedience to the law. Every law that it's possible to disobey must have some sanction. Physical laws don't need sanctions, for the things they govern can't elude their grasp; but whenever the being subject to a law has the power to ignore it, a sanction is required. Otherwise it would be as if the law didn't exist; it could have no influence over the will. For, deprived of any authority, how could the law impose itself on our consciousness?

So the moral law must have a sanction. Do such sanctions exist? They certainly exist in the here and now, where violations are reprimanded and obedience is rewarded. But are these sanctions enough? Or must there be sanctions in the afterlife as well?

There are four kinds of sanctions we encounter in the course of our lives:

1. material sanctions applied by society;
2. moral sanctions applied by our peers;
3. material sanctions resulting from our actions themselves;
4. moral sanctions that we apply to ourselves.

The first consists of civil punishments and rewards. Are these sufficient to guarantee obedience to the law? No, because they're imperfectly applied. How many criminals escape punishment! And how many of the virtuous are ignored and go unrewarded! Good deeds in particular are hardly ever rewarded materially by society. In addition to material sanctions, however, there are moral ones. Many honest men receive no reward whatsoever from society but rather taste the fruit of their morality in the form of the sympathy and respect of their fellow men. The criminal

III. MORAL PROOFS

who escapes public prosecution, by contrast, is treated with contempt and distrust. Unfortunately, these moral sanctions – even when greater than their material counterparts – are still imperfectly applied. It's not uncommon for an unworthy person to receive esteem and respect, while the virtuous person remains unknown, deprived of the moral sanction that should have augmented the even more rare material reward. So moral sanctions aren't enough to guarantee obedience to the moral law.

It's not only society, however, that imposes punishments and rewards. We impose them on ourselves as well. Debauchery is punished by poor health, while good health goes to those who live moderately. In morality, good conduct is rewarded by self-esteem, the satisfaction of having done one's duty. An evil person, by contrast, is always remorseful. These sanctions are much more certain than the ones applied by society, for the individual applies them to himself. But still they're insufficient. Some people manage to preserve their health despite their excesses, while the most sober man may be struck down with illness. And where moral sanctions are concerned, a truly wicked man can silence his conscience and shake off remorse. Remorse is felt only by those who aren't completely depraved. Nor do those who conduct themselves well always experience moral satisfaction. The most honest of men are often afflicted with a refined delicateness that constantly troubles them and makes them say – even when they have acted well – that they should have done even better. Thus they're deprived of the moral rewards of virtue.

So none of the sanctions of the moral law that people can experience in the course of their lives is sufficient to guarantee obedience. Reason demands that happiness flow to the virtuous – something that doesn't always happen in this life. Could it be, then, that this happens later, that after this life ends there's another where the contradictions plaguing our present existence will cease? We have no way of knowing how this sanction might be applied. What we do know is that the harmony between good and happiness – which is hard to attain here on earth – will necessarily be realized elsewhere.

On God. Metaphysical Proofs of His Existence

What's the meaning of the word "God"? While it's been given many different meanings, all refer to a being who's superior to ordinary human beings. But so vague a definition won't do. In our view, God is the absolute, that which exists in and by itself, outside of any relationship with anything else. If God exists, He's a being not limited by any other, determined by nothing outside Himself, completely and perfectly self-sufficient. So to ask if God exists is to ask what reason we have for believing in the existence of the absolute.

Of course, many arguments – sometimes divided into a priori and a posteriori – have been advanced to prove God's existence. But this is too unequal a division, for the vast majority of these proofs are a posteriori. Others have distinguished between proofs that are metaphysical and those that are a priori or between two types of a posteriori proofs – physical (which rest on external observation) and moral (which rest on introspection). But such "physical" proofs have no value without metaphysical support. Like a priori proofs, they rely primarily on the principles of reason. So we'll take a different approach, dividing proofs of the existence of God into only two categories – metaphysical and moral. What follows will demonstrate the need for this distinction.

Let's begin by examining metaphysical proofs for the existence of God. The definition we've given allows us to introduce a certain order into the exposition. Since God is the absolute, for example, proofs of His existence have to show that what's relative can't exist by itself, that phenomena must be explained by something other than themselves; and since the world can be understood from as many different perspectives as there are principles of reason, the goal of any metaphysical proof is to show that phenomena can't exist by themselves from one of these perspectives. The principles of reason most often invoked in this demonstration are those of perfection (which we argued weren't really a priori), causality, and finality.

I. *Proofs by the Principle of Perfection*

There are two such proofs. The first, which was initially proposed by St. Thomas Aquinas, was later revived by Descartes. We noted earlier that beings are more or less good, more or less perfect. But this assumes that there's an ideal perfection against which everything else can be measured. For how could we gauge relative perfections if not by comparing them to an absolute perfection? So the idea of an absolute perfection must exist somewhere within us. But the only way we could get such an idea would be from a perfect being – God. Descartes's attempt to establish that the cause of this idea really is a perfect being begins with the principle – which we reserve the right to examine – that the cause must have as much reality as the effect.

The second proof – this one ontological – has been advanced by St. Anselm, Descartes, and Leibniz. The first form of this proof begins with the observation that we can't conceive of a being greater than God. If He didn't exist, however, we would be able to conceive of a being greater – having more existence – than God. Therefore God must exist.

Descartes substituted qualitative comparisons for this quantitative comparison. "I have the idea of a sovereign and perfect being," he said. But the first and most necessary of perfections is the perfection of existence. Therefore God exists.

II. *Proofs by the Principle of Causality*

Proofs based on the principle of causality employ Aristotelian reasoning. Everything that's in motion has been put into motion by something else. But all the motive forces with which we're familiar have themselves been put into motion by something else. So there must exist outside of what we know a first mover from which the movement comes. We must find the term that begins the series – ἀνάγκη στῆναι (necessary stop). What would bring this infinite regress to a stop? Only if this first mover were to derive his movement from himself, giving movement without receiving it.

Clarke's *a contingentia mundi* (from the contingency of things) argument is similar and has two elements:

1. Something exists. Therefore, something has always existed. If this something hadn't always existed, what exists presently would have had to be created *ex nihilo,* and its existence would lack a cause.

2. This something is God. What else could it be? Could it be the infinite totality of relative and ever-changing beings? This is impossible, for each of the elements of this totality has a cause external to it, so the same is true of the totality itself. So this totality has no internal cause and can't be explained by itself. It thus assumes the existence of an external cause. This cause is eternal in the sense we've described – that is, it's immovable and independent, so it's not included in the series of relative and ever-changing beings. Such a cause would be God.

All these arguments can be reduced to the following form. The causes revealed to us by experience explain their various effects quite well but can't explain themselves. Each can explain itself only in terms of another. But mustn't this regress from cause to cause have some final limit? If not, the world would be inexplicable. So for the world to be intelligible, we must stop at a first cause that itself has no cause, which is God.

III. *Proofs by the Principle of Finality*

There are two ways to present this proof. Without worrying about experience, for example, we might remain entirely in the realm of abstraction and establish the existence of a supreme end, or God, using the principle of finality. Alternatively, there are certain facts given in experience that appear inexplicable unless we acknowledge the existence of an intelligence that has arranged the world toward some end.

1. Reason requires that we conceive of series of causes and effects as each converging toward their ends. But in order for this unity required by the mind to be realized in the world, these ends must be subordinate to one another. Through regress we arrive at a single end – God – who appears to us as the goal toward which the world is tending, the absolute end of things.

2. Nature is an order, a system of things. Observation reveals that the world is governed by a plan. How can this order be explained? Clearly it suggests that the world has a designer, and thus an intelligence that's joined all things together in a harmonious concert toward some end. This intelligence is God.

III. PROOFS BY THE PRINCIPLE OF FINALITY

This proof could be connected to what Leibniz said about the principle of sufficient reason. At the origin of the universe, there was an infinity of logically possible worlds. So who was it who chose from among these? And why was one chosen and the others rejected? This choice implies the existence of an intelligence and will belonging to a supreme being – God. Without Him, the choice would be lacking sufficient reason. God has chosen the present world because it's the best.

SEVENTY FIVE

Critique of Metaphysical Proofs of the Existence of God

In the second part of the "Transcendental Logic" ("Transcendental Dialectic," chap. 3, "The Ideal of Reason"), Kant presented a systematic critique of metaphysical proofs of the existence of God. Each element of this critique was inspired by an idea central to Kantianism. For Kant, the only role of the principles of reason is to regulate experience. So it's a fallacy to rely on them to demonstrate the existence of a being who, by definition, is outside of experience. Reason ties together and organizes the phenomena we perceive; but God is an absolute and doesn't exist within the phenomenal world.

Let's back up and examine the proofs we've just discussed. The first assumes that within us there exists an innate idea of perfection. We've already refused to accept several of the proposed principles of reason, on the grounds that they have no foundation in experience. Yet this proof rests on one of these contestable principles, that the cause has as much reality as the effect. This principle assumes that the effect derives from and is adequate to the cause. But this is a mathematical conception of things that's out of touch with reality. Cause and effect needn't be of the same type – the effect might have quite novel qualities and characteristics. For example, the reality of water is entirely adequate to its cause – oxygen and hydrogen combined by the influence of electricity – but the effect and cause are heterogeneous. Finally, this argument assumes a theory of knowledge that we've already refuted, that ideas are produced in us by the action of an external object. Regardless of whether this object is conceived of as material or transcendental, the theory robs the mind of its own proper activity, which is unacceptable.

Nor is the ontological argument of any value. Even before Kant, Leibniz noted that the argument required a correction. In his version, the existence of God is demonstrated just as we would demonstrate a mathematical truth. He begins with the definition from which the relevant conclusion is drawn, that God is perfect, existence is a perfection, therefore God exists. He notes, however, that when we define a geometric figure in a certain way in order to draw conclusions from it, we know that the figure is logically possible. But here we know no such thing – perfection might be contradictory – so according to him we have to start by demonstrating that a perfect being is possible; and until we do, St. Anselm's syllogism will be useless. But even with Leibniz's correction, the proof remains inadequate. First, as Kant asked, is existence a perfection? To say that a thing exists adds nothing to its concept but merely declares its attributes real. Second, syllogisms don't allow us to deduce a thing's existence from its definition. If the premises don't establish an object as possible, it's absurd a priori – by virtue of the very definition of a syllogism – that the conclusion could deduce the object's reality. This would be a synthetic judgment that syllogisms, instruments of analysis such as they are, can't make. From my affirmation that all perfections are of a piece with God, it follows only that God may exist – not that He really does.

This brings us to proofs that rest on the principle of causality. Their general form is the ἀνάγκη στῆναι (necessary stop) of Aristotle. But does the principle of causality really require that we put an end to the otherwise infinite regress of causes and effects? Not at all. On the contrary, the first cause would contradict this principle, as it would itself be without a cause. To this, some have responded that the first cause is its own cause. But the principle of causality is still violated. A term in a series can be called a cause only if it's distinct from another term, its effect. An object that creates itself is thus beyond the limits of reason and contradicts the principles of reason.

So the principle of causality actually forces the mind into an infinite regress. Nevertheless, this proof of the existence of God, while imperfect, is still better than the others. By bringing the principle of causality together with the principle of number, we begin to get the sense that something must exist outside of phenomena. Everything that's composed of parts is composed of a finite number of parts, so there must be a finite number of effects and causes, and thus the series must have some limit.

But when we try to conceive of the first term of this series – and do so using the principle of causality, which is appropriate only for phenomena that are relative in nature – we descend into the absurdities mentioned earlier. For now, we'll be content with the conclusion that the series of causes and effects does have a limit.

This proof by causality might, on the whole, be better than the others. But the proof by finality has a greater logical value. Indeed, the principle of finality doesn't require the regression of means and ends to be indefinite, as was the case with causes and effects. But this argument isn't decisive either. Why must all the series of causes and effects in the universe form a single system and have a single end? Why couldn't they form many distinct systems, each with its own specific end? If this were the case, we'd have left the realm of the absolute altogether and would be far from having proven the existence of God. Second, even if there aren't multiple ends for the world, there's no proof whatsoever that the world's single end must be transcendent, outside of all things.

Suppose, for example, that man is the end of the world and that the sole *raison d'être* of all phenomena is to promote the realization of mankind, the coming of a being who's both rational and free. If this were so, we wouldn't arrive at the sought-after absolute; and the existence of God wouldn't be demonstrated.

So the argument that tries to prove the existence of God as the end of the world has no value. Yet there remains another way to demonstrate God's existence by invoking the principles of finality and causality – by considering God to be the organizer of the world. We'll move on now to an exposition and critique of this argument, which Kant called the physicotheological proof.

Explanation and Critique of the Physicotheological Proof

Kant summarized the physicotheological argument as follows:

1. Everywhere in the world there are clear signs of an ordering having occurred.
2. This ordering doesn't inhere in things but belongs to them, so to speak, only contingently.
3. Therefore, there must exist one or several knowing causes that have produced the world, not as a force that automatically determines its effect but as an intelligence that acts freely.
4. The unity of this cause can be inferred from the unity of the relationships between the various parts of the world, viewed as different pieces of a work of art.

This proof, for which Kant had special respect, has been subject to numerous objections. To be sure, no one doubts that the universe has a certain harmony. The first element of the proof is thus agreed upon by all philosophers.

But this isn't so with the second element. An entire school of thought, which can be traced back to Democritus, seeks to explain this order without invoking the notion of finality. But it's in the work of Epicurus that, for the first time, the problem is neatly stated and completely resolved. In his view, the harmony we see in the world is due neither to an ordering intelligence nor to scientific necessity but simply to chance. Atoms are endowed with freedom, so the forms of the bodies they make up are necessarily contingent. If atoms are combined to form the world as it is, the cause is chance alone.

Cicero objected that such an explanation is no explanation at all. How can we accept that chance alone has presided over a harmony as complete as that found among the parts of the body? And what likelihood is there that, by selecting twenty-nine letters at random, we would be led to the first verse of the *Iliad*? Still smaller is the likelihood that the present world – so well ordered as it is – was formed and is sustained by chance alone.

To this objection we might respond that there is a reason why, among all the possible combinations, the world we know was produced. Logically, atoms can be grouped together in an infinite number of ways, and in fact an infinite number of different worlds have succeeded each other in the infinity of time. But the present combination brought this succession to a close, for this combination was the only one that was stable, the only one that brought a state of equilibrium to the world. So we shouldn't be surprised either that it came to be formed or that, once formed, it endures.

But what's the nature of this stability, this equilibrium that accounts for the endurance of the world? Epicurus didn't say. If atoms aren't made in order to form a predetermined system, why of all the possible combinations is there only one that allows the world to remain stable? If atoms are indifferent to one form rather than another, why would they change? Why wouldn't they remain in a state of chaos? The equilibrium that Epicurus posits is extremely vague, and if we try to make it more precise, our efforts would take us far beyond his system.

For this reason, no one any longer accepts this philosophy, which does away with finality and puts chance in its place. It's been replaced by a more subtle and learned philosophy that goes by the general name of mechanism and in its most recent and perfect form is called evolutionism.

Let's examine the principle of mechanism.

Defenders of the notion of finality begin with the observation that there's an exact agreement between means and their results, between organs, for example, and their functions in animate bodies. Beginning with this observation, finalists argue that this agreement could have been produced only by an intelligence. Mechanists claim that this agreement came about differently, from the very nature of things. Means produce their results deterministically – things could not have been otherwise. We admire the eye's ability to see light, but it's light that has made the eye, so the perfect agreement between them shouldn't surprise us.

Here's how Herbert Spencer (in *First Principles*) explained the foundations of evolutionism:

Two kinds of harmony and order are seized upon by the finalists. First, there's a marvelous agreement between beings and their environments. Among viviparous organisms, for example, the fetus is such that it can nourish itself from the same food as its mother, but upon its birth it's reconstituted so as to be in perfect harmony with its new environment.

Second, there's a coordination within each being (especially within organized beings) forming an end toward which each of its parts converge.

Whereas finalists believe that these two facts can be explained only by invoking the notion of a higher intelligence, mechanists explain them without finality, through the determinism of efficient causes. Spencer accounts for the harmony between organism and environment through adaptation. As a consequence of what Spencer calls the instability of the homogeneous, the organism is forced to adapt to its environment, for one that hasn't adapted to its environment is in a condition of perpetual instability and disequilibrium. A homogeneous mass is necessarily in an unstable equilibrium, because "the several parts of any homogeneous aggregation are necessarily exposed to different forces; from this it follows that there exist relations of outside and inside, and of comparative nearness to neighboring sources of influence; and from this it follows that unlike changes will be produced in the parts thus dissimilarly acted upon."

This acknowledged, we still have to explain coordination. How do the heterogeneous elements born in this way form a unified system?

It's by means of what Spencer calls segregation. Adaptation has produced aggregates of heterogeneous elements. Now, "if some aggregate, composed of unlike elements, becomes subject to the action of a force, these elements separate from one another in order to form smaller aggregates, each composed of like elements differing from those of other aggregates." A gust of wind, for example, may hurl to the ground the dead leaves of a tree while leaving the green leaves untouched. For Spencer, therefore, segregation involves a kind of sorting that brings similar elements together into distinct systems, producing order and unity.

Such are the principles of evolutionism. Now let's see how well founded Spencer's theories are. The harmony between a being and its environment is produced, he says, by a necessary and mechanical adaptation. An aggregate plunged into an environment that provides food and oxygen is going to live. But suppose that the environment ceases to provide food and that the food necessary to the living being is at a distance. To continue living, it needs organs capable of moving it. But is it this need alone that produces the organs? And even were it so, wouldn't it rather be proof of finality? In fact, either the seeds of the organs existed already, so that the mechanical causes we've been examining only develop them further, in which case the difficulty is merely pushed back, or the modifications necessary for adaptation were produced by chance, in which case things are produced in one way rather than another simply because of the chance situations they've encountered, so that nothing is explained.

We must also ask if segregation can explain the coordination within each being. Physical coordination, yes. Organic coordination, no. An organized whole involves not only a collection of like elements but also their systematization, their subordination to an overall unity. All the parts cooperate to form the whole, and this subordination can be found not only in the body as a whole but also in each organ. But Spencer's theory doesn't explain this adequately. Evolutionism might well be correct, but it doesn't refute the notion of finality. It does a terrific job showing us how causes, means, and their consequences come to be well suited to one another. But this isn't enough to show that the notion of final causes is useless. They only become more necessary when we try to explain the phenomena of evolution and segregation.

Critique of the Physicotheological Proof (Conclusion). Moral Proofs of the Existence of God

Until now we've done no more than establish the existence of an end in the universe. But how should this end be understood? The physicotheological argument views the world as a work of art and sees its finality as reflecting the intelligence of the artist who conceived of and produced the present order. But might this involve an unjustified anthropomorphism? Why assume the intervention of a being who realizes his designs outside himself? Why can't finality, things proceeding spontaneously toward their ends, be immanent? A good example of such finality is instinct, which pushes beings surely and unconsciously toward their ends. It might be the same with the universe. A doctrine of this kind is found in Aristotle's theory of desire, later taken up by Hegel. For Aristotle, efficient causes are merely appearances, for in reality all causes are final causes. The purely ideal end of things exists only at the moment of origin and then comes to realize itself. Things move toward their ends by attraction, not mechanical impulsion. This theory of immanent finality, which can also be found in the work of Hartmann and Schopenhauer, is designed to avoid the anthropomorphism of the theory of transcendent finality. But what's the great advantage of rejecting the assumption that God's intelligence is analogous to that of men? It's true that, by comparing this intelligence to instinct, we avoid the sin of anthropomorphism. But we simply substitute zoomorphism in its place. Yet this isn't the really important criticism of the theory. Its great failing is that it leaves the end of the universe unrepresentable. Finalism assumes that ends can be conceived. But how is conception – a psychological phenomenon – possible in the absence of consciousness? Hartmann believes in the existence of unconscious psychological phenomena and so remains untroubled. Having already refuted Hartmann's theory, however, we're forced to accept the theory of transcendent finality.

So there is order in the world, and this world comes from a transcendent mind. Does it follow from this that the physicotheological argument decisively proves the existence of God? Kant didn't think so and offered two arguments against those who did:

1. The physicotheological argument demonstrates that the universe has an architect but not a creator. It shows that the form of the world – but not its matter – is contingent. Like us, Kant rejects the cosmological view that matter is contingent.

2. The argument is supported by experience but can't rest on it. It begins with the facts of order and harmony that are revealed to us by observation and concludes that God is the cause of this order and harmony. But the cause must clearly be proportional to the effect. If the order and harmony are imperfect, we can't conclude that there exists a perfect cause. And as Kant says, everything given to us in experience is more or less limited, more or less imperfect. So we can't conclude that there exists an all-knowing, all-powerful cause, as the definition of God would suggest, but only that there exists a cause that is, in relation to ourselves, very knowing and very powerful.

To us, this critique seems unassailable. The conclusion to be drawn from it isn't that the physicotheological argument proves nothing but that it merely establishes the existence of an architect of the world – not his absolute grandeur – for experience can't give us the idea of omniscience or omnipotence.

Two arguments are generally advanced under the heading of moral proofs for the existence of God. The first, which dates back to Cicero, rests on the universal agreement of man. All men believe in the existence of God; therefore He exists. But it's not clear that all men do believe in God's existence, and even if they did, it would only establish a presumption in favor of God's existence. For universal agreement, often found on questions considered easily resolved, is often mistaken. This assent, which is at least quite general if not universal, is a fact that we have to consider and can't ignore. But neither can we make it a criterion of truth.

The second argument made under the heading of moral proofs consists of the effort to establish the existence of God as a condition of morality.

There are two moral facts that can't be explained by themselves and that rest on a foundation distinct from morality.

The first fact is that of moral obligation. At the beginning of our discussion of ethics, we established this experimentally but didn't explain it. But how can a law be obligatory? We're never obligated except by someone – so who obligates us to follow the moral law? By itself, an abstract law can't produce obligation. Until now, we've considered the moral law to be only an abstraction, but clearly it must be a living thing. In this sense, the moral law is simply God.

But we have to be more specific about what we mean here. The Stoics saw virtue as consisting in conformity to nature, to the will of God. But this obedience to a being foreign to ourselves isn't what we mean. The moral law isn't the will of God, it's God Himself. So the moral law assumes the existence of God.

The second fact is that of moral sanction. As we've said before, reason demands harmony between virtue and goodness. So this harmony, not found here on earth, must exist elsewhere, in some higher realm. For this, the immortality of the soul is a necessary – but not a sufficient – condition. There must also be a cause capable of assuring this harmony, of rendering nature compatible with the moral law. This cause is God. So God, who appeared to us just a moment ago as the moral law in living form, now appears as the condition for harmony between goodness and virtue.

We've now examined and criticized the proofs of the existence of God that history has bequeathed to us. Metaphysical proofs were of little value, and some were utterly worthless. By conjoining proofs by causality with proofs by the principle of number and finality, however, we were able to show that the absolute must exist. We thus arrived on the shore of the sea spoken of by Littré. Finally, the physicotheological proof revealed God as the architect of the world, and the two moral proofs showed him to be the living form of the moral law and the condition for moral sanction. With these steps we've therefore demonstrated that the absolute exists and – since we've defined God as the absolute – that God exists as well.

SEVENTY EIGHT

The Nature and Attributes of God

Having established that God exists, our job now is to determine His nature – His qualities or attributes. Two methods of doing this are available. The first proceeds by analogy, elevating the attributes of imperfect beings to a state of perfection and then attributing these to God. This method begins with the principle that there must be at least as much reality in the cause as in the effect. But this is an idea we've already refuted, so this method isn't open to us.

The second method is to start from the definition of God and then examine the conditions of His attributes. This method proceeds by straightforward deduction, and it's the one we'll follow.

Our definition of God includes both metaphysical and moral attributes – the first concerning God as a being in general and the second God as a person.

I. *Metaphysical Attributes*

1. Infinity. God, being absolute, can't be finite, for if He were limited, He'd be relative to whatever limits Him.

2. Unity. Something made up of parts is relative to those parts. We can conceive of such a thing, not as existing in and of itself, but only as a function of its constituent parts. But God is absolute, so He must necessarily be one.

3. Perfection. Divine perfection is sometimes understood to mean the sum of all the qualities of beings, elevated to the absolute. But this definition demeans God's divinity, for the qualities of beings are relative. Also, to attribute to God the qualities of beings past, present, and future is to undermine His unity. So by perfection, we mean instead a quality

of a being who's sufficient in and of Himself and has no need of any other. For us, perfection is merely a synonym for the absolute, as in τέλειος (complete), *absolutus*, which has the double meaning of perfect and absolute.

4. Immutability. God is immutable, for change takes place only within the world of the relative. God would be subject to change only if there's something external to Him that makes him change – which is contrary to our definition – or because He changes Himself, which is impossible, for God is what He is.

5. Immensity. God isn't in space – for this idea is unintelligible – but outside of space, which is even more so. Nevertheless, everything that's in space is in one part of space and is therefore relative.

6. Eternity. By the same token, God is eternal, outside of time. For God, there is no past, present, or future.

II. *Moral Attributes*

It's when considering God's moral attributes that thinkers lean most heavily on the analogical method, relying on a kind of anthropomorphism that gives to God – as to man – a sensibility, an intelligence, and a will. Here the method of deduction isn't very helpful, for we can't derive moral attributes from an entirely metaphysical notion of the absolute. But we do know God to be the cause of the harmony between goodness and virtue, and from this we can derive His moral attributes.

For God to judge men with perfect knowledge of the causes of their actions, He must be omniscient. In addition, He must be omnipotent, so that He can execute His judgments unimpeded. Since nature is completely amoral, an unlimited power is obviously required to make it conform with morality. Third, this supreme judge must be completely impartial, perfectly fair. Finally, God's freedom is both a condition of His superior majesty and a consequence of His metaphysical nature. In order to render judgments with perfect justice, it's necessary that God be exempt from all external causes, just as no external cause can act upon Him because He is absolute.

These moral attributes make us see God as a person and together make up the divine personality. It's sometimes been said that there's a contradiction between the metaphysical and moral attributes of God, that the latter lead us to conceive of God in a personal, and the former in an impersonal, way. This objection would have merit if by "infinity" we meant "infinity in extension." But we understand God as having "infinity in comprehension." So divine infinity is simply another form of God's absolute nature.

The same is true of His perfection. There'd be a contradiction if the idea of perfection involved only the conjunction of all real and possible qualities taken to their maximum intensity. But for us, perfection is almost synonymous with the absolute, and there's no contradiction between the idea of personality and that of the absolute. On the contrary – the ideal of the perfect person is precisely the absolute.

SEVENTY NINE

The Relationship between God and the World. Dualism, Pantheism, and Creation

We've now shown that God exists, and we've also determined His nature. What we must do next is examine the relationship between God and the world. It's generally agreed that God is the cause of the world. But how does this cause produce its effect?

Dualists believe that God has done no more than order the world, that when He began His work matter (the χώρα [place] of Plato, the ὕλη [matter] of Aristotle) already existed. According to the dualists, matter has existed for all eternity. But were this the case, matter would be another absolute, one that limits the power of God and thus contradicts His attributes. In addition, no matter how indeterminate we assume this matter to be, it still would function according to its own laws, so that God couldn't organize it completely as He pleased.

But why depict God as being outside of the world? Why couldn't the universe be God Himself? This view, called pantheism, wipes away the existence of individuals. It understands them to be phenomena of a common substance, which is God. So pantheism explains the relationship between God and the world by reducing it to those that obtain between a substance and its phenomena. Of course, there are different versions of pantheism. Materialist pantheism – found in the thought of the Stoics and Ionics – depicts the God-world as material in nature. Hegel's idealist pantheism, by contrast, conceives of it as spiritual and places the Idea at the beginning of all things. This Idea, subject to the law of opposites or reality, realizes itself over time. Spinoza's pantheism, in which God is the principle of both extension and movement (*res extensa et cogitans* [thinking and extended substance]), differs from both.

Three serious objections to pantheism can be raised. First, its conception of God is problematic. A being who contains all beings within himself isn't only monstrous and impossible to come to grips with but also implies a serious contradiction. How could the same being have both extension and thought? Spinoza spiritualizes divine extension as much as he can, but it remains fundamentally material. So the God of the pantheists has no determinate nature – all we can say is that it is a being of some sort. Second, pantheism doesn't explain the existence of the individual. We are free, one, and identical. How can we be so if we're but a moment in the development of the divine? Freedom, like individuality, is utterly irreconcilable with this hypothesis. The pantheists deny these two attributes; but since we've accepted them as real, we can't accept pantheism. Finally, pantheism doesn't explain the multiplicity of sensation. In a system that places all reality in an eternally immobile God, what could be the source of change and movement? Pantheism denies both, and with them all the multiplicity of the sensory world. This was the position taken by the Eleatics like Parmenides and Zeno, for whom there's but one existence – and the rest is merely appearance. So the consequence of every rigorous pantheism is monism.

The conclusion we reach is that God is neither orderer nor spirit of the world. What can be said, instead, is that God created the world. We needn't try to understand the meaning of this phrase, for it defies both imagination and reason. For us it can mean no more than this, that God is distinct from the world and, further, that He's more than its architect.

EIGHTY

The Relationship between God and the World (Conclusion). Providence, Evil, Optimism, and Pessimism

The relationship between God and the world extends beyond the act of creation itself. We reject the view that, after creating the world, God lost interest and abandoned it. The world must remain perpetually connected to the source of its existence – one of the main metaphysical reasons Descartes gave for the existence of Providence.

Providence may be either general or particular in nature. The idea of a particular Providence is that God actually intervenes in the affairs of the world, directing human events and holding the reins of all empires and souls. Bossuet developed and applied this theory in his *Discourse on Universal History*.

To attribute this faculty to God, however, is to deny human freedom and reduce the majesty of the divine. According to this theory, man is but a means in the hands of God. We no longer do what we will but do what God wills for us. Thus it is that in his *Discourse* Bossuet depicts all peoples converging around an end that they don't even suspect – the glory of God. Bossuet accepts that human freedom and divine Providence are equally true but irreconcilable. Yet in our view philosophy can't resign itself to this contradiction. The idea of the quotidian intervention of the Creator in the affairs of his creatures also reduces the majesty of the divine, exalting the power of God at the expense of His dignity. So we can't accept the theory of a particular Providence.

Providence is therefore general. God wasn't content merely to create the world but arranged things so that they'd constitute the best possible world. Providence was exercised at the beginning of time, when the laws that preside over the life of the world were established. Providence represents the perfect wisdom and goodness of God, preparing the future of the beings He created. God maintains these general laws in perpetuity.

He is their guardian, and this is the continual service He renders to creation. So Providence involves

1. Establishing laws in view of the good;
2. Preserving existence in the world;
3. Maintaining the laws thus established.

But a serious objection has been raised against the idea of Providence – the problem of evil. " Si Deus est, unde malum?" ("If God exists whence evil?") asked the Scholastics of the seventeenth century. Bayle, adopting a Manichean approach, maintained that evil must have its source in a principle other than God. Leibniz responded to the same objection in his essays on theodicy, distinguishing, like Bayle, between three types of evil: metaphysical, moral, and physical. Metaphysical evil is the imperfection of all beings. We're finite and limited – as is everything in the world. We know few things well, we're often wrong, and our strength and our intelligence are limited – all this representing a most painful evil. Moral evil is sin. Why didn't God give us a sufficiently upright intelligence and a sufficiently strong will to see the good and act on it? Physical evil, finally, is suffering. Why is there sickness and death? Why are there natural disasters?

But the existence of these evils, responds Leibniz, proves nothing against Providence. Not one of these evils was willed in and for itself, but each is the necessary condition of the good. To best understand this response, we should recall Leibniz's theodicy. At the moment of creation, God imagined the infinity of possible universes, choosing not the absolute best but the best that could exist. So the perfection of this work and the goodness of its creator should be judged not in terms of the details of its various parts but in terms of the totality of its existence.

Leibniz applied this theory to Bayle's three types of evil. With regard to metaphysical evil, Leibniz showed that, as beings that have been created, we can't be perfect, for only the absolute is perfect. So rather than itself being positive, metaphysical evil is simply a negation resulting from a good that's essentially positive. Similarly, moral evil is not something positive that God has willed but the consequence of moral goodness, which can exist only if we're free. For there to be freedom, we must have the power to do good or evil. So evil is a condition of the good.

Physical evil takes the form of various kinds of physical pain. Where does it come from? If we isolate a man from the rest of the world, of course, the source of evil can't be seen. But such an abstraction gives a false idea of things. The evil experienced by the individual is the result of a good for the entire world. The laws of the world may result in a disaster that makes some men suffer, but these laws weren't made for this purpose. Without them, the world couldn't exist. So the suffering of some individuals is a condition of the greater good. Suffering is also a useful ordeal, the best school of morality. Through suffering the soul is tempered and the spirit exalted, acquiring a dignity that could never be obtained by someone who's always happy.

So evil will be considered bad only by those whose perspective is limited. The world isn't perfect, but neither is it bad. It is, according to the expression of Leibniz, the best world possible.

Today, pessimism is back in vogue, but it's become more psychological and moral than Bayle's theological pessimism was. In fact, pessimism – thus understood – has become almost popular in many parts of Europe. The two thinkers it's most associated with are Schopenhauer and Hartmann.

The foundation of Schopenhauer's pessimism is the theory that pleasure is only a negation of pain, that pleasure follows pain, which is the positive and normal sensory state.

Hartmann granted that pleasure is positive but believed that the amount of pleasure we can experience in life is infinitely less than the amount of pain we're promised. On the balance sheet of pleasures and pains, there's a constant deficit in the column of the former.

Hartmann's philosophy is dominated by two ideas. Whether its causes are psychological or physical, pleasure lasts only for a short time. Scarcely born, it disappears; our body can't support it beyond a certain intensity and duration. Pain, by contrast, lasts much longer. Unforgettable, it returns to haunt the mind, so that the foundation of life is pain, with pleasure momentarily interrupting it only on occasion. In addition, not only is the intensity of a pleasure insufficient compensation for its limited quantity – it can't even be considered equivalent to a pain of equal duration. Hartmann believes that there's more pain in listening to disagreeable sounds than there is pleasure in listening to harmonious music, so if we had to purchase this pleasure with pain, we'd never consent. Pain, in short, is the law of life, the nearly constant sensory state. If this is so, the being that made us doesn't merit the name of Providence. And in fact, according to Hartmann, the mysterious principle of all nature, the Unconscious, made us only in order to realize its own personal ends, arranging the world so that we would play the role of its docile means.

To this end, the Unconscious tricks us, making us believe that we're moving toward our own ends, while all we do is serve its own. Believing that we're moving toward our ends, we also believe that we experience pleasure, but this appearance crumbles under philosophical analysis. If human beings opened their eyes, they'd perceive that our fate is suffering and that we can enjoy ourselves only by allowing ourselves to be fooled.

The first error of the pessimists is to treat pleasure as an objective, impersonal phenomenon. For it's entirely individual. The balance sheet of which Hartmann speaks may be valid for him but not for others. He regards violent pleasures as disagreeable, but not all people are as likely to feel the same way about the nirvana that charms him. We can't say that pains are quantitatively greater than pleasures. Such objects don't lend themselves to mathematical evaluation.

Next, if it's true that pleasure is fleeting, mustn't pain be equally so? Our sensory life is constantly in flux, and isn't there room in our hearts for many feelings at once? But, says Hartmann, pain haunts the mind even when it isn't present. But isn't it the same with pleasure? "When the wise man suffers," Aristotle says, "he need do no more than recall a past pleasure in order to experience joy." This is an exaggeration, but it's still true that memory and hope – which Hartmann sees as too deceptive – can make pleasure last longer, no matter how fleeting it might be in itself. As for Hartmann's second argument, it's too subjective. Many people find that a pleasure more than compensates for an equal pain and would happily purchase an hour of good music at the cost of an hour of discordant noise. It's purely a matter of personal opinion.

Pleasure is not *in medio,* ready to appear in all men in a quantity greater than that of pain. But the victory of pleasure over pain isn't impossible, and we mustn't lose hope if there are times when we're not happy. Happiness is an art, and any art can be learned.

APPENDIX

Biographical Glossary

Abelard, Peter (1079–1142). French philosopher, logician, and theologian. A student of the nominalist Roscelin, Abelard attacked a variety of realist theologies of the early twelfth century.

Alceste. A character in Molière's play *Le Misanthrope* (1666) who has high ideals and rigid standards and is as blind to his own faults as he is acutely aware of those of others.

Anaxagoras (c. 500–428 B.C.E.). Pre-Socratic philosopher. He reacted sharply against the monism of Parmenides, insisted against Zeno of Elea that matter must be infinitely divisible, and argued that even the mind is corporeal.

Anselm, St. (1033–1109). Scholastic philosopher and one of the first medieval thinkers to apply Aristotelian logic (inherited from Boethius) to the solution of theological problems. In the *Proslogion*, he introduced what has since been known as the "ontological argument for the existence of God" (later embraced by Descartes and attacked by both Hume and Kant).

Aquinas, St. Thomas (c. 1224–74). The greatest Scholastic philosopher of the "High Middle Ages." In the *Summa Theologia*, St. Thomas dismissed Anselm's ontological argument, embracing instead what have come to be known as "the five ways" – that is, various formulations of both the "cosmological" and "teleological" arguments.

Arcesilaus (c. 316–242 B.C.E.). As sixth head of the Academy of Athens, Arcesilaus introduced a skepticism (derived either from Socrates or from Pyrrho of Elis), refusing either to accept or to deny the possibility of certainty in knowledge.

Aristippus of Cyrene (early fourth century B.C.E.). Close friend and follower of Socrates and the traditional founder of the Cyrenaic school of hedonism. Like Socrates, Aristippus was interested almost exclusively in practical ethics, whose end he understood to be the enjoyment of present pleasure (leavened by a Socratic element of self-control).

Aristotle (384–22 B.C.E.). Greek philosopher, student of Plato, and teacher of Alexander the Great. His unparalleled significance in the history of Western thought is amply testified to throughout all of Durkheim's works. (See Douglas Challenger, *Durkheim through the Lens of Aristotle*, 1994).

Bacon, Francis (1561–1626). English statesman, philosopher of science, and first in the great line of British empiricists extending through Locke, Hume, and J. S. Mill. The works to which Durkheim elliptically refers include *The Advancement of Learning* (1605), the *Novum Organum* (1620), and the *New Atlantis* (1627).

Bain, Alexander (1818–1903). Scottish philosopher and psychologist. An associate of J. S. Mill who assisted with the editing of the latter's *System of Logic* (1842). Author of *The Senses and the Intellect* (1855) and *The Emotions and the Will* (1859) and founder of the journal *Mind* in 1876.

Bastiat, Claude Frédéric (1801–50). French political economist, advocate of free trade, and editor of the journal *Le Libre Échange* (1846–8). His posthumously published *Harmonies économiques* (1850) argued – like Adam Smith's *Wealth of Nations* (1776) – that the division of labor was important primarily because it transformed the pursuit of private interest into public goods. It was to displace this preoccupation with the purely *economic* benefits of the division of labor, of course, that Durkheim would later write *De la division du travail social* (1893).

Bayle, Pierre (1647–1706). French lexicographer, philosopher, and critic. Raised a Protestant, Bayle became a Catholic and then reverted to Protestantism before finally becoming a religious skeptic and fideist. His *Dictionnaire historique et critique* (1697) ridiculed every rationalist effort to make sense of human experience.

Bentham, Jeremy (1748–1832). English economist, political and moral philosopher, leader of the Philosophical Radicals, and the father of British utilitarianism. His *Introduction to the Principles of Morals and Legislation* (1789) advanced the "hedonic calculus" as the standard by which to adjudicate alternative courses of action and policy.

Bernard, Claude (1813–78). French experimental physiologist and the author of *Introduction à l'étude de la médecine expérimentale* (1865). An absolute determinist, Bernard insisted that a set of conditions (a cause) will invariably produce the same phenomenon (an effect).

Bonald, Louis Gabriel Ambroise, Vicomte de (1754–1840). French publicist, royalist, and philosopher. Against the eighteenth-century view that language was a human invention, Bonald revived Rousseau's notion that – since an invention requires thought and thought is internal speech – language could not have been invented but was placed in man's soul at the creation.

Bossuet, Jacques Bénigne (1627–1704). French theologian and moralist. In his *Traité de la connaissance de Dieu et de soi-même*, Bossuet combined Thomistic theology with sympathy for the reassuringly authoritarian side of Cartesian philosophy, even as he denounced the dangers of individual reason and inquiry.

Bouillier, Francisque (1813–99). French philosopher. The author of the *Histoire de la philosophie cartésienne* (1854), *Du plaisir et de la douleur* (1865), and *De la conscience en psychologie et en morale* (1872).

Buffon, Georges-Louis Leclerc, Comte de (1707–88). French naturalist and the author of the monumental *Histoire naturelle* (44 volumes, 1749–1804). The first three volumes, which included his *Theory of the Earth* and *History of Man* (both published in 1749), contained views that ran counter to Genesis and thus incurred the wrath of the Sorbonne.

Caesar, Julius (102?–44 B.C.E.). Roman leader and statesman who conquered Gaul.

Carneades (c. 213–c. 128 B.C.E.). A leader of the Academic Skeptics who, as the head of Plato's Academy, developed its antidogmatism far beyond the point to which Arcesilaus had brought it.

Cato, Marcus Porcius (95–46 B.C.E.). Roman statesman and Stoic philosopher, the grandson of Cato "the Elder" (234–149 B.C.E).

Charles I (1600–49). King of England from 1625 to 1649. Charles I was at the helm when Cromwell rose to power.

Cheselden, William (1688–1752). British surgeon who developed improved procedures and instruments for the removal of cataracts. In 1728, in a case that is still famous, he gave sight to a boy aged thirteen or fourteen by removing his highly opaque congenital cataracts.

Cicero, Marcus Tullius (106–43 B.C.E.). Roman orator and statesman. During periods of forced retirement from public life, Cicero wrote a number of philosophical treatises – for example, the *Tusculan Disputations, On Duties, On the Nature of the Gods*, etc. – reflecting the influence of various schools at the time, including the Stoics, Peripatetics, and Academics.

Clarke, Samuel (1675–1729). English theologian, philosopher, friend and disciple of Newton. Against Hobbes and Spinoza, Clarke's two sets of Boyle lectures – "A Demonstration of the Being and Attributes of God" (1704) and "A Discourse Concerning the Unchangeable Obligations of Natural Religion" (1705) – attempted to prove the existence of God by largely mathematical means.

Clodius Pulcher, Publius (93–52 B.C.E.). Roman politician and enemy of Cicero.

Comte, Auguste (1798–1857). French positivist philosopher, whose six-volume *Cours de philosophie positive* (1830–42) traced the development of human thought and society from its theological and metaphysical stages to its positive stage – the last characterized by the systematic collection and correlation of observed facts for the purpose of establishing scientific laws.

Condillac, Étienne Bonnot de (1715–80). French philosopher who, though an ordained priest, associated himself with the secular and rationalist tendencies of the Encyclopedists. An admirer of Locke, his *Essai sur l'origine des connaissances humaines* (1746) and *Traité des sensations* (1754) traced all human faculties back to their origins in sensation.

Corneille, Pierre (1606–84). French dramatist. His play *Le Cid* (1637) marks the beginning of classical tragedy in France.

Cousin, Victor (1792–1867). French eclectic philosopher who, as minister of public instruction, established the institution of the *cours de philosophie* – of which Durkheim's Sens lectures afford a later example.

Cudworth, Ralph (1617–88). English scholar and a leading member of the Cambridge Platonists. His *True Intellectual System of the Universe* (1678) and the posthumously published *Treatise Concerning Eternal and Immutable Morality* (1731) reflect the group's concern to establish a reasonable philosophical justification for Christian theology.

Darwin, Charles (1809–82). British biologist. In *The Origin of Species* (1859), he advanced a theory of evolution by natural selection that revolutionized Western science, and *The Descent of Man* (1871), which extended that theory to the evolution of the human species, similarly revolutionized the social sciences.

Democritus of Abdera (c. 460–c. 370 B.C.E.). Greek pre-Socratic philosopher. A younger contemporary of Leucippus, Democritus was a materialist and atomist who advanced the first rigorously naturalistic system of ethics.

Descartes, René (1596–1650). French philosopher and mathematician. He withheld his *Le Monde* (1632) from publication after learning of Galileo's condemnation by the Inquisition, but by 1637 he was ready to publish a selection of his scientific views – the *Dioptric, Meteors,* and *Geometry*. To this he added a philosophical introduction titled *Discours sur la Méthode*, which became his best known work and established the foundations of French rationalism.

Epicurus (341–270 B.C.E.). Greek atomistic philosopher, a disciple of Democritus to whose materialistic philosophy he added the famous "swerve of atoms" to explain their combination and interaction. Extending his metaphysical views to ethics, Epicurus proposed a hedonistic system in which all moral judgments are derived from the human experience of pleasure and pain.

Espinas, Alfred (1844–1922). French sociologist and philosopher. Influenced by his early reading of German social science and its emphasis on the group rather than the individual, Espinas' *Les sociétés animales* (1877) argued that all the really essential attributes of human society – solidarity, dominance of the social bond over individual will, the social basis of individual reactions to the natural world, etc. – are to be found in the social organizations of animals.

Euler, Leonhard (1707–83). Swiss mathematician and physicist, one of the founders of pure mathematics. His interests were broad, and his *Lettres à une princesse d'Allemagne* (1768–72) provided an admirably clear exposition of the basic principles of mechanics, optics, acoustics, and physical astronomy.

Faust (sixteenth century). German astrologer memorialized in works by Marlowe and Goethe, among others. The fictionalized Faust sold his soul to the devil.

Fechner, Gustav Theodor (1801–87). German physicist and philosopher who was a key figure in the founding of psychophysics. In his *Elements of Psychophysics* (1860), he suggested that mind and body, though appearing to be separate entities, are actually different sides of one reality. He developed experimental procedures, still useful in experimental psychology, for measuring sensations in relation to the physical magnitude of stimuli, and he devised an equation to express the theory of the just-noticeable difference (advanced earlier by Ernst Heinrich Weber).

Fichte, Johann Gottlieb (1762–1814). German philosopher. Strongly influenced by Kant, Fichte's *Versuch einer Kritik aller Offenbarung* (1792) described religion as the belief in the divinity of moral law. But his later *Wissenschaftslehre* departed from Kant, anticipating Hegel's absolute idealism as well as some aspects of existentialism.

Flaubert, Gustave (1821–80). French novelist, author of *Madame Bovary* (1857). Flaubert aimed at a strictly objective and impersonal work of art, presented in the most perfect form. Because of his meticulously accurate documentation, he was hailed as a realist and even naturalist, but he detested such labels and explained his painstaking detail as the means to an end rather than the end in itself.

Flourens, Marie Jean Pierre (1794–1867). French physiologist who was the first to demonstrate the general functions of the major portions of the vertebrate brain. A disciple of Georges Cuvier, Flourens conducted experiments that led him to conclude that the cerebral hemispheres are responsible for higher psychic and intellectual abilities, that the cerebellum regulates all movements, and that the medulla controls vital functions, especially respiration.

Foucher, Simon (1644–96). French philosopher and one of the foremost critics of Malebranche and Descartes. A skeptic and antirationalist, Foucher insisted that we can't have knowledge of the external world if it doesn't come to us through our senses.

Galileo, Galilei (1564–1642). Italian mathematician, astronomer, and physicist who founded modern experimentalism and mechanics and defended the Copernican, heliocentric theory of the universe in his *Dialogue on the Two Chief World Systems* (1632) – for which he was subjected to the Inquisition and placed under house arrest.

Garnier, Adolphe (1801–64). French philosopher, author of *De la peine de mort* (1827), *La Psychologie et la phrénologie comparées* (1839), *Critique de la philosophie de Thomas Reid* (1840), and the *Traité des facultés de l'ame* (1865). In the early nineteenth century, Garnier was among several French philosophers – including Royer-Collard, Cousin, and Jouffroy – to be influenced by Scottish philosophy.

Girardin, François Saint-Marc (1801–73). French literary critic and professor of poetry at the Sorbonne. An antiromantic, Girardin's writings include *Essais de littérature et de morale* (1845), *Souvenirs de voyages et d'études* (1852–3), and his collected lectures on the treatment of the passions in dramatic literature, published as *Cours de littérature dramatique* (5 vols., 1843–68).

Hamilton, Sir William (1788–1856). Scottish philosopher. In his main work, published as *Lectures on Metaphysics and Logic* (1859–60), he argued that perception gives us direct (rather than representative) knowledge of objects, while still maintaining that this knowledge is relative rather than absolute. The critique of this position in Mill's *Examination of Sir William Hamilton's Philosophy* (1865) effectively marked the end of the distinctively Scottish school of philosophy that had begun with Hume and Reid.

Hartmann, Eduard von (1842–1906). German philosopher whose *Die Philosophie des Unbewusstsein* (1869), a philosophical investigation of the unconscious mind, brought him early and widespread scholarly recognition. The work was particularly noteworthy for its third volume, which contained a justification for philosophical pessimism based, not on Schopenhauer but on Kant.

Hector. Known as the bravest of the Trojans, Hector, a figure in Greek mythology, was depicted by Homer in the *Iliad* as a paragon of virtue, strength, and courage. He came to symbolize such qualities in Renaissance art and literature and remained an icon through the nineteenth century. Hector was killed by Achilles, and all of Troy mourned his death.

Hegel, Georg Wilhelm Friedrich (1770–1831). A key philosopher in the German idealist movement, alongside his predecessors Fichte and Schelling. Opposing Kant's efforts to ground all knowledge in human reason, Hegel proposed an organicist conception of reason as coextensive with reality and saw the goal of human beings and their institutions as being to contribute to reason's unfolding.

Hobbes, Thomas (1588–1679). A towering intellectual figure in seventeenth-century Britain whose major contribution to political theory was the argument that the right of a soveriegn to act as he will is based on a transfer of power from the people, who wish to escape the brutality of the state of nature. An adviser to the British aristocracy, Hobbes's most famous tract, *Leviathan* (1651), gave ideological support to monarchism.

Horace (65–8 B.C.E.). Roman poet whose satires treated the full range of human experience and who was known for his perfection of lyrical form.

Hutcheson, Francis (1694–1746). Spearhead of the eighteenth-century Scottish Enlightenment, Hutcheson argued against the view that humans always act out of self-interest. In *A System of Moral Philosophy*, published posthumously in 1755, he not only insisted on the reality of benevolence but held that humans have a God-given natural capacity to distinguish right from wrong. Hutcheson's views influenced Bentham, Kant, and Smith.

Jacobi, Friedrich Heinrich (1743–1819). German critic and novelist whose interpretation of Kant and sympathy for the ideas of Reid may have influenced Cousin, who studied with him briefly. Against what he saw as the dominant strain in German philosophy, Jacobi sought to defend an expansive conception of reason compatible with the demands of God and individual conscience.

Jouffroy, Théodore Simon (1796–1842). A student of Royer-Collard and Cousin, Jouffroy sought to develop a philosophical psychology around the Scottish commonsense philosophy of Reid and Stewart, whose works he translated for a French audience.

Kant, Immanuel (1724–1804). Author of such enormously influential works as the *Critique of Pure Reason* (1781), *Critique of Practical Reason* (1788), *Critique of Judgment* (1790), and *Metaphysics of Morals* (1797), Kant expounded a philosophy of critical idealism, which had at its center a critical analysis of human reason and which aimed to reconcile Newtonian scientific determinism with the autonomy of morality.

Kepler, Johann (1571–1630). A pioneering figure in the history of astronomy, Kepler brought together the careful empirical observations of Tycho Brahe with a Copernican cosmology to introduce three laws of planetary motion. These laws, which explained elliptical planetary orbits as a function of physical forces, represented an enormous advance over medieval astronomy, which was for all intents and purposes a branch of theology.

La Bruyère, Jean de (1645–96). French writer and moralist whose 1688 book, *Les caractères ou les moeurs de ce siècle*, was a catalogue of the human condition as it existed during the *ancien régime*, containing detailed observations about the psychology, manners, and morals of people from all walks of life.

Laplace, Pierre Simon de (1749–1827). An astronomer, mathematician, and philosopher, Laplace was a supporter of the French revolution and held one of the first posts at the École Polytechnique. A great believer in Newtonian mechanics, Laplace devoted much of his career to resolving some of the anomalies in Newton's theory and to working out the details and identifying the practical implications of an early version of probability theory.

La Rochefoucauld, Duc François de (1613–80). La Rochefoucauld was a fixture of the seventeenth-century Parisian salons. His 1665 book, *Maximes*, argued that self-interest is at the base of most human action and that passions and bodily urges often get the better of us.

Leibniz, Gottfried Wilhelm (1646–1716). A German philosopher with wide-ranging interests whose metaphysical views intrigued the early Durkheim. Leibniz accepted a mechanistic view of the phenomenal world as a site of cause-and-effect relationships but held that beneath this world lies another, in which reality is composed of simple mindlike entities called monads. According to Leibniz, the monads composing the mind and body are constituted by God so as to always act spontaneously in "preestablished harmony" with one another.

Lélut, Louis François (1804–77). French physician who argued, most famously in *Du démon de Socrate* (1836), that many of the giants of intellectual and religious history suffered from hallucinations.

Lemoine, Albert (1824–74). Philosopher and psychiatrist, author of *Du sommeil du point de vue physiologique et psychologique* (1855), Lemoine held that consciousness does not vanish during sleep but merely diminishes in intensity.

Lewes, George Henry (1817–78). A writer and philosopher, Lewes helped popularize the positivist philosophy of Comte in England. A committed naturalist, Lewes urged that traditional metaphysics be scrapped and replaced by a science centered on the empirical verification of hypotheses.

Littré, Maximilien Paul Émile (1801–81). Founder of the journal *La philosophie positive* and author of *Auguste Comte et la philosophie positive* (1863), Littré was one of Comtean positivism's most ardent French champions, seeking – after a dispute with the master in 1852 – to save it even from itself, that is, from what he saw as the errors to which Comte, late in his intellectual career, had been prone.

Locke, John (1632–1704). A key figure in the tradition of British empiricism, Locke denied that any ideas are innate and identified experience as their true source. His political theory, worked out in *Two Treatises of Government* (1689), departed from that of Hobbes insofar as it founded the state on a transfer of the natural rights of individuals, broadly conceived thus limiting its power.

Louis XIV (1638–1715). King of France from 1643 to 1715, he ruled with an iron fist but presided over a great cultural efflorescence.

Lucretius, *in full* **Titus Lucretius Carus** (c. 94–c. 55 B.C.E.). Roman poet in the Epicurean tradition who held, in line with the general Epicurean insistence that a mechanistic metaphysics is the key to a simple and secure life, that there is nothing to fear in death, for the soul does not pass over into a mysterious world of gods.

Maine de Biran, *real name* **Marie François Pierre Gonthier de Biran** (1766–1824). French philosopher who criticized the empiricist tradition for its failure to properly grasp the nature of the will. An influence on Cousin, Maine de Biran suggested that the will could best be understood through introspection.

Malebranche, Nicolas (1638–1715). French philosopher who drew out the theoretical implications of Cartesianism. Malebranche reconciled the problem of evil versus God's benevolence by asserting that God's perfection consists in using the simplest means possible to obtain the universe such as it is, which may sometimes lead to imperfect results. He also explained knowledge as a function of God's will.

Malthus, Thomas Robert (1776–1834). A British economist and philosopher, Malthus argued, against various utopian visionaries, that increasing misery rather than progress is society's fate over the long run because human population growth always tends to outstrip gains in the size of the resource base.

Mansel, Henry Longueville (1820–71). A British philosopher influenced by Cousin who held that empirical knowledge is dependent on psychological knowledge of the self, which, by its very nature, always remains somewhat elusive.

Mill, John Stuart (1806–73). Writing in opposition to both Scottish commonsense philosophy and to German idealism, Mill pushed the bounds of empiricism by arguing that all knowledge, including knowledge of logic and mathematics, is known inductively through experience, but that this need not be seen as undermining its certainty. A utilitarian when it came to ethics and a fervent supporter of individual rights and champion of liberalism in his political philosophy, Mill also believed, following Comte, that a society's institutions generally correspond with its overall level of philosophical development.

Milo, Titus Annius (d. 48 B.C.E.). Roman politician accused of murdering his rival Clodius. Milo had been responsible for bringing Cicero back from exile, and Cicero unsuccessfully came to Milo's defense at trial in his *Pro Milone*.

Montaigne, Michel Eyquem de (1533–92). Most famous as the author of the *Essais* (1580), Montaigne helped revive the skepticism of the ancient Greek philosopher Pyrrho. Montaigne held that human knowledge is fundamentally faulty, that most philosophy is based on error, and that only by restricting ourselves to that which is certain can we be assured of following in the path of God.

Müller, Friedrich Max (1823–1900). A pioneering figure in the field of comparative philology, Müller, a German, emigrated to Britain in 1846, where he was given a professorship at Oxford. Müller specialized in the study of Sanskrit and advanced the hypothesis that the growth of language is a function of natural laws.

Newton, Isaac (1642–1727). Revolutionary figure in the history of modern science, Newton – for many years a professor of mathematics at Cambridge and then member and president of the Royal Society – was the first to formulate the theory of universal gravity and is credited, along with Leibniz, with having discovered the infinitesimal calculus.

Parmenides (early to mid fifth century B.C.E.). Teacher of Zeno, Parmenides is one of the earliest known Greek philosophers. The only work of his that survives, an approximately 150-line fragment from a philosophical poem, asserts that there exists no such thing as not-being and that the world is, despite appearances, actually continuous, homogeneous, and unchanging.

Pascal, Blaise (1623–62). A French philosopher and scientist, Pascal is remembered today not simply for his contributions to theology, where he argued that there is nothing to lose and everything to gain by believing in God, but also for his work on vacuums and for the experimental procedures on which this work was based. Against the Aristotelian view that nature abhors a vacuum, Pascal showed that the level of mercury in a barometric tube is a function of air pressure.

Peisse, Jean Louis Hippolyte (1803–80). According to Françisque Bouillier, writing in *Le principe vital et l'âme pensante* (1873), Peisse offered in *Rapports du physique et du moral* (1848) – also the title of a work by Cabinis – an underappreciated vitalist critique of Jouffroy's attempt to distinguish between physiology and psychology.

Plato (427–347 B.C.E.). Student of Socrates and recorder and champion of his views, Plato argued for the benefits of a life lived according to the teachings of philosophy. A realist, Plato held that philosophy should aim to elucidate the real timeless essence of things, which he termed their Forms. As philosophers alone are in a position to understand the Forms of Beauty, Truth, and the Good, Plato urged in *The Republic* (c. 380–67 B.C.E.) that philosophers should be society's rulers.

Ravaisson-Mollien, Jean Gaspard Félix (1813–1900). A student of Cousin, Ravaisson is best known for his 1867 book, *Rapport sur la philosophie en France au XIXe siècle*. Criticizing Cousinian eclecticism for its arbitrariness and for misunderstanding the importance of Maine de

Biran's thought, Ravaisson argued that philosophy fails when it cannot adequately account for the fact that humans are active causes.

Reid, Thomas (1710–96). Scottish philosopher and formulator of the philosophy of common sense, Reid rejected the view, associated with Hume, that all objects of thought are represented by the mind in the form of ideas. According to Reid, this view – like many other philosophical theories – displays an obvious sign of its weakness: that it finds no support in common sense, that is, in that body of judgment that is part of the very nature with which God has endowed us.

Renan, Joseph Ernest (1823–92). French historian and philosopher. Embracing Hegel's emphasis on the historical development of the mind but wishing to give a more scientific account of the process than either Hegel or Comte, Renan argued that the philological study of language and religion held the key to uncovering the true laws governing history and progress.

Rousseau, Jean Jacques (1712–78). One of the central figures in the French Enlightenment, Rousseau held that society is a corrupting influence on human morality. Although Rousseau admitted that exiting the state of nature by forming a social contract may be in our best interests because it helps overcome the limitations of individual self-sufficiency, he insisted that a just state would be one whose powers are limited, that is governed by the general will of the people, and in which invidious political and economic differences would be minimized.

Royer-Collard, Pierre Paul (1763–1845). French statesman and, for a short time, professor of philosophy at the Sorbonne. Royer-Collard helped popularize in France the commonsense philosophy of Reid. Only fragments of his work survive.

Schelling, Friedrich Wilhelm Joseph von (1775–1854). A contemporary of Hegel, Schelling built on the ideas of Fichte and Kant to argue, as part of the doctrine of subjective idealism, that human knowledge is grounded in the ego but that there is no unbridgeable chasm between the ego and the objective world, for they have force – that is, attraction and repulsion – as their common ground.

Schopenhauer, Arthur (1788–1860). An influential German philosopher, Schopenhauer advanced the metaphysical claim that the world is will, a mystical life force, and that this force powerfully shapes human life, despite the fact that we are unconscious of it. Schopenhauer's ideas are often said to have formed part of the backdrop to Freud's development of psychoanalysis.

Smith, Adam (1723–90). Deeply influenced by the thought of Hume, Smith put at the center of his philosophical program the notion of imagination, by means of which the mind searches for order amid the chaos of physical reality and, in its dealings with other humans, allows their thoughts and actions to be sympathetically understood. In his contributions to political economy, Smith held that a commercial economy offers more liberty to the laborer than does feudalism, for in it particularistic relationships of dependence are replaced by relationships based on universalistic market principles.

Socrates (469–399 B.C.E.). Athenian philosopher famously tried and executed for his impious views about the Greek gods. A champion of reason and virtue, Socrates engaged in extended public dialogue with the prominent men of his day on matters of ethics, questioning them until the logical flaws in their positions came into view. Socrates argued, subtlely, for the unity of the virtues and for the position that genuine knowledge of what is good or right necessarily entails virtuous action.

Spencer, Herbert (1820–1903). British writer and philosopher who sought to apply Lamarckian evolutionary theory to, among other things, psychology, biology, and sociology. Noting the tendency of all things to evolve, through adaptation, from the homogeneous and undefined to the heterogeneous and well defined, Spencer asserted that intelligence is the outcome of human evolutionary adaptation and not innate.

Spinoza, Baruch (1632–77). A Dutch philosopher who made his living as a lens grinder, Spinoza believed that all things in the universe have a causal origin that can be understood by human beings, that these causes are logical and natural rather than final, that mathematics is the key to understanding them, and that God and nature are one and the same. Forced out of his synagogue early in his life, Spinoza advanced ideas so heretical that many had to be published posthumously.

Stahl, Georg Ernst (1660–1734). A German physician, Stahl is remembered today for his theory of phlogiston, which posited the existence of a new chemical principle responsible for combustion, and for his argument that organisms are made animate by soul.

Stewart, Dugald (1753–1828). Stewart, a philosopher at the University of Edinburgh, extended the commonsense philosophy of Reid and developed ideas that would be enormously influential in nineteenth-century French and American academic philosophy. Stewart argued that Reid's philosophy, while important, was apt to be misunderstood. The fact that common sense – understood to mean the views of the common man – might disagree with a philosophical position has no bearing on its validity, Stewart asserted. What does matter is whether the position violates basic laws of human reason to which all men are, in principle, subject.

Taine, Hippolyte Adolphe (1828–93). Taine's urge was to reconstruct philosophy in accordance with the findings of empirical science. Author of scores of popular essays and books, including one about the eclectic spiritualists, Taine took comfort in Spinoza's naturalism and sought to produce a philosophical vision of the world in which contingency would be "banished."

Tiberius, Caeser Augustus (42 B.C.E.–37 C.E.). Second emporer of Rome.

Weber, Ernst Heinrich (1795–1878). Pioneering German experimental physiologist who sought to derive a formula that would precisely state the relationship between a stimulus and least perceptible differences in sensation.

Wundt, Wilhelm Max (1832–1920). A founding figure in experimental psychology, Wundt started the first psychology laboratory at Leipzig in 1879 – a laboratory to which many important thinkers in the then nascent social sciences, including Durkheim, came to study. Wundt's experimental work mostly centered around sensation and perception, reaction times, and attention. His thought ranged widely, however, and he also produced a two-volume work (*Völkerpsychologie*, 1900–20) that sought to use the materials of human history and culture to contribute to an understanding of the mind.

Zeno of Elea (c. 450 B.C.E.). In support of his friend Parmenides' claim that the world is homogeneous and unchanging, Zeno, whose ideas are recorded in the work of Plato and Aristotle, sought to show the paradoxes inherent in any effort to understand plurality and motion.

Index

a priori, 4, 9, 272, 278
Abelard, Peter, 135
absolute, 34, 104–105
abstraction, 133–134
action, residual categories of, 25; voluntary, 156
activity, 57, 148–150, 252–253, 268–271, 289
aesthetics, 138–147
agrégation examination, 1
altruism, 12, 64–65, 258
analogy, 210
analysis, 33, 179, 205–206
Anaxagoras, 74
animism, 286–287
Anselm, St., 293, 297
antinomies, Kantian, 116–117
Aquinas, St. Thomas, 293
Arcesilaus, 181
architecture, 147
Aristippus, 233
Aristotle, 16, 34, 45, 59, 61, 85, 151, 200, 246, 293, 297, 303–304, 309, 314
art, 126–127, 146–147, 229; 17th century, 143; ancient Greek, 143
artists, 71, 126
association of ideas, 119–121, 131, 154
associationism, 106–109

attention, 123, 132–133
axioms, 207

baccalauréat examination, 13, 16
Bacon, Francis, 197, 199, 202
Bain, Alexander, 76
Bastiat, Claude Frédéric, 259
Bayle, Pierre, 157–158, 312–313
beauty, 65, 66, 138–147; 17th century conceptions of, 141; 19th century conceptions of, 141
beaux-arts, 146–147
Bentham, Jeremy, 233–234
Bernard, Claude, 211, 258, 280, 285
bodies, metaphysics of, 277
Bonald, Louis de, 222–223
Bossuet, Jacques, 34, 69, 258, 311
Bouillier, Francisque, 61, 97, 286–287
Boutroux, Emile, 11
Brooks, John, 3, 7
Buffon, Georges, 133

Carneades, 181
Cartesianism, 33, 127
causality, 42–43, 93, 99, 101, 103–104, 107–109, 113, 115, 118, 159–160, 162–164, 201, 297–298
certainty, 12, 169, 172–180, 182
charity, 161, 264, 270–271
Charles I, 119
Cheselden, William, 75

Christianity, 65
Cicero, 16, 34, 36, 196, 300, 304
cities, 65
Clarke, Samuel, 293
classification, 213–214; artificial, 213–214; natural, 214
common sense, 12, 37–38
communism, 254
comparison, 133–134, 214
comprehension, 185, 191
Comte, Auguste, 7, 43
Comteans, 19
conception, faculties of, 72, 119–131
conceptualism, 135
Condillac, Etienne de, 58, 90, 132–134, 149, 150, 205, 225
consciousness, 24, 52, 94, 129; conditions of, 86–88
contract, 158
contradiction. *See* identity and contradiction, principle of
Contrat social, Rousseau, 260
Corneille, Pierre, 143–145, 157
cosmological argument, 304
courtesy, 267
Cousin, Victor, 7, 12, 14–16, 19, 23, 36–38, 46, 77, 92, 97, 103, 136, 248
creativity, 124, 126
crime and punishment, 24, 259–260, 265–266, 290–291
criticism, 184
Critique of Judgment, Kant, 145
Critique of Pure Reason, Kant, 116
Cudworth, Ralph, 284
Cyreanics, 233

Darwin, Charles, 110, 149–150
De Legibus, Cicero, 16
De Vita Beata, Seneca, 16
deduction, 190–197, 200, 203, 207–208, 278
definition, 188–189, 207
Democritus, 106, 299
demonstration, 207–208
Descartes, René, 16, 46, 69, 85, 123, 130, 139, 149, 153, 172, 197, 203, 280, 284–285, 293, 311

desire, 157–158
determinism, 11, 157, 159–165
Discourse on Method, Descartes, 16
Discourse on Universal History, Bossuet, 311
discoveries, 206
disinterestedness, 142; relationship to beauty, 140
division of labor, 8, 259
Division of Labor, The, Durkheim, 3, 6, 25
"Doctrine of Right," *Metaphysics of Morals*, Kant, 255
documents, 219
dogmatism, 181, 183–184
doubt, 172
dreams, 119, 129–130
duration, measurement of in psychology, 54
duty, 161, 246–271; civic, 249, 258–262; domestic, 249, 254–257; individual, 249–253; negative, 263–264; positive, 263–264; social, 249

eclectic spiritualism, 7, 15, 19, 21, 36–38
École Normale Supérieure, 1, 4, 6, 11, 13, 15
education. *See* higher education in France
effervescence, 12
egoism, 12, 63–64, 258
Eleatics, 310
Elementary Forms of Religious Life, The, Durkheim, 4, 12, 27
Émile, Rousseau, 256
emotion, 67–71, 123; classification of, 67–68; relationship to inclinations, 67
empiricism, 8, 22–24, 39–40, 75, 106–109, 116, 201, 272
end, 101
Epicureanism, 46, 60
Epicurus, 95, 106, 233–234, 236, 272, 299–300
epigraphy, 219

essentialism, 9
Ethics, Spinoza, 68–69
ethics, 27–29, 46–47, 229–273;
  practical, 229, 249; theoretical,
  229
ethnographic data, 8
Euler, Leonhard, 191–194
evidence, 172–173
evolutionism, 110–114, 300–302
experience, 94, 96, 113, 115;
  constitutive principles of,
  99
experimentation, 9, 23–24, 39–40, 43,
  211–212, 220
explanation, 41–42
extension, 82–84, 185, 191
externality, origin of the idea of, 77–79;
  objectivity of, 82–85

Fabiani, Jean-Louis, 21
faculties, definition of, 57; discursive,
  179; intuitive, 179; relationship to
  states of consciousness, 58
fallacies, 202–204
family, 8, 24, 64–65, 254–257
fatalism, 159, 164–165
Faust, 146
Fechner, Gustav, 23, 52–54
Ferry, Jules, 17–18
Fichte, Johann, 38
finalism, 26–29
finality, 99, 103–104, 164, 214,
  245–248, 273, 298, 303–304
First Principles, Spencer, 110, 301
Flourens, Pierre, 279, 282
force, 84
freedom, 156–165, 173, 231, 243–244,
  248, 261, 268–269
functional explanation, 8

Galileo, Galilei, 37, 127
Garnier, Adolph, 221, 223
generalization, 134–135
genius, 206
geometric figures, 102–103
Germany, 6, 16
Girardin, Saint-Marc, 142

glory, passion for, 70
God, 277, 292–295
God, existence of, metaphysical
  arguments for, 292–295; argument
  from common consent, 304;
  argument from moral obligation,
  305; argument from moral sanction,
  305; argument from the principle of
  causality, 293–294, 297–298;
  argument from the principle of
  finality, 294–295, 298; argument
  from the principle of perfection, 293,
  296; critique of metaphysical
  arguments for, 296–298; critique of
  physico-theological argument for,
  303–304; moral arguments for,
  304–305; physico-theological
  argument for, 298–302
God, nature and attributes of, 292,
  306–308; as creator, 310; dualism,
  309; metaphysical attributes,
  306–307; moral attributes, 307–308;
  pantheism, 309–310
God, relation to world of, pessimism,
  313; evil, problem of, 312–313;
  providence, 311–312
good, 65, 66; relationship to beauty,
  139, 246–248
government, 259
*Groundwork of the Metaphysics of
  Morals*, Kant, 240

habit, 69, 87, 107, 124, 148, 149,
  151–155
hallucination, 73, 130–131
Hamilton, William, 61, 79, 194
Hartmann, Eduard, 61, 86–88, 92,
  303–304, 313–314
hedonism, 233
Hegel, Georg Wilhelm Friedrich, 28,
  38, 303, 309
higher education in France, 18
history, 24, 216–220; method, 218–220
Hobbes, Thomas, 64, 66, 119, 247–248,
  258
honor, 267
Horace, 145

Hutcheson, Francis, 237
hypotheses, 210–211, 220; role of imagination in formulating, 128

ideal, 143, 157
idealism, 36, 38–40, 85, 97; in art, 146; transcendental, 27, 116–117
ideas, 185, 224–226; abstract, 153, 225; general, 225; particular, 224; Platonic, 134
identity, 42, 93
identity and contradiction, principle of, 117, 208
imagination, 33, 125–128, 207, 210–211, 219, 238
imitation, 222
imperative, categorical, 233, 240–242; hypothetical, 240–241
Impersonal Reason, Bouillier, 97
inclinations, 63–66, 121
induction, 198–201, 203–204, 212, 278
infinite, 83, 104–105, 117–118
instinct, 87, 148–152; relationship to physiology, 149
intellectuals, 60, 71
Intelligence, Taine, 226
intelligence, 24, 58, 72, 153, 169, 251–252, 267–268, 270, 288–289
interest. *See* self-interest
interpretation, 219
introspection, 9, 19, 23, 55–56
inventions, 206–207, 209–211
Ionians, 309

Jacobi, Friedrich, 237
Janet, Paul, 15, 16
Jouffroy, Théodore, 37, 129, 161
judgment, 95–97, 135–137, 185–187; qualitative, 186; quantitative, 186
justice, 263–271

Kant, Immanuel, 27, 44, 97, 99–101, 115–117, 136, 138, 145–146, 156, 158, 161, 163–164, 205–206, 233, 240–242, 245–247, 255, 269, 272, 273, 296–299, 304. *See also* antinomies, Kantian

Kepler, Johann, 126
knowledge, divisions of, 72; regulative principles of, 99

La Bruyère, Jean de, 141
laborers, 60
Lalande, André, 2, 6, 8–10, 21
language, 135, 221–226; artificial, 224; origin of, 222–224
Laplace, Pierre de, 199
LaRochefoucauld, François de, 64, 66
law, science of. *See* social science
laws, 198, 213, 229; civil, 230; demonstration of, 209, 211–212; invention of, 209–212. *See also* moral law
legends, 218–219
Leibniz, Gottfried, 16, 36, 85–86, 100, 119, 130, 160, 221, 285, 293, 295, 297, 312–313
Lélut, Louis François, 130
Lemoine, Albert, 74
Lettres à une princess d'Allemagne, Euler, 191
Liard, Louis, 18
liberalism, 260–261
Literature, ancient, 140; classical, 139, 145; modern, 127, 140
Littré, Emile, 105, 305
Locke, John, 106
Logic, Mill, 107, 198
logic, 46–47, 172–226, 229; applied, 229; general, 229; nature of, 169–171
Louis XIV, 141
love, familial, 65; maternal, 66
Lukes, Steven, 2
Lycée de Puy, 1
Lycée de Saint-Quentin, 2, 10
lycée philosophy class, 2, 13–14
lycées, 1, 13

madness, 126, 130–131
Maine de Biran, 58, 79, 92, 103, 152
Malebranche, Nicholas, 127, 243, 284–285

Malthus, Thomas, 150
Manicheism, 312
Mansel, Henry, 108
marriage, 255
Marx, Karl, 5, 28
materialism, 281–283
mathematics, 103, 207–208; explanation in, 42
matter, qualities of, 82–83
Mauss, Marcel, 4, 6
mechanism, 300
Mémoire sur l'habitude, Maine de Biran, 152
memory, 56, 122–126, 153
metaphysics, 35, 46–47, 277–314
meteorology, 212
method, 43, 170, 205–206
Mill, John Stuart, 22, 77–79, 106–109, 121, 160, 197–199, 234–237, 272, 273
mind, 98
Monadology, Leibniz, 16
money, passion for, 70
monism, 310
Montaigne, Michel de, 196
monuments, 219
moral consciousness, 245
moral law, 27, 158, 230–248, 250, 263–265, 270–273
moral responsibility, 230–231, 245, 272–273
moral sentiment, 237–239, 247, 264
morality, secular, 15
motives, 159–161
Müller, Friedrich, 135
music, 147

Napoleon, 14
nativists, 75
natural history, 212, 213
nature, state of, 247–248
New Academy, 36, 181
Newton, Isaac, 126
Nicomachean Ethics, Aristotle, 16
nominalism, 134–135

norms, 12, 25
noumenal world, 116

observation, 220
Of Pleasure and Pain, Bouillier, 61
ontological argument, 293, 297
opinion, 172–173, 175, 176
organicism, 285–286
Origin of Species, Darwin, 149

painting, 71, 147
Parmenides, 310
Parsons, Talcott, 25–26
Pascal, Blaise, 64, 107, 127, 130, 182, 198, 211–212, 238
passion, 67–71, 87, 127, 153
patriotism, 65
Peisse, Louis, 286
perception, external, 73–79; faculties of, 72; internal, 86–88
perceptionists, 79
perfection, 104–105, 293, 296; relationship to beauty, 139–140
personality, 28, 241, 243–244, 250, 260–261, 265, 269–271
persons, 93–94
phenomenal world, 115
philology, 215–216
philosophical spirit, 33–34
philosophy, definition of, 33–35; divisions of, 45–47; method of, 36–40; object of, 34–35; relationship to science, 41–44; role in French educational system, 3
philosophy of science, 10–11
Philosophy of Sir William Hamilton, The, Mill, 107
Philosophy of the Unconscious, The, Hartmann, 61, 86, 92
physics, 45
physiology, 213
Plato, 16, 45, 58, 61, 65, 97, 104, 134, 215, 231, 254, 258, 309
Platonic philosophy, 34
pleasure/pain, 51, 57–58, 60–62, 67, 142, 152
poetry, 147

political economy, science of. *See* social science, political economy
politics, science of. *See* social science, politics
Port-Royal logicians, 188–189, 203, 206
positivism, 7, 34
prettiness, 146
Primitive Classification, Durkheim and Mauss, 4
Pro Milone, Cicero, 196
probabilism, 181
progress, 155
property, 268–269
propositions, 185–187
psychology, 46–47, 51–165, 273, 279, 282; relationship to history, 56; relationship to logic, 169; relationship to physiology, 44, 51–52
psychophysical school, 52–54
psychophysiological school, 54
punishment, 158. *See also* crime and punishment

rational choice theory, 25
rational ideas, 101–105
rationalism, 4
Ravaisson, Felix, 152
realism, 85, 134–135; in art, 146
reason, 143, 264; definition of, 95–97; objectivity of, 115–118; origins of, 26, 110–114; principles of, 98–100
Reid, Thomas, 12, 160, 200, 216
religion, 33, 65, 169, 173
Renaissance, 197
Renan, Ernest, 223
Renouvier, Charles, 19
Republic, Plato, 16, 215
responsibility, civil, 231
Ribot, Théodule, 19
rights, 247–248, 269
Rodrigue, 146
Rousseau, Jean-Jacques, 12, 28, 64, 237, 251, 256, 258, 260, 264, 267
Royer-Collard, Pierre, 122
Rules of Sociological Method, The, Durkheim, 10, 11

Schelling, Friedrich, 38
Schmaus, Warren, 7, 9
scholasticism, 186
Schopenhauer, Arthur, 10, 61, 86, 303, 313
science, 41–43, 170, 209–212, 215–217, 229
Scottish philosophy, 200, 216, 221
sculpture, 147
self, 51, 52, 59, 66, 69–70, 73, 84, 116, 136, 143; identity of, 124, 231, 243; nature of, 92–94; noumenal, 163–164; origins of the idea of, 89–91; phenomenal, 163–164
self-interest, 236–239, 241
Seneca, 16
Sens, 1
sensation, 52, 68, 132, 140, 143; least perceptible differences of, 53; measurement of, 52–54; possible and actual, 77–78
senses, 73–76; relationship to extension, 75–76
sensibility, 12, 58, 115, 152, 163, 182–183, 242, 252, 267, 270, 288; relationship to intelligence, 175–176
sensualism, 36, 106
signs, 221–226; artificial, 221–222; natural, 221
skepticism, 176, 181–184
slavery, 268
sleep, 119, 129–130
Smith, Adam, 237–239
social facts, *sui generis* reality of, 3
social morphology, 8
social realism, 7, 10
social science, empirical, 19; German, 7, 215–217; of laws, 215; political economy, 215; politics, 215
socialism, 260
society, 64–65, 258–262
sociology, 8, 10; empirical science of, 4–6; relationship to philosophy, 3–4
sociology of knowledge, 3
sociology of religion, 3, 9, 11–12
Socrates, 45, 130, 138

solidarity, 21
Sorbonne, 6
soul, 57–59, 277; immortality of, 288–291; materialism and, 281–283; relationship to the body of, 284–287; spirituality of, 279–280
space, 79, 98–99, 101–102, 117–118
special creation, doctrine of, 110–111
Spencer, Herbert, 24, 102, 105, 110–114, 149–150, 232–235, 237, 272, 301
Spinoza, Baruch, 38, 58, 68–69, 152, 158, 172, 178–179, 309, 310
spiritualism, 85, 280
Stahl, Georg, 286, 287
statistics, 8
Stewart, Dugald, 106, 154
stoicism, 46, 60, 65, 106, 305, 309
Structure of Social Action, The, Parsons, 25
sublime, 139, 145–146
substance, 99, 101, 103–104
sufficient reason, principle of, 295
Suicide, Durkheim, 3
suicide, 12, 250–251
syllabus, official, 16
syllogism, 190–197, 200, 208
sympathy, 238–239
synthesis, 33–34, 179–180, 205–206

Taine, Hippolyte, 89–90, 123–124, 130, 134, 226
terms, 185
Thèse, Ravaisson, 152
Thesis on the Origin of Language, Renan, 223

thought, 224–226
Tiberius, Caesar, 119
time, 98–99, 101–102, 117–118
Tiryakian, Edward, 2
tolerance, 177, 267–268
Traité de la connaissance de Dieu et de soi-même, Boussuet, 69
"Transcendental Logic," *Critique of Pure Reason*, Kant, 296
truth, 65, 66, 172–174; relationship to beauty, 139

unconscious, 51, 54, 86–88, 313–314
understanding, 125, 127, 175; categories of, 4, 9, 115, 163
University of Bordeaux, 6
utilitarianism, 233–239
utility, relationship to beauty, 138

virtue, 139, 246
Vital Principle and the Thinking Soul, The, Bouillier, Francisque, 286
vitalism, 286

Weber, Ernst, 23, 52, 54
Weber, Max, 25
will, 60, 67, 93, 130, 132, 148, 153, 156–161, 175–176, 182–183, 245–246
World as Will and Representation, The, Schopenhauer, 61, 86
writers, 71
Wundt, Wilhelm, 7, 23, 54

Zeldin, Theodore, 14
Zeno, 310